How to sell to Europe

How to sell to Europe

Peter Danton de Rouffignac

Pitman

Pitman Publishing
128 Long Acre, London WC2E 9AN

A division of Longman Group UK Limited

First published in Great Britain 1989

©Longman Group UK Ltd 1990

British Library Cataloguing in Publication Data
Danton de, Rouffignac, Peter.
  How to sell to Europe.
  1. Great Britain. Exports to European Community Countries
  I. Title
658.8'48

ISBN 0-273-03149-X

Printed in Great Britain at The Bath Press, Avon

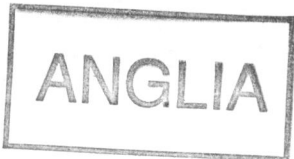

For Andrew

Contents

Foreword

In preparing this book I have tried to draw on my experience of working with British – and some European – companies who are attempting to get to grips with the European market as it will look after 1992. That Europe has been largely neglected by exporters up until now is a constantly recurring theme, and although 1992 is not a magic formula for success, it is hoped that the attendant publicity will help to concentrate the minds of company managers on this virtual home market of 320 million consumers.

In a book of this size it has not been possible to cover all the issues relating to the new, open Europe but I have tried to include as much practical advice as possible that is equally applicable to companies selling capital equipment, consumer goods and services. Indeed each category has a special section of its own, as well as being covered in general chapters on selling and promotion. I have also touched very briefly on the history of the Common Market and the main European institutions, as I find the level of ignorance among business people generally alarming. Those interested in studying in greater depth the work of the Commission, the Parliament etc. and how they can be influenced are directed towards my book *Presenting your case to Europe* which examines the delicate art of European lobbying.

I am grateful to a number of people for help in preparing this book (although the views expressed in it are entirely my own, as are any omissions and shortcomings). I would like to thank in particular the various information sources cited and hope that readers will be encouraged to use them for their own researches. They include the helpful staff of the European desks inside the Department of Industry and of the European Commission and European Parliament information offices; the Commercial Counsellors in British embassies in Europe who kindly provided information about their services and about typical problems of intending exporters; and the Chambers of

Commerce, trade and professional associations and official United Kingdom and European bodies who kindly responded to my requests for further information.

I wish all readers and potential European exporters the best of luck in their endeavours and hope they will find this book helpful.

Peter Danton de Rouffignac
Dolphin Square
London SW1V 3LR   December 1989

1 You too can do it

Europe as an export market – before and after 1992

This book is not primarily about the new, free, open Europe that is the dream of the Brussels-based Commission by the end of 1992. Of course there will be frequent references to 1992 and the effect that it will have on your business – and that of your competitors. Later in this chapter we will be discussing in some detail how after 1992 the process of doing business in Europe will be that much easier, again both for you and for your competitors. But with or without the Common Market, geographical Europe has always been with us and yet has been a surprisingly neglected export market for British businesses. The advent of 1992 may simply make it more fashionable. The question is, for how long?

British performance

Britain's poor export performance, both in Europe and elsewhere, is seen by many observers as symptomatic of the overall decline in this country's economic fortunes. The evidence has been well documented by other writers but can be observed in:

- The decline in manufacturing output, that is the amount of goods that this country makes. This should not be be confused with improved productivity, largely brought about by automation and job losses.
- Rising levels of unemployment, despite manipulation of the official statistics. (Nearly 20 different methods of counting have been introduced since 1979.) At the same time, the active workforce (those wanting to work) has been expanding, so aggravating the problem.
- A drift from manufacturing into services. However, the service

sector cannot compensate for the equivalent output lost in manufacturing. Britain simply cannot survive as a service economy.
While Britain has suffered a 30% decline in manufacturing employment, in the same period Japan has increased by 5%.

- A decline in overall export performance, which is of particular
  concern to readers of this book.

Much has been written about Britain's widening trade gap with the
rest of the world – the difference between what Britain exports and
what it imports – and the figures are indeed alarming. It is worrying
to recall that just thirty years ago, in the 1950s, Britain commanded
around 25% of all world trade, and imported just 5% of its requirements. By the mid-1980s the position had changed dramatically:
Britain's share of world trade had fallen to under 10%, and imports
risen to 30%. In a purely European context, in manufactured goods
alone Britain now has an annual deficit of more than 8 billion pounds
just with its Common Market neighbours. The overall trade gap is
of course much larger.

So while 1992 should not be seen as an isolated event similar to the
City's Big Bang, it is, as this book will explain, a unique marketing
opportunity, an ideal time for companies to review their export
performance in what is after all Britain's closest overseas market. To
date Britain's record has not been good. Britain joined the European
Community in 1973 and since that date there has been a steady
upward trend in her exports to West Europe. This improved performance, however, is invariably balanced by a rising tide of imports
from the Twelve, as the figures all too clearly demonstrate. By 1973
the Community was taking around 30% of Britain's manufactured
exports – but provided nearly 40% of her imports. Ten years later,
Britain's performance had indeed improved – to 40% exports, but
again offset by 50% imports!

By the late 1980s the Common Market took around 50% of total
British exports, worth an estimated 40 billion pounds. Even these
figures are distorted by extremely high quantities of North Sea oil
and gas, and we should also not forget that in 1986 the market was
enlarged with the addition of Spain and Portugal, or that the rest of
the Community still accounts for more than half of Britain's total
imports.

In terms of overall export performance within the Community, the United Kingdom today ranks in only fourth place behind West Germany, France and the tiny Netherlands. So why is Britain's export performance in Europe (and the rest of the world) so poor and what can be done to improve it?

Inhibitions

Like so many other aspects of Britain's economic decline, the roots are historical and can be traced back over a hundred years. These include Britain's failure to innovate even in the late 19th and early 20th century, when industrial rivals in America and Europe were developing electricity and the automobile. Britain was also slow to react to competition in and from overseas markets. Too great reliance was placed on the old Empire and later the Commonwealth; on ailing traditional industries such as iron, steel, coal, shipbuilding and textiles; on a myth that 'British quality' was sufficient to hold on to declining markets; and a confusion between the export of British-made goods and services (trade in invisibles) and direct investment in overseas countries. The latter trend, which continues and was increasing in the 1980s, is not a substitute for exporting and arguably works against British interests. More (foreign) manufactured goods enter as imports from British-owned investments overseas, to the detriment of home-manufactured products that could be sold inside the country – or exported. It should be remembered that, when balancing the country's books, a home sale against foreign competition is as valuable as an export sale in a foreign market.

It is against this historical background, which I have attempted to describe as briefly as possible, that British business must face up to the challenge of exporting to Europe. My own researches, among mainly medium sized companies, indicate that a number of factors still inhibit their export performance. They include:

- **A lack of commitment to exporting**. Such an accusation would be vigorously denied in many companies, who point proudly to their lists of agents in over fifty countries. But how many countries are actually visited during the course of a year? How many are actually sold-to out of the fifty? What is the level of investment in exporting – personnel, sales literature, overseas exhibitions – compared with home sales?

- **The lure of distance** – allied to spreading the effort too thinly Export managers have enviable jobs. Big budgets, lots of foreign travel. And it is this attitude that seems to generate a misty-eyed approach to export markets: the further you go, the more likely you are to make a sale. Not long ago it was the Middle East, with tales of executives camping out in the ballrooms of luxury hotels not yet completed, while they hung around for days on end for an appointment with some elusive Arab minister. Then it was Eastern Europe. Today it is China. All this to the neglect of the biggest single market lying just 25 miles across the English Channel!

- **The language barrier**. Britons are notoriously bad at learning foreign languages. Perhaps this is also a throwback to the old Empire mentality and the naive assumption that 'everyone speaks English'. The common language is probably the single most potent reason for Britain's so-called special relationship with the United States. Again, always to the detriment of Europe and our relations with our nearest neighbours. The lack of fluency in foreign languages is reflected also in basic problems like not producing foreign sales brochures, which are repeatedly reported by British embassy commercial staff as a serious barrier to export performance.

- **British insularity**. Is it inevitable that living on an island should breed an insular mentality? It is worrying that while more and more Britons visit Europe on holiday, they do not take the trouble to get to know their continental neighbours. Stereotypes continue to gain ground: the smooth Frenchman, the stubborn German, the lazy Spaniard or the untrustworthy Italian. Such attitudes may represent extremes but they reflect to an extent much official thinking, from prime ministerial xenophobia to distrust of Common Market institutions and motives – a classic case of joining the club late and then complaining about the rules.

Other observers, including the British Overseas Trade Board, have identified further barriers to exporting. Among them is the feeling that a company's products are 'not suitable for exporting' reported by nearly 30% of those recently surveyed. These, coupled with 'lack of experience of exporting' (10%) and 'lack of market information' (13%) indicate that many more companies are failing to exploit their export potential in Europe.

Exporting is not just for large firms

Small and medium sized companies sometimes feel that exporting is not for them. Export successes, and even Britain does have her fair share of those, are often only known about and publicised when they relate to the achievements of the very largest companies. This is laudable, and indeed the Awards for Export Achievement people have done much to publicise the efforts of medium and smaller firms in foreign markets, and reinforce the message that exporting is not just for large firms. The Institute of Export note that irrational fears frequently prevent many smaller companies from achieving their export potential, and that a further five billion pounds of export sales could be made by these British companies overseas.

The recurring theme throughout this book is that Europe is, and always has been, the obvious first place to try for the company new to exporting. After 1992 the procedures for doing business there will be greatly simplified, making it an even more attractive market. The mechanics of doing business in Europe are explained throughout, together with guidance on the wealth of information, advice and assistance that are readily available. However, 1992 is not a one-way event, and what will become simpler for Britain will also be simpler for her European neighbours. Perhaps because of their less rigid frontiers, the ease of overland travel from one country to the next, and their greater facility in languages, Britain's mainland European competitors have a head start. They are already demonstrably more European in their outlook, and their export performance, as already noted, is better than Britain's. Even at the level of small and medium sized companies their record is superior. Whilst this is on the one hand discouraging it should also indicate to managers of similar sized British companies that it really can be done.

Your European competitors

The export success of small and medium sized firms is sometimes the result of having to operate in a very small home market (such as Denmark) but this is not always the case, as examination of small firms' performance in France and Italy indicates. Denmark has a large number (92%) of small firms of up to 50 employees. In France and the United Kingdom where 'small' is used to describe firms with up to 100 employees the figures are 99% and 98% respectively. My own recent research suggests that taking the definition of 'small and medium firms' to mean those employing up to 500 people, then 98% of all European businesses come within this wider category and it is these who are the significant exporters.

Where home markets are extremely small – as is the case in Denmark, Eire, the Benelux and Portugal – a proportion of small and medium enterprises remain essentially local or regional, content to satisfy only their home markets. However, others react by becoming exporters. In Denmark, with its 5 million population, small businesses export an average 30% of their turnover, and 'large businesses' (which are still small by international standards) export up to 55%.

In France, nearly half of all small firms are involved in exporting some of their output, and this rises to 70% of firms employing up to 200 people, and 90% of those with more than 200. In Italy a similar pattern emerges, with at least 30% of the smallest micro-firms (1-19 employees) involved in some overseas sales, and this figure rises to more than half of 'small firms' (20-99 employees) who export at least some of their output. Among medium sized Italian firms (up to 499 employees), 80% are engaged in export, a quarter of them selling more than half their output overseas. The Italian scene is particularly well documented and further research shows that of the exports by the small firms, 60% go to Europe – their nearest and most obvious market. As the size of firms increases, there is less dependence on Europe, with the proportion of exports to the Community reducing to 55% among medium firms, and 50% in large firms – the balance going to the rest of the world's markets.

If Britain's small business competitors in Europe are already performing well now, how much better will they be after 1992? As in

Britain they can benefit from 1992 aid packages that invariably include advice and assistance, export guarantees, soft loans, promotional services. The take-up can sometimes be patchy, as it is in Britain, and many exporters succeed without any kind of government aid or intervention. It is often a result of entrepreneurial spirit or simply of accident (a chance enquiry from an overseas customer) or whim (the owner has personal or business connections abroad).

What the performance of European small and medium sized businesses shows is that they are in general already more active in reaching out to their European neighbours (often a simpler process than crossing the English Channel); they can take advantage if they wish of a similar package of assistance as that available to intending British exporters; and that while they demonstrate that exporting is not just for the large firm, the mainland Europeans pose a serious threat to British business after 1992 when the remaining barriers to free trade are lifted. It is a message both of encouragement and concern.

You too can do it!

Research undertaken by the CBI indicates that the greatest export potential lies among British firms in the medium-sized category of 21 to 50 employees. Many of the companies surveyed were already exporting, but exports represented a comparatively small percentage of turnover – around 25% of total sales, but with engineering companies generally doing better. Exchange rate fluctuations were seen as the greatest problem facing exporters, followed by lack of market information. The CBI has been a champion of the European Monetary System, which would reduce wide variations in the exchange rates and promote greater use of the Ecu, the European unit of account (both topics are discussed later). It is clear that medium-sized firms are hampered by lack of knowledge about Europe and it is hoped that this book will go some way towards bridging the gap and among other things help point the intending exporter towards the wide range of advice and assistance available.

Europe is the obvious choice for the first time exporter

West Europe has a lot going for it as an export market in addition to the specific benefits (detailed below) that will accrue after 1992. First is its size and similarity. It is a market of 320 million people, including the United Kingdom and the rest of the Twelve, plus a further 30 million if we add the remainder of West Europe (Scandinavia, Austria and Switzerland) who are not members of the EEC. All of them with slight variations having more or less the same or similar tastes in food, cars, clothes, holidays, lifestyles. Journeying through Europe one is impressed by the uniformity rather than the diversity, and this feeling is reinforced by standardised international hotels, and the presence of hundreds of familiar brand names wherever we go.

Although language is a barrier that can and must be overcome in many situations, the British are fortunate that the influence of American and English language television is all pervasive, and that English is widely spoken and understood, particularly in business circles. The presence of this pan-European television further reinforces life-styles and consumer spending, on everything from soap powders to do-it-yourself gadgets. So in dealing with our continental neighbours we are for the most part talking to people who have the same outlook, needs, aspirations and mode of living as themselves. It is truly an extension of Britain's domestic market.

As will be seen later in the brief geographical studies of Europe, the majority of potential customers tend to live in towns, and distinct groupings can be found similar to Britain's south-east, midland, north west, northern and Scottish conurbations. This facilitates research, and subsequent coverage of the market, with the potential for regional experimentation. It means also that, again, the European customer is very like his or her British counterpart, lives in a similar type of house or apartment, and buys the same types of product. A French or German household is as likely to contain a washing machine, a refrigerator, a microwave oven, a dishwasher, a vacuum cleaner as its British equivalent, while offices are equipped with the same types of word processors, photo-copiers, facsimile machines and answering machines. The Europeans have by and large the same taste for instant coffee, lunchtime snacks, soft drinks and fast food, despite surviving pockets of regional gastronomy.

From a practical point of view, Europe offers the unique advantage of proximity – a mere 30 minutes by Hovercraft, still less when the Channel Tunnel opens in the mid-1990s. It has to be easier to sell to someone close to home rather than on the other side of the world, and as the businessman gets to know Europe he will be surprised to find that he can travel as quickly to Paris or Frankfurt (by any means of transport) as he can to Manchester or Scotland. In Chapter 4 on field research we talk about exploring the market, but it must be said at once just how easy it is to get around Europe. It is blessed with an excellent motorway network, in many ways superior to and less congested than the roads in Britain. These make it possible to cover large distances in a single day particularly outside the principal holiday seasons (when you will not be travelling on business anyway). Unlike Britain, the European rail network has not been downgraded and excellent fast services run to all the major cities. Although European air fares remain artifically high, services are frequent and rapid, and the prospect is held out that fares will come down as a result of Commission pressures and competition from direct high-speed rail links.

Because Europe is so close and easy to get around, it is easier to explore and research the markets for British goods and services. It costs considerably less to spend a week in exploratory visits to an exhibition or to size up potential distributors in Belgium or Spain than to undertake the equivalent task in the Far East or America. And when you are eventually established in the market, distribution channels are shorter, customers can be visited more easily and more often, complaints dealt with more rapidly, spare parts and/or your technicians despatched more swiftly: in all, the European market is so much easier to control.

So much so that for many operations you can effectively market to Europe direct from the United Kingdom. Clearly, as we will discuss in later sections, some operations require the use of agents, distributors and representatives, but these people can be supported, visited and generally supervised simply and cost-effectively from a British base. There is frequently no need to set up a branch office or other permanent presence in order to sell capital goods, and as we shall see many consumer items can be sold direct from the home country to retail groups, buying chains and cooperatives – in essence, just as you would service your home market.

All these benefits – proximity of the market, similarities in lifestyle and consumption, ease of communications – alone have always made the European market worthwhile for British exporters. With the advent of 1992, a whole range of measures designed to make doing business with Europe even easier will be added to these advantages. Unfortunately, as already mentioned, they will apply to everyone, so making life easier but at the same time more competitive for the businessman. The principal changes are examined in the following sections.

1992 and the exporter

In order to understand the impact of 1992 on business it is useful to look back briefly at the history and development of the Common Market and why it was in June 1985 that the twelve Member States formulated a White Paper, which in turn led to the signing of the Single European Act in 1986. This Act listed over 300 legislative proposals designed to remove the last remaining barriers to free trade throughout Europe. The fact that it has taken so long – 30 years since the creation of the Common Market (or European Economic Community to give it its correct title) – to bring about a genuinely open market is both an indication of how far short of the original ideals enshrined in the Treaty of Rome the European idea has been allowed to drift; and of the pressures that have been brought by various Member States anxious to promote their own national interests.

Some European history

If we look back to 1957/58 and the original Treaty of Rome, many of the proposals now put forward in the Single European Act were stated objectives then. They included removal of restrictions on:

- movement of goods within the Community,
- movement of individuals throughout the Community,
- freedom to sell services throughout the Community,
- free movement of capital.

In addition, the Treaty of Rome pledged that there would be progress towards the harmonisation of indirect taxes (such as VAT and excise duties), and formulation of a genuine competition policy that would do away with many of the artificial barriers (such as quotas) which were seen as hampering free trade.

The need for some kind of European common market was recognised in principle soon after the end of the second world war. As early as 1947 Belgium, the Netherlands and Luxemburg got together in what has been a highly successful free trade area, the Benelux Union. In April 1951 the European Coal and Steel Community was formally established, and comprised the three Benelux countries, plus France, West Germany and Italy (the original Six). Involving only coal, iron and steel, but with a central administrative authority, the ECSC set out to remove all customs and other artificial barriers that prevented free movement of these commodities within the member countries. It was a success both in terms of improved performance within these sectors, and when the time came in the late 1950s, in helping redress some of the worst effects of the rundown of the coal industry.

The concept of the ECSC was the basis for the foundation in March 1957 of the European Economic Community, the Common Market as we know it today. Its objectives included the gradual removal of internal customs barriers; the application of a common external tariff (a 'customs union'); freedom of movement of people, goods, services and capital; and coordination of policies for transport, energy, agriculture and manufacturing industry.

Meanwhile some other trade groupings were taking place. In 1959 seven countries – United Kingdom, Sweden, Norway, Denmark, Switzerland, Austria and Portugal – formed EFTA, the so-called European Free Trade Area. This was partly a reaction to the success of the Six, whose economic progress contrasted sharply with Britain's stagnation in the late 1950s and early 1960s. All this occurred in a period when Europe – including Britain – lost at least political control over most of their former overseas colonies, cutting off not only a favoured source of raw materials but also diminishing many traditional markets for finished goods.

Britain continued to view with alarm the growing discrepancy between her own performance and that of the Six and negotiations began in 1961 for her to join the EEC. Britain's entry was blocked for several years by France's General de Gaulle and did not in fact occur until several years after his death (April 1969). Negotiations which had temporarily lapsed were re-opened, and on 1 January 1973 Britain's Prime Minister Edward Heath led Britain into the European Community, together with Eire and Denmark. The Community, now the Nine, was further enlarged in 1981 with the arrival of Greece, and in 1986 by Spain and Portugal, finally making the Community of Twelve.

Despite or perhaps because of its numerical growth, some of the original ideals of the Common Market have got lost along the way. As countries saw their domestic trade affected by the general economic decline of the 1970s (the OPEC price rises date from 1973), national concerns rapidly overtook the European ideal. As a result progress towards the goals originally set out in the Treaty of Rome – and now reinforced under the Single European Act – has been uneven and at times painful. There are some who argue even now that the free European market will not be a reality by the end of 1992, the date set for completion. However, given the economic threats from the super-powers of America and the Far East, it is difficult to envisage any other mechanism for ensuring Europe's survival into the twenty-first century.

The cost of not going ahead with 1992

Before considering in some detail the programme of liberalisation envisaged in the Single European Act, let us look briefly at the cost of non-Europe as it has been described. In presenting its case for 1992, the Brussels based Commission of the European Communities in 1988 produced a report outlining the main defects of the present Common Market. Backed by Commission President M. Jacques Delors and the then vice president Lord Cockfield (subsequently recalled by Mrs Thatcher), the Commission undertook a two-year research programme. This involved using nearly thirty outside agencies (research groups, consultancies) who spoke to more than 11,000 European business people. The result was a 1988 report presented by Mr Paolo Cecchini of the Commission. (The full text is available in English, published by Gower).

The Cecchini Report makes interesting if alarming reading. Citing some of the typical problems associated with doing business in Europe, it calculated:

- that the cost of controls and delays associated with border crossings was equivalent to a penalty of up to 25% of profits in some industries;
- that as a result smaller companies were effectively debarred from engaging in European trade;
- that the cost of varying technical standards in engineering and electronics annually cost companies billions of pounds;
- that public purchasing instead of being free was restricted – limiting competition and therefore putting up the price of goods and services bought under this system;
- and that wide price variations – up to 300% – distorted the value of many essential goods and services between member countries.

Starting with the question of *physical movement* within the Community, the Commission found that road journeys within Europe took on average twice as long as a result of border crossing delays and that hauliers' restrictions on cabotage (the right to bring back a return load) was an expensive and unnecessary restraint on competition. Horror stories were recounted of personal computers being confiscated from businessmen on their way to an international conference and of lorry drivers being delayed at frontier posts and heavily fined for minor errors in their paperwork. There was even talk of bribes and other inducements offered to frontier policemen.

Invisible barriers to free trade were also cited. They include differing technical standards and the need for duplication of certification, which add to the cost of research and development, design and tooling, and led to delays in submitting products approved for use in one country to the equivalent certification body in another. By judicious manipulation of such national regulations individual governments could effectively restrict free trade in machinery, spare parts, machine tools, electronics.

The report found that *delays in obtaining type approval* for equipment such as private telephone switchboards could take up to a year in Belgium, France, Germany and Italy, and was expensive – up to £100,000 in the United Kingdom. In the automobile sector it was found that different technical requirements between member states prevented the mass manufacture of over 90 components surveyed, so adding considerably to their cost.

Packaging and labelling requirements were found to affect up to a third of food items. Almost the same number were restricted by laws governing content or specific ingredients. The Germans, for example, attempted to restrict imports of beer by citing their country's purity regulations while France and Spain have used their national regulations to restrict the import of certain kinds of soft drinks. The Danes cited their national recycling laws in order to insist that such drinks were imported only in re-fillable containers. The Italians have restricted certain types of plastic containers. And so on.

Fiscal barriers were also widely noted. Different levels of purchase tax on cars (12% in Luxemburg up to 200% in Denmark and Greece) as well as Value Added Tax and their treatment in business accounts produced wide distortions in prices to the consumer. When consumers got wise to this, other 'technical' barriers were raised, as occurred when British customers tried to buy right-hand drive cars from dealers in Belgium at well below equivalent British prices.

The need for some sort of *currency harmony* was dramatically demonstrated by a group in Belgium who set out with BF40,000 and sent it on a journey through the Community's bureaux de change. On its return to Belgium what remained was worth less than 50% of the original sum.

The *non-recognition of national qualifications* – such as an engineering degree or design diploma – was again seen as an effective barrier to the free movement of people seeking to work anywhere within the Community. What movement there had been was predominantly among the unskilled or semi-skilled. Building labourers were able to find temporary jobs in West Europe but a British architect or civil engineer was effectively prevented from setting up a practice outside his home country.

Looking at this situation, the European Commission decided to set itself an immense task of reform for completion by the end of 1992. Its proposals are wide ranging and will affect virtually every area of our business and private lives. To bring these into perspective, however, in this section we concentrate on the changes most likely to have an effect on the way business will in future be conducted in Europe.

Removal of physical barriers to trade

The Commission has rightly recognised that frontier controls are the most visible and frustrating signs of the restriction on free movement of goods and people within the Community. Widespread changes are therefore proposed. Frontier controls have always existed for a number of purposes. They are needed to monitor the movements of people at entry and exit, including the detection of terrorists and criminals, and others considered undesirable. Such controls will have to remain but at the outer edges of the Community only, and the Member States will have to agree on a common policy for the treatment of non-Europeans (visa requirements, etc.) and the control of terrorism and drug trafficking.

Control of goods has a number of objectives. These include the collection of VAT and excise duties, carrying out health and hygiene checks on animals and foodstuffs, and compiling various trade statistics. By deciding on common policies applicable within the Community (covering hygiene, harmonising VAT and excise duties, etc.) it is intended to remove the need for most of this frontier activity. The transport of goods across national borders is already greatly simplified by the use of the Single Administrative Document (SAD) which has replaced the hundred or so forms previously used in European trade. By further standardising data requirements and the increasing use of computers it is hoped that the process will continue to be speeded-up.

Considerable work is being done in the areas of animal health, hygiene standards for meat and meat products, poultry, fish and plants. In addition, a number of framework directives are proposed covering virtually all aspects of food and food production – additives, ingredients, labelling and packaging. These detailed proposals are outlined in documents such as the Department of Industry's *Single Market* package which is available free on demand; or from relevant trade associations to which the intending exporter is likely to belong.

It is intended that international road haulage within the Community will also be liberalised by the end of 1992. All permits and quotas for trade between Member States will be abolished, following their progressive harmonisation up to 1992. If all of the Commission's proposals are accepted hauliers should be able to operate freely within the Community, carrying on their business wherever they wish.

Similar deregulation will be applied to shipping, civil aviation and road passenger transport. At the time of going to press the question of a Common Shipping Policy was still under review, but the intention was to liberalise the industry in a way similar to the proposals for road freight. In air transport, the Commission's Transport Council (1987) agreed a series of measures intended to lead to greater competition between airlines, to open up more new routes (including 60 out of the United Kingdom), to effectively bar cartels and price fixing, and to reduce passenger fares as a result. The present national restrictions on passenger coach services are also being tackled.

Finally, the advent of the Channel Tunnel will provide a boost to rail transport, with international through-train services expanded to and from Europe. These should speed the flow both of people and goods, as well as improving road links between Britain and mainland Europe.

The existing transport regulations and their progressive liberalisation are both complex areas. In addition to outline material available from the Department of Trade and Industry, a comprehensive set of guides is available from the Department of Transport, International Road Freight Office, Newcastle upon Tyne. These include detailed guidance notes and all the regulations applicable to each European country (including non-EEC). In addition, the exporter can consult the Road Haulage Association and/or the Freight Transport Association for more information and advice. Practical help can also be obtained from the Routiers Drivers Club. All these bodies and their addresses are listed in the Department of Transport's comprehensive booklet *A Guide to Taking your Lorry Abroad* which is essential reading for the exporter.

Harmonisation of technical standards

As we have seen different national standards are an effective barrier to free trade within Europe. They add to the cost of product research and development, and prevent the mass manufacture of many simple components that could benefit from economies of scale. The problems arise as a result of the non-recognition of each others' national standards by certification and regulatory bodies such as the British Standards Institute (BSI), France's AFNOR or West Germany's DIN organisation.

The Community's approach is twofold. It encourages moves towards mutual recognition of national standards so that products passed as acceptable in one country will also be allowed into another without further testing and approval, and it promotes a harmonised European Standard under the auspices of the European Standardisation Committee (CEN) and the European Standardisation Committee for Electrical Products (CENELEC). These bodies will recognise the existing national standards of the Member States (and also of the EFTA countries) and eventually a relevant European Standard will supplement the individual national standards.

A considerable amount of detailed work is still required at the European level, and the Department of Industry has pointed out that the British have not been as active as the French and Germans in joining the working groups of CEN and CENELEC. As a result they fear that British Standards, where these are superior, will not become the norm in Europe, and Britain will have only itself to blame. A comprehensive service of information, advice, consultancy and publications is available from Technical Help to Exporters, British Standards Institute, Linford Wood, Milton Keynes. Exporters should also consult their relevant trade and technical associations, particularly about volunteering to work with one of the European standards committees.

No discussion on technical standards is complete without mentioning European legislation covering the consumer and the environment. In the area of consumer protection a number of directives have been published. They cover misleading advertisements, product liability, safety of toys, price marking of goods, and regulations covering doorstep selling (mainly allowing a cooling-off period for certain sales contracts) and consumer credit (similar to Britain's current regulations). Further proposals are expected to cover product safety, with a general obligation to market only safe products, and such sectors as package holiday travel and electronic payment systems using credit and charge cards.

The Commission has for a long time expressed concern about protecting the European environment. Over 100 directives are already in force covering water and air pollution, and noise levels. Detailed advice should again be sought from the BSI and trade and technical associations.

Freedom to follow most trades and professions

One of the most significant benefits of 1992 will be the freedom it gives to both people and companies to set up business and work anywhere they wish within the Community. Not only does this mean the mutual recognition of personal qualifications, but also reforms of company laws and agreeing new regulations allowing the setting up of businesses in the financial and services sectors.

Working anywhere within Europe has traditionally been easier at the lower skills level while Professionally qualified people have found it difficult to practice where they wish. At the lower levels, the Community is already at work attempting to agree compatibility of national vocational qualifications, through the European Centre for the Development of Vocational Training (CEDEFOP). They have so far tackled qualifications within hotels and catering, construction, electrical and electronics, agriculture, and textiles, with further areas still to be covered. In addition new directives are being issued to ensure that Member States recognise the national qualifications (known as 'certificates of experience') of another state. Sectors already covered include insurance, some transport services, retailing, some areas of manufacturing and hairdressing.

Furthermore, those seeking work can make use of British Jobcentres to enquire about vacancies anywhere within the Community, and employers in the Community can notify vacancies to Jobcentres. Further information about mutual recognition of certificates or experience is available from the Internal European Policy Division of the DTI. Information on jobs abroad is obtainable from Jobcentres, and on social security from the Overseas Branch, Department of Social Security, Newcastle upon Tyne respectively.

At the professional level, moves towards mutual recognition of qualifications have been making slower and more uneven progress. A directive has been proposed requiring Member States to recognise each other's qualifications, with the object of opening up the market for the professions in Europe. Some aptitude testing or a period of supervised practice may still be required where standards are regarded as widely differing. The situation has been brought about partly as a result of the differing attitudes towards regulating the professions in Britain and the rest of Europe. Whereas in Britain many occupations are self-regulated by (chartered) associations to which membership access is more or less difficult, in the rest of Europe the tendency is for more of these occupations to be state regulated. There is also the question of agreeing definitions and titles: the term 'engineer' for example can, in Britain, mean either a fully qualified specialist with an advanced degree, or the man who comes to repair the washing machine. In Germany and France these definitions are more precise, and it is likely that the Europeans will move in this direction rather than adopting Britain's more laissez-faire attitude.

Accordingly, there are powerful arguments for British people to secure recognised national professional qualifications if they intend to practice in Europe, as this should automatically give them the right to enter even the 'restricted' occupations. This applies whether the appropriate United Kingdom body is a chartered association or not.

The Commission's proposals extend also to the provision of services not generally described as 'professions'. These include the more recent occupations such as computer consultancy or – in the Commission's words – 'activities of an industrial character, activities of a commercial character, activities of craftsmen and activities of the professions'. Firms or individuals carrying on such activities in their home country will have automatic right of establishment in another European country and/or the right to provide such services without actually setting-up an office in the host country. Two sorts of situations typical of those likely to occur are: the case of a British project engineer who temporarily supervises a construction site in, say,

Denmark; or a consultant who travels occasionally from Britain to advise clients in a number of European member states. While qualifications may be seen as desirable in all these occupations, the fact that a person is entitled to practice in his home country (and can provide documentation if required to show that this is the case) invariably means that he or she will have the right to follow that occupation in all the other Member States.

Further information should be obtained from the relevant professional association in the United Kingdom or the Internal European Policy Division of the DTI. The Commission's own booklet *The Professions in the European Community* by J.-P. de Crayencour is the definitive guide in this area and describes a number of test cases which have reached the level of the European Court.

As much business is conducted through the means of the private or public limited company, the Commission has published a number of directives aimed at harmonising the company regulations of the Member States. They include some less popular proposals such as employee participation, which is commoner in Europe than in Britain, but most of the regulations apply to accounting practices, publication of annual figures, qualifications of auditors, operation of branches and subsidiaries, and the conduct of mergers. The creation of a new legal entity the 'European Economic Interest Grouping' has been proposed to enable closer cooperation between companies in joint ventures such as research and development or marketing, without the need for the companies to merge or form a joint subsidiary. (See further Chapter 10).

Another proposal is for the single person company. At present most Member States require a minimum of two people to form a private company. The new proposal would enable a single person to do so, hence reducing his or her liability in the event of failure, and providing a useful alternative to sole proprietorship.

Practical information about the type of company options available in the Member States is given later in this book on a country by country basis. Qualified accountants and solicitors should be consulted at all stages about the existing and proposed legislation.

Capital movements and other benefits

Although exchange controls had been abolished (at the time of writing) in the United Kingdom, some controls were applied by other Member States. A directive removing all controls was adopted in June 1988. This applied to all the Member States with effect from July 1990 with additional time extensions (to the end of 1992) for Spain, Portugal, Greece and Ireland. These measures are designed to facilitate the freer movement of capital within the Community. Practical benefits would include the right of a French person to borrow from an English bank or a Spaniard to invest his or her funds in another country.

Progress on the European Currency Unit or Ecu is less satisfactory. The value of the Ecu is calculated as a basket of set amounts of Community currencies, which are periodically reviewed. The Ecu is central to the operation of the European Monetary System (EMS) and its associated Exchange Rate Mechanism (ERM), which are designed to avoid wide fluctuations in exchange rates. Regrettably, at the time of writing, the United Kingdom, Greece and Portugal did not participate in the ERM.

In the area of fiscal reform, the Commission has put forward various proposals which will enable banks and insurance companies to operate more freely and across national borders within the Community. Among the practical benefits for the exporter will be a wider choice as consumer of these services.

The removal of border controls within Europe will necessitate harmonisation of VAT and excise rates – to discourage illegal trade in items which attract high rates in one country but not in another. Proposals include one for a two-tier VAT system to operate at Basic and Standard rates and agreement will have to be reached that some Zero-rated items (such as children's clothes and books in Britain) will in future be subject to VAT.

Finally, the opening up of public purchasing will allow all companies a fair chance of competing to supply the goods and services required by government and other public bodies within Europe – currently reckoned to be worth some 15% of the Community's gross domestic product. Although in the past lip service has been paid to the principle of open competition in public purchasing, numerous invisible but nonetheless effective barriers have frequently been placed in the way of would-be suppliers. These include failure to advertise tenders publicly, complicated specifications and tendering procedures, and policies of 'buying national'. Among the proposals are those for greater transparency in public purchasing, through wider advertising of tenders and advance publication of public procurement programmes. Further proposals are designed to help small and medium firms compete for public tenders. Information would be made available through the Small Firms Task Force and their BC-Net information service (discussed later).

Making yourself heard in Europe

The above programme has not and will not come about by accident. Rather it is the result of deliberations by the Common Market Commissioners and their staffs, who in turn are influenced by soundings taken among Euro MPs, the Economic and Social Committee and others, who hopefully find themselves listening at grassroots level. It is a terrible indictment of the European Community and its institutions that businessmen on the whole know so little about them. Who can name his European Member of Parliament, let alone the Director of DG XII (the directorate responsible for Science, Research and Development)? The Commission has itself to blame for much of the lack of interest in its operations. A recent report showed that, although a mass of information emanates from Brussels, much of it goes un-read. There was criticism of the Commission's own 'Official Journal' which was universally regarded as dull, badly laid out and poorly written. Much of the output from Brussels has been described as un-read and unreadable, put out by people with the best of intentions but lacking in communications skills.

However much this is true, the serious exporter has a duty to inform himself about Europe, to learn what is going on and what he or she can do to influence the decisions that have serious and long lasting implications for business life. There are numerous excellent books (plus the 1992 information pack freely available from the DTI) which describe the working of the various European institutions – the Commission (the Community's 'civil service'), the Councils (of

Ministers, Working Groups and Permanent Representatives), the
European Parliament and the Court of Justice. The exporter should
have a basic understanding of the legislative process, how Regulations, Directives, Decisions and Recommendations are formulated
and subsequently applied.

There are a number of points of information and influence. They
include United Kingdom offices of both the Commission and the
European Parliament (both located close to each other in Westminster). Both publish booklets and information packs, many of which
are free, and have a library and enquiry service. If it is necessary to
make direct approaches to the Commission in Brussels, the staff of
the United Kingdom Permanent Representative's Office can help
with information and contacts. They act rather like a permanent
British embassy to the Commission, working both as a listening post
and a channel of influence.

Up-to-date detailed information about proposed and actual Community legislation and much practical information is available on the
DTI's Spearhead Database. This is a computerised information bank,
which can be accessed online. Details are given in the DTI 1992
information pack.

Almost weekly there are seminars and conferences dealing with
1992. They are a useful, if sometimes expensive, way to get a first
taste of European issues.

It is likely that the exporter already belongs to a local Chamber of
Commerce and to one or more trade or professional associations.
Their role in market research is discussed later, but almost all of them
have active sections dealing with every aspect of Europe, as do
bodies such as the CBI and Institute of Directors. It is through active
participation in his or her representative body that the exporter can
and should both be informed about Europe and participate in the
policy formulation process.

The European institutions

This book was being completed in June 1989, around the time of the
Elections to the European Parliament. Despite the publicity surrounding that event and confirmed by informal researches among

British business people, there still appears to be a measure of ignorance about the main European institutions and how they work. This section is intended only as a brief guide to the workings of the European Community. It covers the Commission, the Councils of Ministers, the European Parliament, the Economic and Social Committee and the European Court.

The Commission

Politicians are fond of referring to 'the Brussels bureaucrats' who are portrayed as interfering, faceless men and women who are determined to control every aspect of our lives. The reality does not accord with this view. The European Commission, based at the Berlaymont Building in Brussels, can be regarded as the *Community's administrative organisation*. It is in fact quite small, comprising just over ten thousand employees, of whom one thousand are translators and interpreters. It is headed by seventeen Commissioners, drawn from each of the Member States (two each from Britain, France, Germany, Italy and Spain; one from each of the other Members). The President (currently M. Jacques Delors) is also a Commissioner who, together with his colleagues, is allocated a portfolio which includes a number of responsibilities (for example, Competition, Small Firms, Regional Policy). Each Commissioner is assisted by a small private office.

The Commission includes a Secretariat General, Legal Service, Statistical Office, Joint Interpreting and Conference Service, Euratom and a Publications Office. The work of the Commission is split between a number of Directorates-General comprising a permanent staff of officials and advisers. There are currently 22 Directorates General covering:

Directorate General I   External Relations
              II Economic and Financial Affairs
              III Internal Market and Industrial Affairs
              IV Competition
              V   Employment, Social Affairs and Education
              VI Agriculture
              VII Transport
              VIII Development

IX Personnel and Administration
X Information, Communication and Culture
XI Environment, Consumer Protection, Nuclear Safety
XII Science, Research and Development
XIII Telecommunications, Information Industries and In-
novation
XIV Fisheries
XV Financial Institutions and Company Law
XVI Regional Policy
XVII Energy
XVIII Credit and Investments
XIX Budgets
XX Financial Control
XXI Customs Union and Indirect Taxation
XXII Coordination of Structural Instruments

The names of principal staff inside each DG (together with the Commissioner with overall responsibility) are published periodically by the Commission. It is important to know who does what, as Commissioners and officials cannot intervene outside their areas of competence. The main role of the Commission is in proposing policy, which is then considered, accepted or rejected by the Councils of Ministers and the Parliament. It is responsible for implementing policy once it has been agreed.

Council of Ministers

The Councils of Ministers are more or less ad hoc bodies, comprising the Ministers from each Member State, depending upon the subject currently under discussion. Europe's Foreign Ministers attend Council meetings concerned with foreign affairs, the Agricultural Ministers those concerned with agriculture and so on. All the Community Prime Ministers meet in Council, for example when they all signed the Single European Act.

European Parliament

Initially known as the Assembly, the European Parliament comprises a single chamber of 518 MEPs elected from all twelve Member

States. The power of the Parliament has increased considerably since the Single European Act, and MEPs feel they are now starting to have a real influence on Community policy.

Members group together according to political persuasion rather than along national lines. The Parliament has the power, so far not excercised, to demand the resignation of the entire Commission. It can also influence budget expenditure. An up-to-date list of MEPs is available from the European Parliament Offices.

Economic and Social Committee

The Economic and Social Committee comprises a group of experts (just under 200) drawn from trade unions, trade and professional associations, consumer groups, etc., who meet monthly in full session and also divide their work among a series of ad hoc working parties. They have advisory status only, but are regarded as another point of influence on the Commission and other institutions. They deliver over a hundred Opinions every year and are a useful target for lobbyists and others seeking to influence European policy. A list of UK committee members is available from the Commission's London Offices.

The European Court of Justice

This body is located in Luxemburg, and should not be confused with the International Court at The Hague or the Court of Human Rights in Strasbourg. The Court comprises a panel of European judges and its task is to interpret and apply Community laws and make rulings in the case of disputes. Details of its rulings are widely published.

There has never been a better time

From what has been said already it should be clear that British companies are at the threshold of a unique, never-to-be-repeated marketing opportunity. 1992 has been described as a process of evolution rather than revolution, with some of its main effects not likely to be felt for ten or twenty years, well into the twenty-first century. The changes taking place will have profound effects on companies, changing the way they look at production, sales, marketing, distribution, finance, product development.

Among the key production related questions to ask are those concerning economies of scale, alterations to production processes, rationalisation of the product mix, switching from manufacture to buying-in, changing standards to comply with European norms. In sales and marketing, the export-led company will be looking at the new customers that can be reached, how they can be reached, what competing products exist, what are the promotional requirements, whether agents and distributors should be used. A study of distribution requirements will involve examining quantity and frequency of deliveries, utilisation of different transport services, possibly setting up European warehouses. Company purchasing policies may also be revised, as more goods and services become available from mainland European suppliers. In the professional and services sectors, as we have seen, new business opportunities also abound.

It is only by informing themselves about Europe and the opportunities for business that British companies will reap the benefits when 1992 opens up for business.

2 A first look at Western Europe

Treating the European market as a whole

The changes that are taking place between now and 1992 mean that the West European market can and should be treated by the British exporter as a single unit – an extension of his home market, with a total combined population of 320 million. This figure includes the United Kingdom's nearly 57 million and the remaining members of the Common Market of the Twelve – Republic of Ireland, Denmark, Netherlands, Belgium, Luxemburg, France, West Germany, Italy, Spain, Portugal and Greece.

This market can be considered as a geographic whole, and once the exporter starts travelling within mainland Europe he gradually becomes less aware of cross-border variations in architecture, lifestyle and patterns of spending. Indeed even before 1992, crossing borders was itself a matter of routine, with little more required than to slow down at a Customs post. It is this ease of movement into and out of countries that makes the United Kingdom's Continental neighbours so much more European in their outlook than the average Briton. Many Germans or Frenchmen are accustomed to visiting customers across national boundaries or simply doing their personal shopping in another country, the distances involved being no more than travelling from London to the West Country or Yorkshire. It is this 'European-ness' that many British business people lack and it can be cured only by frequent travel to mainland Europe and a genuine willingness to get to know the neighbours.

That said, in considering the European market as a whole, it is unfortunate that it is necessary to present much of the available statistical information needed to study the market on a country by country basis. This is because historically such information has always been collected this way. Record keeping and statistics are part of the systems of national government that will remain in place after 1992, but in dealing with the population structures, employment trends and major industries, although drawing on national statistics, we will continue to try and present a picture of Europe as a whole, as indeed it is. National boundaries are artifical demarcation points at best and can sometimes be ignored.

It must also be pointed out that the first-time exporter or the business person looking for an extension of activities inside Europe will probably want to approach the markets on a regional basis. Language differences alone, although these are blurring, may dictate this approach. It is also likely that the exporter will not wish to tackle all of the national markets at once. The emphasis in this book is therefore on the larger markets where business opportunities are considered to be greater (France, West Germany, Italy and Spain) and to a lesser extent on Benelux and Denmark, followed by Ireland, Portugal and Greece. The first four countries have similar sized populations and in the author's view offer the best opportunities for the export of both goods and services.

Getting to know West Europe

In Chapters 3 and 4 we shall explain how the exporter can set about getting to know West Europe by means of desk-based and field research. This chapter presents an over-view of Europe, attempting to highlight the principal demographic features (area, population, major conurbations, patterns of employment) and economic factors (unemployment, decline of traditional industries, rise in services, retailing patterns) that make West Europe in so many ways similar to Britain today. The fact that Britain's European partners have done generally better in solving their economic problems is also recorded. Each section concludes with some indications of where the best market opportunities are thought to lie.

But before getting into such essential detail the exporter should do everything he can to 'get a feel for Europe'. If he does not have the opportunity for regular European travel on business or pleasure, he should at least buy a large map of Europe, hang it on the office wall, and make a point of studying it regularly. To check out your knowledge of Europe try a simple test. Without looking at the map try and locate the cities of Arhus, Utrecht, Hannover, Koblenz, Mannheim, Rennes, Narbonne, Toledo, Verona and Rimini. If you scored less than five out of ten, you clearly need to brush up your knowledge of Europe!

Europe's population structure

The combined population of the European Community, including Britain, is 320 million. This represents less than 7% of the total world population. However, the combined populations of the Community are greater than the Soviet Union (279 million), the United States (239 million) and Japan (121 million) but less than those of India (over 700 million) and China (over 1,000 million inhabitants). It is convenient to consider the European Community market as roughly equivalent to the combined populations of USA and Japan. Broken down by country the populations are as follows:

Country	Male Population	Female Population	Total	No. of households
Belgium	4.81	5.04	9.85	3.72
Denmark	2.5	2.6	5.1	2.2
France	26.8	28.3	55.1	19.6
West Germany	29.2	31.8	61.0	26.4
Greece	4.73	5.01	9.74	2.98
Ireland	1.7	1.8	3.5	0.98
Italy	27.8	29.4	57.2	19.9
Luxemburg	–	–	0.37	–
Netherlands	7.2	7.3	14.5	5.5
Portugal	4.9	5.2	10.1	3.4
Spain	18.5	19.2	38.7	10.8
United Kingdom	27.6	29.19	56.8	21.3

Table 2.1 Population (in millions) per country
(*Based on Statistics of the Community, 1988*)

As can be seen there are wide variations in population, from the five Common Market Members (Germany, Italy, United Kingdom, France and Spain) who dominate the Market, down to countries with extremely small populations (the Netherlands, Portugal, Belgium, Greece, Denmark, Ireland and Luxemburg). However, for marketing purposes there are recognisable groupings such as Spain and Portugal and the Benelux (Belgium, Netherlands. Luxemburg) that help to balance these extremes of size. For those looking at geographical Europe, the addition of five (currently) non-EEC states adds a further 31 million people:

Country	Population
Finland	4.75
Norway	4.04
Sweden	8.30
Austria	7.5
Switzerland	6.5

Although geographers plot precise national areas and population densities, the latter are distorted by the high numbers of people living in large conurbations where the population density exceeds 350 people per square kilometre. Looking at the map of Europe (the Community) overall, the most densely populated areas stretch along a broad diagonal line which starts in North West England, passes through London and the South East, Southern Holland/Northern Belgium, Germany's Rhine/Ruhr conurbation, through to industrialised northern Italy (see p.32). Outside these areas three other major population centres occur – Greater Paris, Madrid and Barcelona, and the area around Naples.

In terms of populations the main conurbations are given in Table 2.2 and, as the Table shows, only Germany's Rhine/Ruhr industrial area and Paris have populations equivalent to that of London. Some seventeen towns are grouped together in the Rhine/Ruhr. Their suburbs tend to merge, creating one enormous conurbation.

Population densities in Europe are generally much higher than in the United States and Soviet Union, the highest being in Belgium,

Figure 2.1 Densely populated diagonal

United Kingdom	London	7 680 000
	West Midlands	2 360 000
	Manchester	2 340 000
	West Yorkshire	1 480 000
	Glasgow	1 210 000
	Tyneside	780 000
	Liverpool	750 000
Ireland	Dublin	920 000
Denmark	Copenhagen	1 370 000
Netherlands	Rotterdam	1 030 000
	Amsterdam	940 000
Belgium	Brussels	1 280 000
West Germany	Rhine/Ruhr	7 790 000
	West Berlin	1 870 000
	Munich	1 840 000
	Hamburg	1 620 000
France	Paris	8 710 000
	Lyon	1 220 000
	Marseille	1 110 000
	Lille	940 000
Spain	Madrid	4 170 000
	Barcelona	2 700 000
	Valencia	850 000
Portugal	Lisbon	1 300 000
Italy	Milan	2 810 000
	Rome	2 790 000
	Naples	2 520 000
	Turin	1 480 000
	Genova	800 000
Greece	Athens	3 030 000

Table 2.2 The main conurbations
Source – Eurostat, Luxemburg

Netherlands and Germany; followed by the United Kingdom, Denmark, Portugal and France. France and Spain are roughly twice the geographical area of the United Kingdom, with smaller populations and considerably less (average) population density.

Another trend to note is the decline in the European birthrate, compared with the United States and the Soviet Union. Since the mid-1960s the European birthrate has slumped. Only Ireland and Spain are achieving zero growth (population replacement by equal numbers of births to deaths) while in Germany each new generation is smaller than its predecessor. Predictions from 1985 to 2005 are for a population growth rate of only 2%, compared to 17% in the United States and Soviet Union, 8% in Japan and a world average as high as 36%

A study of the 'age pyramid' for Europe shows an increasingly elderly population compared with the rest of the world, with fewer younger people available to support them. Among the reasons given for the declining population are the demands for higher living standards and the hard work needed to achieve them; the employment of women; the decline of the family unit; and attitudes to birth control.

The low birth rates of the 1960s mean there are fewer children in school in Europe today than a decade ago. The numbers peaked in 1977/78 to around 72 million, but fell ten years later to around 68 million. The shortages of teenagers currently available for work are finally being noted by government and employers, and the shortages are being made more acute by the fact that in some European countries children are staying longer in full-time education. Of these there are now almost equal numbers of girls and boys in secondary education, and significant increases in the number of girls at the higher education and university levels. Succeeding generations will on the whole be better educated than their parents.

Of the subjects studied in schools and colleges, there has been an increase in the social sciences, followed by the arts and teacher training courses. Medical, engineering and the natural sciences come next. Over six million European students are now attending universities or higher education colleges, almost double the number in 1970.

Languages form an important part of European education, with generally greater numbers of Europeans able to speak English and other foreign languages. These compare unfavourably with the average Briton's lack of fluency in French, German, Spanish or Italian which is a serious draw-back when conducting European business. The following table shows the main trends:

Belgians	26% speak English, 71% French, 68% Flemish, 22% German
Danes	51% Speak English, 48% German
French	26% speak English, 13% Spanish, 11% German
Germans	43% speak English, 18% French
Irish	12% speak French, 2% German
Italians	13% speak English, 27% French
Dutch	68% speak English, 67% German, 31% French
Spanish	13% speak English, 15% French
British	15% speak French, 6% German

Table 2.3 *Source – Gallup (survey of adults over 18)*

Employment and unemployment

The overall patterns in Europe are remarkably similar to the problems faced in the United Kingdom. As a result of the post-war baby boom, the adult working population increased by some 12% between 1970–85. The problem has been compounded until recently by the smaller numbers of people just reaching retirement age, that is, those who were born during the First World War. At the same time there has been an increase of nearly ten per cent in the active population (those seeking work) combined with job losses in many sectors of the economy. The result has been widespread unemployment, which over the same period has risen from 3 million at the start of the 1970s to more than 14 million or more than 10% of the active population during the 1980s. Many of those seeking work are women, reflected in the rise of 18% in the female active population (45 to 53 million).

In contrast with the United states and Japan, fewer new jobs have been created in Europe. America has succeeded in creating overall 21 million jobs, of which 4 million are in industry; and the Japanese 6 million (1.5 million in industry). Industrial job losses in 1981/82, around the time of the second oil price rises, were equally severe in Europe (over 3 million), the United States (2 million) and Japan (0.5 million). However, in comparison with population numbers, Europe has failed to make up the deficit by creating more non-manufacturing jobs. Despite its size Europe has created only 10 million new jobs in services. This is still less than the 17 million new service jobs in America and contrasts poorly with the 4.5 million in Japan.

Many service jobs are either temporary and/or part time, although regarded by some as a first step up the employment ladder. Women now account for 37% of the 124 million jobs available in the Community, but only one job in six is held by a person under 25. This is a reflection of the small number of 'real jobs' being created. Industrial jobs now number 41 million of the total 124 million jobs within the Community (or 33%), while the services sector numbers 73 million jobs (or 59% of the total). Of these service jobs, nearly half are held by women. Part-time jobs are also increasing and now total around 14 million within the Community, most of them being held (70%) by married women.

Overall the rate of unemployment in Europe rose from 5 million in 1975 (2.9%) to around 16 million (average 11%) in 1986. There have been a number of distinct phases in the rise in unemployment, but the rate of increase is reckoned to have slowed down. However, larger numbers of people are still seeking work as part of the 'active population'. The highest levels – around 20% – have been seen in Ireland and Spain, the lowest in West Germany (7.1%) (and Luxemburg with just 2.5%). Belgium and Italy have also suffered rates of around 15% and France, Netherlands and the United Kingdom all at around 11–12%.

Within each Community State unemployment levels vary geographically, but tend to be high in the (former) heavy industrial areas and in major centres of population. A worryingly universal trend is the length of time people have been out of work. Overall, more than half have been unemployed for more than a year, one third for more than two years. This proportion is higher in the United Kingdom, Belgium, Netherlands and Italy. Young people under 25 appear to fare worst, accounting for 23% of the jobless total. This problem is particularly acute in Italy.

Prosperous Europeans?

In spite of high levels of unemployment, the average European in work has enjoyed a rise in living standards resulting from a doubling of his or her income since 1960. Europe's increased gross domestic product (GDP) compares with a fourfold increase in Japan and only 60% in the United States, but wide variations tend to distort these figures. Coming from a lower base, the economies of Greece, Portugal and Spain have shown the fastest annual increases (4.5% to 5% annually). But it should be borne in mind that the five largest member states are together responsible for nearly 90% of the Community's GDP. Variations also occur within countries, with greater prosperity observed in northern Italy compared with the south; north eastern Spain (Basque country), Barcelona, Madrid compared with the rest of Spain; Britain's south east compared with the industrial north and north west. Again some Community countries such as Germany and Denmark enjoy considerably higher GDPs than Greece, Portugal and Spain. And even the highest Community consumption levels are lower than those in the United States, but roughly on a level with Japan's.

Consumption patterns also vary widely between countries. In prosperous Denmark above average amounts are spent by households on accommodation and heating, transport, communications and recreation, whereas in Greece nearly half of the household budget goes on food, drink and tobacco. Danish consumption is similar to the American pattern and in general spending on transport and recreation is growing fastest (by 75% between 1970 – 1985) in the developed economies of Europe. However, prices for accommodation, medical care, energy and fuel have tended to rise faster than the costs of food and clothing. This has a corresponding effect on spending patterns and on the statistics used to illustrate them.

Consumption by the government stands at around 20% in most countries, although it is higher in Denmark at 30% (compared with Japan's 15%). Household spending is also conditioned both by taxation (what is left of take home pay after taxes) and wage levels. Table 2.4 illustrates the average proportion of take-home pay after taxes in the Community states.

As can be seen, with the exception of Denmark which has a higher proportion of government spending, the remaining EEC countries pay approximately the same amount of salaries and wages in taxation, with or without the inclusion of various forms of family

	Avge. take-home pay as % of gross earnings	
	Excl. family benefit	Incl. family benefit
Belgium	70%	82%
Denmark	60%	64%
France	85%	82%
West Germany	72%	77%
Ireland	75.5%	79%
Netherlands	65%	74%
Spain	86%	87%
United Kingdom	73%	82%

Table 2.4 Average take-home pay after taxes
Source – Eurostat

benefits. Even the Netherlands' system redresses the balance when family credits are included.

Industrial and white collar pay levels tend to be higher in Europe than their equivalents in the United Kingdom. Making direct comparisons is not always easy, but recent executive salary surveys put pay levels in the developed European countries at one-and-a-half to two times the British equivalent. Obviously this is not true for all jobs and Europe has pockets of extreme poverty similar to those in Britain. But given the similar levels of taxation, it is possible to observe that Britain's European neighbours are in general better off. This can be noted by even the casual observer in the quality of homes and furnishings, newer cars on the road, clothing, etc., as well as in the (generally) superior quality of public services such as railways and roads. With some glaring exceptions there is considerably less of the squalor that characterises so much of Britain today.

European industry

As was noted in the study of unemployment patterns, European industries have shed large numbers of jobs in the last ten to fifteen years. Losses have been most severe in the traditional 'smokestack' industries. Among the worst affected are heavy metals with nearly 35% reduction of the workforce, textiles (28%), chemicals (20%), vehicle manufacturing (14%), oil refining (12%) and general and electrical engineering (each 9%). Among the reasons for the decline is Europe's reliance on imported raw materials (oil, copper and iron ore, etc.) which were subject to price rises from the early 1970s, leading to balance of payments problems. The result was higher prices for finished goods which led in turn to lack of competitivity, industrial restructuring and subsequent job losses. As a result an overall 13% of industrial jobs have vanished (4.3 million).

However, despite both its losses and cutbacks, European industry is still a world leader in some sectors. The Community produces over 30% of private cars – around 10 million vehicles annually, putting it ahead of Japan and the United States; nearly 20% of steel (again ahead of Japan and the United States), 20% of synthetic textiles (USA 24%), 10-11% of man-made textiles (similar to Japan, United States), and 15% cement (Japan 10%). Europe lags behind in production of commercial vehicles, however, at just over 10%, against contributions to world production of 30% by the United States and 40% by Japan.

Although some industries are declining and newer ones coming to the fore, export opportunities arise across all sectors and a view of Europe needs to be tempered with an understanding of the import-ance of each sector to national economies. Some of these are now examined.

West German industry

Since the early 1980s there has been a shakeout in West German manufacturing industry. After thirty years of near unparalleled growth, the industrial economy, though still accounting for half of the gross national product, has been faced with a number of prob-lems. These include very high labour costs – German workers are among the best paid in the world – and too rigid reliance on tradi-tional industries with some evidence of a reluctance to change. Large scale industry closures tend to have a knock-on effect in areas of already high unemployment, and political and social considerations have sometimes been balanced by purely economic judgements. However, many companies have shown considerable resilience in their response to decline through measures such as concentrating on specialised products for niche markets, and improving profitability. Although the number of manufacturing establishments has been reduced by two-thirds since the mid-1960s to under 40,000, many of these are still small and medium sized companies who have reacted more swiftly to the changing industrial climate. Growth industries include those in higher technology. There is generally less movement towards services in Germany than is evidenced in other European countries and overall jobs in manufacturing have still risen.

Despite cutbacks in both manpower and output, West Germany's *iron and steel industries* remain the world's third largest behind those of the United States and Japan. The workforce has been halved from over 300,000 in the late 1970s to around 150,000, with the process of slimming down being somewhat eased by government assistance and the cooperation of the trade unions. There was a temporary boom in 1984/85 but this was then affected by the strength of the D-mark which reduced exports, and an increase in cheaper steel imports which gradually took 40% of the home market. Today the industry's fortunes are governed by Community quotas for steel output, which forces many plants to operate at less than capacity. The industry's response has been a predictable mixture of mergers, diversification into other products areas, specialisation and the manufacture of higher added-value products such as special, coated steels.

Similar restructuring has taken place inside the *chemicals industry*, which is still dominated by the giant companies Bayer, BASF and Hoechst. There has been some over-capacity but by switching product emphasis, new investment, aggressive marketing overseas and increased expenditures on research and development, the chemicals industries have not had to cut back on jobs. Just under 600,000 are now employed in this sector.

Germany's *motor vehicle industry* remains under threat from imports, with Japanese cars accounting for nearly half of the 30% of imported cars. However, the reputations of companies like BMW, Porsche and Daimler Benz have ensured that output has been around 4 million new cars annually, over half of which go for export. The industry's problems include again high labour costs and the competition from Japan and Japanese-owned plants within the EEC. Germany's car makers have reacted by promoting their own overseas investments in countries with cheaper labour costs both inside the Community (Spain) and further afield (South Korea).

The country's other core manufacturing industry, *general engineer-*

ing, has again had to face problems of imports (from Japan) but dominance by small/medium-sized companies (90% employing less than 500 people) has enabled the industry to react by diversification, investment in automated machine tools, and specialised marketing. Germany's larger engineering companies have reacted in similar ways, though some have suffered job losses.

Dominated by Robert Bosch and the Siemens group West Germany's *electrical industries* have tended to remain within the traditional sectors such as electric motors, while losing ground to the Japanese and the Americans in higher technologies. They are, however, fighting back. Much of the impetus has come from Siemens who have set up a large research and development base near Munich, employing some 7000 technicians. There are also several cooperation and collaboration agreements, such as between Siemens and Philips of Holland for the manufacture of semiconductors, and with various European partners in defence electronics. There is less growth in consumer electronics, but evidence of specialisation in areas such as process control systems, medical and laboratory equipment, advanced manufacturing and telecommunications.

Britain remains a major supplier of goods and services to West Germany. Among the opportunities for British exporters of capital goods, the British Overseas Trade Board lists:

Advanced manufacturing equipment in electronics
Automotive components
CAD/CAM equipment
Educational software
Electrical equipment
Environmental protection
Heating and ventilation equipment
Machine tools
Office machinery
Opto-electronics
Passive components
Printing machinery
Process plant
Scientific instruments
Security equipment

Semiconductors and semiconductor manufacturing equipment
Telecommunications

Industry in France

France's industries contribute significantly less (around 30%) to the country's gross national product, which is supported by a large services sector (40%). Services now employ nearly 5 million people, equivalent to the numbers working in industry. Many of the industrial problems noted in West Germany are to be found in France. The French state, however, plays a major role in industry through planning, ownership (banks, some industries) and generally through closer involvement by such means as taxation, investment, interchange of government and industry personnel.

Cutbacks have taken place in such sectors as coal mining, steel, shipbuilding, and textiles, although some traditional industries (engineering, vehicles, railway equipment) have survived and new ones such as aerospace and telecommunications expanded. However, these last two sectors are increasingly related to defence projects. Some of the threats from Japan have been countered by restrictions on imports, such as a ceiling on the number of cars. About half of France's total exports go to the Community (with West Germany her major trading partner), with the United States the second most important market. In some areas such as machinery and machine tools France faces stiff competition from West Germany, Italy, the United States and inevitably Japan.

France's *steel industries* have been cut back, and two state-owned companies Sacilor and Usinor merged. Lack of demand has been due to the overall reduction in heavy engineering and shipbuilding, which is now reduced to one major yard at St-Nazaire. Motor vehicle output is also down, at around 3 million cars annually, and there have been a number of mergers – Peugeot with Citroen/Chrysler, and Renault's stake in American Motors. The two major groups, Peugeot/Citroen and Renault each have about about 30% of the French car market and around 10% of the rest of Europe. Ford, Fiat and Germany's Audi/BMW each have around ten per cent of the French new car market.

France's major *chemical companies* are state-owned and include Rhone-Poulenc, Atochem (a subsidiary of Elf) and CDF Chimie.

France is a net exporter of chemical products, including agro-chemicals, petrochemicals and plastics. Competition in traditional areas such as fertilisers comes from East Europe and there is considerable over-capacity in synthetic fibres and some bulk chemicals. There has been some investment in the newer sectors such as biotechnology, and the market for pharmaceuticals is strong. Many French-based pharmaceutical companies are in fact subsidiaries of foreign (usually Swiss or German) parents.

As already noted much of France's involvement in aerospace is defence related, and this sector comprises some 200 companies. The industry is dominated by Thomson-CSF and Aerospatiale (the makers of Exocet missiles). Major projects include nuclear weapons, radar, communications, nuclear powered submarines, missiles (Matra) and fighter aircraft (Dassault). The joint European Airbus in which France, Germany, Spain and the United Kingdom each have a share is the main civil aerospace project, with nearly 40% stake held by the French (including Snecma engines). The sector is highly competitive with Boeing and McDonnell Douglas in the United States.

The boom in *telecommunications*, albeit from a very low base 20 years ago, has resulted in a strengthened industry producing modern digital switching equipment, satellite systems and fibre optics. One of the industry's greatest successes has been Minitel, which is similar to Britain's Prestel but has many more users as a result of the widespread free issue of basic Minitel sets to telephone subscribers.

France's *high-technology sector* has been encouraged and now comprises 500 or more companies producing systems and software. The industry is dominated by IBM France (more or less independent). Other major companies include Burroughs, Bull, Digital and Hewlett Packard. The government has been heavily involved in promoting both national and Community sponsored research programmes, although joint ventures with overseas partners and more in-house research can be expected in future.

No discussion of French industry is complete without at least passing reference to the importance of the country's *agriculture, food and wine industries*. The export of cereals, oilseeds and sugar have in particular helped to boost French agricultural exports by nearly 100% in recent years.

Opportunities for British exporters in the capital goods sector include many types of machinery and process equipment (for example in textiles, printing, converting); electronics components, laboratory and scientific equipment; and automobile components. French investment in capital equipment continued at very high levels during 1988, with much of the emphasis on equipment designed to improve productivity. However as wage levels remain lower than in Germany, French companies are succeeding in competing against their industrial neighbours. As a boost to the domestic economy, some VAT levels have been reduced and incentives created towards helping the unemployed and encouraging job creation.

Industry in Italy

The casual visitor to Italy can easily gain an incorrect impression of business prospects in a country of extreme contrasts. The poverty and lack of industry in the middle and south of the country bear little relation to the visible signs of enterprise and prosperity found around Milan and Turin in the north. Here are many small firms, often working in the shadow of giants like Fiat and Olivetti, located in well-equipped factories run by dynamic young entrepreneurs. Indeed, the country is distinguished by the large number of small and medium enterprises as many former workers become bosses, leaving larger companies to set up their own businesses often with considerable encouragement and support from socialist regional governments.

There is also a considerable state-run sector in the form of IRI (Instituto per la Ricostruzione Industriale) which owns over 600 companies in all sectors of industry, including steel, engineering and services such as banking and air transport. Created by Mussolini in 1933 as a reaction to the Depression IRI started life as a rescue service for ailing industries, and gradually rose to become Italy's largest industrial concern with over 1000 companies. At its height it owned Europe's largest steel company, Italy's television network, the airline Alitalia, car makers Alfa Romeo – and suffered losses equivalent to 8% of turnover! As an employer of over half a million people IRI was and remains a major factor in the Italian economy.

Since 1981 it has undergone considerable reorganisation. There have been staff reductions and replacements, a hiving-off of some parts, a mixture of privatisation and joint state participation, and considerable improvement in the group's fortunes. IRI still owns several of Italy's major banks, the airline Alitalia, Autostrade (high-ways), Italtel (switching systems) and major companies in engineer-ing, steel making, shipbuilding, aerospace and electronics. Alfa Romeo has been sold to Fiat, and numerous mergers and cooperation agreements have been negotiated. Its high-technology arm STET is a major force, sometimes in partnership with IBM, in telecommunica-tions, micro-electronics and robotics.

The state-run company ENI is also involved in hydro-carbon fuels and EFIM in light engineering. ENI has shares in nearly 300 com-panies, and employs around 100,000 people; EFIM has 140 share-holdings and 60,000 employees. IRI's semiconductor company ERS now cooperates with Thomson (France) on developing a new super memory chip. IRI has also extended its activities overseas, and has over a hundred companies abroad which it controls or has a major stake in. Overall, its activities rank IRI fourteenth in the world in turnover, and it is the third largest company outside the United States. Losses have been reduced and, where they do occur, tend to be in the traditional sectors such as steel and shipbuilding.

As noted elsewhere Italy does have serious unemployment prob-lems, particularly among the young, and due in part to the disparity between north and south and the country's share of Europe's declin-ing industries. A special government fund helps compensate those who find themselves out of work as a result of company restructur-ing or industry decline. Any lack of support for those out of work is partly eased by help from close knit and extensive family ties and a thriving black economy. The spread of industry is, however, un-even.

Northern Italy – around Milan with its 4 million population – houses the country's major industries including steel, heavy en-gineering, plastics, machine tools, oil refining, electronics and domestic manufactures (clothing, shoes, furniture etc.). Despite the decline in some of the traditional industries, living standards are as high or higher than in the United Kingdom, and 40% above those in the rest of Italy. The region boasts 130,000 manufacturing establish-ments and is responsible for 40% of Italy's industrial output.

Another important manufacturing centre is Turin, home of Fiat, of much of Italy's aerospace and robotics industries, and of high technology. Fiat's interests are wide ranging and in addition to cars and commercial vehicles include tractors, earth moving equipment, railway rolling stock, machine tools, civil engineering, energy, and services. Olivetti with 21 factories in Italy and abroad manufactures a full range of office equipment, including computers. Fiat has been the subject of an extensive turn-around since the late 1970s. It now has joint ventures with Iveco/Ford in trucks, with Lucas and Matra in components, with General Motors in manufacturing systems, and with Rolls Royce and Pratt & Whitney in aerospace. Fiat also joined with United Technologies to buy a share in Westland helicopters. Fifty per cent of Italy's industrial robots are in Fiat's Turin factories (1600 of them). Fiat Auto now dominates the Italian motor industry and is Europe's leading and most profitable car maker.

Other industries located in a broad arc from the French borders in the west to Venice and the Adriatic in the east include ports and shipping, engineering, paper making, printing, textiles, clothing, and household manufactures. As one moves south industries tend to be smaller scale (clothing, ceramics, electronics, medical equipment) in the region between the industrial north and the capital Rome. Rome itself houses the head offices of many Italian companies and nationalised industries, and is the seat of government. There is some light manufacturing but the main employment is in the services sector.

The southern part of Italy has been the subject of government action to reduce reliance on agriculture. As a result major industries have been set up, including petrochemicals, iron, steel, shipbuilding, aircraft (around Naples), motor vehicles. These heavy industries tend to be concentrated, so that there are pockets of prosperity alongside regions of extreme poverty.

Nearly half of Italy's total export trade is with the rest of the EEC, her principal partners being France and West Germany. These two countries are also Italy's main suppliers: Germany has around 15% of Italy's imports and France 12%. These contrast with Britain's less than 5% share. The British Overseas Trade Board have identified a number of promising areas for British exporters. (These opportunities are explained fully in the BOTB's Country Profile booklet on Italy). They include:

- telematics;
- telecoms equipment;
- software;
- automation;
- robotics;
- CAD/CAM;
- medical and hospital equipment (all regarded as high priority);
- microcomputers for education, electronic components, energy conservation, anti pollution, waste recycling (priority);
- chemicals, clothing, heating and ventilation, railway equipment.

Industries in the Benelux countries

The Benelux Union comprises the countries of Belgium, Netherlands and the Grand Duchy of Luxemburg, although all three countries are independent Member States of the European Community of the Twelve. They are therefore discussed separately below.

The Netherlands has a history of trade dating back to before the 17th century and the country's major port of Rotterdam has long been regarded as the gateway to Europe. Because of the country's entrepreneurial spirit and small size, few heavy industries were created until the early part of the twentieth century, with the advent of coal mining. This was followed by post-war discoveries of oil and natural gas in the Dutch sector of the North Sea, the phasing out of coal mining and government moves to encourage the establishment of foreign companies in Holland. The Netherlands now plays an important role as major international importer/exporters.

Industrial expansion has taken place mainly in the west (coastal) regions, where population densities are high. Over 65% of the country is still given over to agriculture, principally dairy farming, and horticulture.

There are a number of international companies such as Philips, Unilever and Shell, with considerable emphasis on *oil, natural gas and petroleum, chemicals, shipbuilding;* and more recently *paper manufacture and processing, printing, mechanical engineering, energy*. The Netherlands are the fourth largest producer of natural gas in the world, with both off and onshore reserves that will last into the twenty-first century. A third of the labour force work in industry. The decline in world demand for large tankers has reduced the numbers working in shipbuilding and associated industries. Steel making at the Hoogovens plant has been cut back, in line with Community quota requirements. The chemicals industries based near Rotterdam are, however, generally buoyant.

In *electrical and electronics manufacturing* the industry is dominated by Philips, based at Eindhoven. The company operates in virtually all sectors from heavy electrical equipment to instruments, medical equipment, telecommunications, computers, television, video recorders and domestic appliances.

There is also a growing *services sector,* not only supplying the country's native industries, but also in the form of head offices of major civil engineering, consulting, accountancy and financial services companies whose operations extend throughout the Community and the rest of the world.

Not surprisingly, the Netherlands trades actively with other Members of the Community, who together account for 80% of total exports and 70% of imports. Despite the country's small size with just 5% of the Community's population, the Netherlands accounts for 10% of all Community foreign trade. Her main trading partner is West Germany, with whom she enjoys excellent communication links along the river Rhine, and by road, rail and air. It is the Netherlands' entrepot functions that make it attractive to the British exporter, in addition to the country's major native manufacturing and processing industries. Apart from petroleum products and chemicals, the main trade is in office machinery and data processing, electrical and process machinery, and road vehicles. There has been a significant rise in the number of computers sold to The Netherlands, along with software and services, and systems connected with automation and control of manufacturing plants. Another predicted growth sector is in equipment for power generation and distribution, and all types of equipment needed by the oil and gas industries.

Belgium is also well placed to serve the needs of the European exporter. Not only does it have important native industries of steel making, petrochemicals, materials processing and food, but the country enjoys a high standard of living and is readily accessible to the rest of the Market. Nearly two-thirds of the Community's population are within 200 miles of Brussels and can for the most part be reached by direct, fast motorway links.

This favoured location has led to considerable investment in Belgium by companies such as Wiggins Teape (at Nivelles, south of Brussels) and Ford at Antwerp, and companies seeking a European distribution point for their (consumer) goods.

Belgium's natural locational advantages have to some degree offset the declines in the textiles industries located to the northern (Flemish speaking) part of the country and mining and iron and steel making to the south (Wallonia, where French is spoken). However, the northern part of the country (Flanders) is benefiting also from more recently established industries, and the activity at the port of Antwerp. Unemployment has been on a par with the rest of Europe but inflation somewhat lower.

About 75% of Belgian exports are to the rest of the Community, and her principal suppliers are West Germany, France, The Netherlands, Italy and the United Kingdom. Devaluation of the Belgian franc in 1982 led in part to Belgium's first trade surplus for several years in 1986. There is a steady demand for most capital goods: process equipment, NC machine tools, automation systems, container and port equipment, medical equipment and domestic electrical items.

The tiny **Grand Duchy of Luxemburg** has a number of industries, including steel making which still accounts for some 40% of its exports. The state, subsidised Arbed company has suffered losses and cutbacks, but workers have been re-employed in the public sector and elsewhere, giving the Duchy one of the lowest levels of unemployment in the Community. Major industries have also been attracted, including Goodyear, Du Pont and General Motors, and there are important high technology processing industries in the northern part of the country (around Wiltz). British industrial exports to Luxemburg include machinery and process equipment.

Spanish industry
Spanish industry has been enjoying a recovery in recent years, much of it promoted by the socialist government elected in 1982, and given the added stimulus of Spain's entry into the Common Market in

1986. Two basic needs were identified: to reduce Spain's reliance on the traditional industries, in decline as elsewhere in Europe; and to make the country's remaining old industries more competitive, as well as encouraging new ones. The programme has included extensive modernisation and privatising some of the public companies formerly part of the state holding company INI. Spain also participates in a number of the European joint research programmes.

Like its counterpart in Italy, INI is a vast state-owned conglomerate, with wide ranging interests in traditional and heavy industries within Spain. Amongs its interests, where it owns generally close to 100%, are Iberia, the Spanish state airline; Aviaco, another airline; Seat cars; ENASA (automation); ENDESA (energy); and numerous companies involved in shipping, oil and gas exploration, steel, aluminium, minerals, fertilizers, food, defence and 'industrial promotion' of new and related enterprises. INH is a similar state-owned group, specialising in oil, gas, petroleum and petrochemicals. In 1981 the Spanish government also took over the RUMASA group, itself owning or controlling some 600 further enterprises.

The Spanish government is not totally happy with its status as a major industrial conglomerate, and over the last decade has drawn up rules for the conduct and management of state enterprises, including worker participation, decentralisation where appropriate, acquisitions and divestments, and the joint operation of some enterprises with the private sector (the Moncloa Pacts). There is also concern about the concentration of industry in certain provinces, to the economic detriment of others, and major manufacturers such as car makers have been encouraged to spread their operations as far as possible throughout Spain.

The country benefits from extensive receipts from 50 million tourists annually as well as exports of wine and food, which help to make these reforms possible. However, although public expenditure has been reduced and inflation controlled, these have been at the expense of unemployment, which at times has affected about one-fifth of the active population.

The need to modernise inevitably brings a requirement for capital goods across virtually all sectors, particularly those concerned with automation, control, environmental protection. The rise in the numbers attending schools and higher education has created a demand for equipment and materials for this sector. Spain is currently Britain's ninth largest export market and repays closer examination. With recognisable concentrations of people and industry around Madrid, Barcelona and the north east coastline the markets are relatively simple to manage in spite of the country's overall large size.

Portugal

Portugal is still a basically undeveloped economy, with nearly a quarter of the workforce employed in agriculture, although its output is small (6% of GDP). Industry employs a further 25% of the workforce and contributes 30% to GDP and 85% to total exports. These figures give an indication of this small (population 10 million) country's industrial status. However, the country's accession to the EEC in 1986 means that changes must take place and there is already considerable international investment in the country in industries connected with pulp and paper manufacture, textiles, (light) engineering and pharmaceuticals. The country has an important tourist industry, and some investment is evident in this sector.

Portugal's industrial base is in the north of the country, with Porto as its centre. Internal communications are still not particularly good nor are the road and rail links with Spain. Yet new small businesses are starting to appear alongside a new breed of independent entrepreneur.

Britain's exports to Portugal have declined dramatically, from being a major supplier of 50% of the country's imports in 1920 to less than ten per cent in recent years. There are nevertheless opportunities for the supply of manufacturing equipment, computers, water supply, pollution and environmental control equipment, communications systems. Industrial expansion is a mixture of both traditional industries and the newer technologies, with high levels of state involvement in many sectors. The market is small but worthy of further investigation and effort.

Denmark

Another even smaller market – of just 5 million people – is Denmark. It is, however, at the opposite end of the scale in terms of prosperity and industrial development. Denmark benefits from extensive natural resources of oil, fish and land for agriculture. Its industries are specialised and sometimes small, but they include shipbuilding, and internationally known names such as Lego, Bang & Olufsen, Grundfos (pumps), Danfoss (control equipment) and Novo (insulin).

West Germany and Sweden are the principal exporters to Denmark, followed by the United Kingdom. Growth areas include, among others, factory automation equipment and business systems and equipment.

The retail sector

With the convergence in consumer lifestyles it is in the retail sector that manufacturers of consumer goods face some of the greatest opportunities and challenges in the Europe of 1992 and beyond. The selling of consumer goods is discussed fully in Chapter 7 but a number of basic principles can be stated at this stage.

As noted in earlier sections one of the effects of de-regulation after 1992 will be the removal of physical barriers throughout the Community. The result is that transport and physical distribution of goods will become easier, with many companies already establishing mainland European warehouses, for example in Belgium. These are strategically sited to take advantage of Europe's extensive trunk road networks. From such locations consumer goods can be transported by road within a matter of hours to every part of West Europe. This is already happening and even from further afield (e.g. Spain), fresh fruit and vegetables – already washed, sorted and packaged – can now be transported by road to be on the shelves of British supermarkets within 48 to 72 hours of processing.

It is a willingness to cooperate with the retail outlet that will determine the success of many consumer products. As will be shown later, the pattern of retailing throughout Europe is moving towards greater concentrations on multiple groups, cooperatives, supermarkets and hypermarkets. This makes the exporter's task easier, as he sells to fewer buyers, and the traditional distribution chain via distributor, wholesaler, retailer is now considerably shortened. The power of such retailers is enormous and already there is talk of supermarket groups getting together in European joint ventures that may apply even greater pressure on manufacturers. Competition for shelf space is likely to intensify. However, the growth of the supermarkets' own brand products means that (smaller) manufacturers can supply such outlets without the need to promote their own individual brand identities on a pan-European basis. There will also be opportunities for manufacturers to cooperate with companies in Europe who manufacture similar or related products, in order to take advantage of each other's distribution channels.

Careful consideration will need to be given to *branding, promotion* and *pricing*. As has been noted many consumer brands already cross frontiers, as lifestyles in the developed west-European economies become virtually identical. Among the important trends are the predominance of young people with considerable spending power; the greater use of the English language and the adoption of English/American popular culture; the use of strong visual images and of music to sell brands worldwide (for example, Coke, jeans). Young people are also becoming better educated, more sophisticated in their tastes, and tend to travel further and more frequently than their parents. In the older age groups Europe is distinguished by its large numbers of people who live in large conurbations, the growth of single parent families, smaller families (a sacrifice to consumption and lifestyle), increased leisure and recreation, more spending on the home, greater numbers of working women and the arrival of the new liberated woman.

Any brand promotion needs to reflect the modern European outlook while continuing to respect national cultures. Cultural differences occur in advertising and relate to the use of images, colours, concepts, wording, so that an advertisement which appeals in one country may not necessarily do so in another. The advent of European satellite television will not necessarily provide the answer, as many European countries already spend more on newspaper and magazine advertising than on television. Not only do patterns of television viewing vary widely, but also the quality of the viewing audience – a reflection of the quality of programme output. The proliferation of channels has already demonstrated that more is not necessarily better and viewers may simply turn away. Among their alternative interests are greater participation in sports and leisure activities, ownership of a second home, longer and more frequent holidays. In warmer countries where more life is lived on the streets, in bars and pavement cafes, television has less appeal than it has for those surviving through a typical British winter.

Among the constraints that the exporter needs to be aware of will be those concerning advertising restrictions, both in terms of the amount of advertising that is permitted and the type of products that are not permitted to be advertised on television or elsewhere. National laws may still apply in the areas of consumer protection and in packaging and labelling. Wording may have to be in the national language and is sometimes obligatory in the case of descriptions, instructions or directions for use. There are growing trends towards the use of secure packaging, to deter product counterfeiting, and tamper evident packs that reassure the purchaser that the product has not been interfered with between manufacture and arrival on the supermarket shelf.

Pricing structures will have to take account of differences in national income levels and the price of similar competing products. Indirect taxation will also be relevant. At present levels of VAT within the Community range from zero to 38%, greatly distorting the price of some goods. The current Commission proposal is for closer approximation between Member States, with a basic rate of between 4% and 9% and a higher 'standard' rate of between 14% and 20%. These are essential to the working of a free market and to prevent excessive buying in one country to avoid paying a higher rate of VAT in another.

Which consumer goods will sell across Europe? The answer to this non too easy question is that there are probably two basic types: goods that emphasise their strong national identities (such as Scotch whisky or English tweed) and those whose sameness makes them saleable in virtually any market (household goods such as sheets and towels, men's socks and shirts). The fact that a certain British flair can be brought to retailing is evidenced by the arrival of Marks & Spencer and Conran/Habitat in Europe (although the American JC Penny chain have pulled out). Between the two extremes of Britishness and sameness many products can be sold as they are in the home market and will reflect – possibly with slight variations – the growing convergence of European tastes. This is already evident in the sale of mineral waters, health foods, fast foods, chocolates, clothes, DIY and many more similar items throughout West Europe.

The services sector

As has been seen there is considerable growth in employment and turnover within the services sectors of some European economies, with services equalling or even overtaking manufacture. The services sector therefore represents an expanding market both for capital goods (from new buildings down to personal computers) and of consumer goods to those working within services and enjoying an increasing standard of living. Many services are of course already involved in the process of buying and selling goods across Europe. They include export/import agents, shippers, transport and distribution companies, as well as market researchers, advertising agencies, designers, lawyers and management consultants. All these occupations will grow as a result of increased levels of trade after 1992.

The Commission's proposals will also extend opportunities for setting up services businesses in Europe as professional qualifications are subjected to mutual recognition and the freedom to practice is established. A further effect will be increased competition for all forms of business and professional services, and a corresponding reduction in price to the user. Wide variations in the cost of providing services are detailed in the Cecchini Report which looked at banking, insurance, and brokerage services. Divergences as high as 50% are noted, the widest margins being in the cost of providing motor insurance, home loans, consumer credit and securities.

Although controls on capital movements will gradually be phased out, the Report notes that restrictions still applied to Spain, Greece, Portugal and Ireland, and to a lesser extent in France and Italy. Although banks were technically free to set up overseas branches, their services could sometimes not be extended to nationals of the countries where they were sited. This effectively limits the range of services that they can offer in competition with local banks.

Similar restrictions used to apply to insurance companies and others wishing to seek business in another country, and on the operations of stock brokers who have simply not been licensed to practice. Discriminatory taxes have also been applied to transactions involving foreign securities. By gradually removing all such barriers to the provision and use of services the Commission reckons that the overall price of professional services would fall by as much as 21% in

Spain (the highest) to 10 – 14% in Italy, France, Belgium and Germany; by 7% in the United Kingdom, and just 4% average in the Netherlands.

Despite these price reductions, countries which already have a strong financial services sector – Britain, Germany, Italy, France and Spain in that order – will benefit from increased levels of business following liberalisation.

More general business services which are reckoned to account for 4% of Community GDP were seen in the Cecchini Report to be subject to fewer overt restrictions. Among barriers noted, however, were restrictions on the right to raise capital (German advertising and PR firms), television advertising regulations, differing technical standards (computers and consequently software); and nationalistic government and other public sector procurement policies which restrict competition.

Freeing services from these barriers would produce not only considerable savings to purchasers but open up the market to all those qualified and willing to establish their operations anywhere within the Community. (The promotion and sales of Services is discussed fully in Chapters 7 and 8).

3   Look before you leap

Market research before you leave your desk

This chapter is designed to show the exporter how he can and should undertake a considerable amount of desk-based research before he or she contemplates making a business trip to Europe. This may sound like stating the obvious but among the commonest criticisms by commercial officers in British Embassies abroad is that business people arrive without adequate preparation. They fail to make use of libraries and other reference sources in the UK which contain much of the information they need on the country they are visiting. As a result the business trip does not achieve all it could and exporters are consequently discouraged from persevering in the market. An ill-planned business trip is also wasteful of time and money, even though the costs of visiting Europe are less than those for more distant overseas markets.

Chapter 4 will consider how such visits can be planned and undertaken. This chapter concentrates on the essential information sources that should be consulted first. By preparing in advance the exporter will clarify just what he or she is hoping to gain from the visit. This may range from visiting a trade fair to looking at competitors or searching for agents. Whatever the purpose of the eventual business trip, careful prior planning will pay dividends.

Any company serious about Europe should start by getting together a basic library of information material, a great deal of which is free of charge. As will be shown in the following paragraphs a wealth of information about Europe is now available from the Department of Industry as a result of their 1992 initiative. Further valuable sources of information are:

- the principal export intelligence libraries which can be visited without charge;

- the information services of the European Community;
- the (activities of) Chambers of Commerce and Trade and professional associations;
- published books and surveys;
- a number of online information services which can be accessed from a desk-top computer terminal in your own office.

Getting to grips with just what information is available is not easy but this chapter will offer guidelines about basic reading on Europe through to the more complex and precisely focussed information sources. In selecting books and other information sources, these are based on my own researches. There may well be omissions as no doubt readers will discover for themselves.

General books

We have already recommended use of a large wall map of Europe that can be hung in the office and consulted frequently. The exporter should also undertake some leisure-time reading about Europe to get a feel for the market and its people. A good starting point is Anthony Sampson's *The New Europeans*. Sampson is the author of the well known *Anatomy of Britain*, and although his European study is now getting slightly dated it is none the less a classic. It offers a first insight into the Brussels institutions, Europe's major industries, geography, people, travellers, tourists, consumers, politics, television, press, education, employment.

Among a number of excellent general country guides I would cite two by John Ardach. First his *France Today* which is an update of his original *France in the 1980s* and his similar treatment of West (and East) Germany *Germany and the Germans*. Ardach's French study includes chapters about the economy, regional reform, the problems of agriculture and the cities, daily life and attitudes. He uses a similar treatment for Germany, with background about the rise of West Germany, the 'economic miracle' through to politics and daily life in both East and West Germany.

The French also come under the microscope in Theodore Zeldin's *The French*, which is a highly personal insight into the French character. A useful book on the French economy is *L'Economie Francaise* by

J and G Bremond. This books covers its subjects in clear factual style, which includes up-to-date figures and graphs.

John Hooper has written a very readable account of 'the new Spain' in *The Spaniards*, which traces the making of modern Spain from the era of the civil war, General Franco and the accession of King Juan Carlos. Hooper looks at many of Spain's modern problems, including housing, the shift to the cities, young people, the sexual revolution, the separatist movements. You will know Spain better after reading this book. *Spain: A Guide to Political and Economic Institutions* by Peter Donaghy and Michael Newton cover these subjects in some depth. Two books written in Spanish are also recommended: *Introducción a la Economía Española* by Ramon Tamames is a readable yet comprehensive guide. *Diez Anos en la Vida de los Españoles* by Juan Maria Laboa and others is an account of the changes that have taken place during the last decade or so.

The Italian Labyrinth is explored by John Haycraft in this excellent book that looks at the geography, economy, politics and lifestyles of the Italians. *Contemporary Italy* by Donald Sassoon covers much of the same ground, with more emphasis on politics and political parties.

For a view about the development of Portugal since the bloodless revolution of 1974 try *Revolution and Counter Revolution in Portugal* by Martin Kayman, or *Insight on Portugal* written soon after the event by the Insight Team of the Sunday Times.

More general guides to Europe and to specific countries include those designed for the tourist or traveller, published by Baedeker, Michelin, the Automobile Association or Berlitz. Essential while travelling by road, they make good general reading for the exporter anxious to get a feel for areas and towns in Europe. Most of them contain country maps, and some detailed town plans. Other useful guides to Europe can sometimes be found in bookshops selling school textbooks. Because they are written for schools' use they are essentially brief and to the point and can make unashamedly useful reading for the business person.

The more specialist bookshelf

More business-oriented background to Europe is available in a num-

ber of books, some of them recently published and with the accent
on Europe after 1992. Some general reference books on Europe as an
export market include: *Europe: an Exporter's Handbook* by Paul Jen-
ner. Slightly out of date today, the book offers maps, population,
geography, economy, markets and marketing advice on the principal
European countries, including non-EEC. The *Business Traveller's
Handbook: Europe* (1981) edited by Jane Walker is very comprehensive and includes guides, travel details, health regulations, etc. for
Europe's main countries and cities from Albania to Yugoslavia.

Despite its title *An Accountant's Guide to Europe* (Dennis Evans),
this book makes interesting reading for non-accountants as well. An
introductory section deals with the history of Europe and the Community, explains the workings of the various European institutions,
the economics of the Community, the Community budget and how
it is spent, company legislation across Europe, accounting practices,
and Community involvement in social policies, agriculture, industry, trade, education and research. Altogether a comprehensive and
readable guide.

Among more recent volumes on Europe I would cite the following as some of the most useful (again based on personal experience
and research). John Palmer has written *Trading Places* (1988), as a
companion volume to a series from Granada Television, which takes
a critical look at Europe, the removal of trade barriers envisaged in
1992, and some of the practical consequences. Palmer is European
editor of *The Guardian* and his style is eminently readable. *Business in
Europe: Opportunities for Companies within the EEC* by Keith Perry
(1987) sets out to cover the ground implied in the title. The book
examines the Community's major markets of West Germany,
France, The Netherlands; the smaller markets (the author's definitions) of Denmark, Benelux, Italy and Ireland; and the new Community members Greece, Portugal and Spain. There are useful sections on Community policies affecting business, information
sources, how to break into the market, and a chapter on what Britain
needs from a revived Community. This book is strongly recommended.

1992: Strategies for the Single Market (1989) by James W Dudley
touches on the principal European issues and then launches into more
general advice on export market strategy, product development,

pricing, international advertising, distribution etc. that can be applied to other overseas markets as well. An export primer that should be on every manager's bookshelf.

Although strictly speaking a Commission publication (discussed below), Paolo Cecchini's *1992: The Benefits of a Single Market* (1988) is a graphic account of the costs and problems associated with not going ahead with 1992, together with an update of existing and proposed changes in freedom of movement of people, goods and services and the likely gains in real money terms. An ideal book for waverers not yet fully convinced about the benefits of 1992. Should be on Mrs Thatcher's bedside table.

Two shorter guides are *Europe's Domestic Market* by Jacques Pelkmans and Alan Winters (1988) and *1992: The Facts and the Challenges* (1988) produced by the Industrial Society and accountants Ernst & Whinney. The first book contains a good deal of supplementary information about the costs and benefits associated with the new Europe, while the second is a rapid rundown of the principal measures proposed and their likely benefits to business. An excellent reference guide entitled *Europe in Figures* is available from the Commission's Statistical Office and is an excellent source (used extensively in compiling this book) of facts and figures about Europe's populations, demographic trends, employment and unemployment, gross domestic product, principal industries, intra–Community trade and relations with the rest of the World.

An insight into how Community policies are affecting business rather than a how-to guide is John Drew's *Doing Business in the European Community* (1979, 1983). The book discusses the impact of various Commission policies, how they can be influenced, how they affect business and relations within and outside the Community. The Community's institutions are well explained in Stanley Budd's book *The EEC: A Guide to the Maze* (1985), and the book is just that. Very readable, there are sections on overall policy formulation and detailed chapters on individual trade sector directives and proposals. A very good chapter entitled 'Getting Money from Europe' summarises the main European funds and their availability, and the further information section is extremely comprehensive. Michael Palmer has also written a useful guide to *The European Parliament: What It Is, What It Does, How It Works* which fully justifies its title. The book traces the history and functions of the Parliament, and includes a full list of Members (as at 1981) and a graphic account of how an MEP spends his time.

Owners of small and medium-sized businesses will be interested in *Small Business in Europe* edited by Paul Burns and Jim Dewhurst. Written by experts from Denmark, France, Great Britain, Ireland, Italy, West Germany and Switzerland, the book describes the experiences of the smaller business sector in relation to government assistance and their continued survival. Some useful comparisons of export performance are given.

The Economist has published a useful series of guides including *France on Business, Germany on Business, Italy on Business* with other titles to follow, in their world series of business travel guides. Each book contains information about the country's economy, principal industries, politics and methods of doing business, as well as comprehensive guides to hotels and other facilities within the capitals and main regional cities.

Another up-to-the-minute series is that prepared by CBI Initiative 1992. The full set of 12 volumes, written by experts within each sector, includes:

> *Mergers, Acquisitions and Alternative Corporate Strategies;*
> *Tax: Strategic and Corporate Planning;*
> *Finance for Growth;*
> *Company Law and Competition;*
> *Marketing: Communicating with the Customer;*
> *Information Technology;*
> *Marketing to the Public Sector and Industry;*
> *Transport and Distribution;*
> *Property;*
> *Employment and Training.*

The books are very reasonably priced, highly detailed and authoritative, and should be on the shelf of every exporter contemplating Europe. They are linked to a series of CBI seminars on Europe.

The European Commission as an information source

The information emanating from the various Common Market

institutions is both prodigious in volume and complex in content – so much so that at least one book has been written about this subject alone. Edited by Michael Hopkins *European Communities Information: Its Use and Users* (1985) attempts to catalogue just how information is gathered and published, to whom it is directed and what use is made of it. In a chapter by Jim Hogan on Europe and the Business Community, its author has to admit that there is something of a communications gap between the various institutions and the constituencies they are supposed to serve. While praising Commission officials for their detailed knowledge and willingness to help, many are seen as highly specialist within a narrow field. They also tend to move around just at the time they are getting to grips with a particular function, to be replaced by less competent people. The result is that overall performance can be patchy within departments of the Community. Hogan also blames the business sector for not making itself sufficiently well informed, but does concede that finding your way round the Commission's information sources is not easy. The book goes a long way to pointing out just what is available, classified by sector (grants and loans, statistics, agriculture and so on), and where in general it can be found. The next few paragraphs will also attempt to do the same thing.

Both the European Commission and the European Parliament have United Kingdom representative offices located in Westminster, just a few steps from another essential information source (discussed later), the British Overseas Trade Board. The public can visit libraries at both the Commission and Parliament offices, where virtually all official publications are lodged. It can sometimes be difficult to find information if you do not know precisely what you are looking for – a common fault in most libraries. However, the staff are knowledgeable and helpful, handle telephone enquiries and make available photocopies of documents as required. Among the free publications available from the Commission office is a booklet entitled *The EC as Publisher* which lists by subject all the current publications.

EC Publications

It is not particularly helpful to the researcher that Commission publications are classified into either European *Files* or *Documents*. Both are available, usually free of charge for single copies, from Commission offices. European files generally cover a subject in brief outline (10 pages) while documents tend to be longer (up to 100 pages). Commission documents are used mainly to communicate the overall policy objectives of the Commission and include suggested and proposed legislation as well as updates. Some of the information may have been overtaken by events, but the most recent documents give an early warning signal about what the Commission is thinking. Both series cover a wide range of topics from the handicapped to waste recycling, from fisheries policy to research. Some contain valuable market research data, as for example a document on *The Textile Machinery Industry within the EEC*, prepared externally for the EEC and containing virtually all one would need to know about this subject. The simplest method of research is to select your subject and then enquire whether it has been covered in either a document or a file.

The day to day affairs of the Commission are chronicled in the *Official Journal* and in a monthly digest called the *Bulletin*. Neither makes exciting reading, but the *Official Journal* is essential for checking advertised public tenders and can be bought on subscription or studied at the Commission offices. Abstracting services and the more serious daily and Sunday newspapers use the *Official Journal* as an information source for reporting European events.

In addition to seeking out specific information on your relevant sector, some more general Commission publications make useful reading. They include *The Single Act: a New Frontier* (published as a supplement to the bulletin of January 1987) which contains the text of the Act and outlines what the Commission feels is required to complete reform of the internal market by the end of 1992. It makes interesting and uplifting reading. There are also documents entitled *Completing the Internal Market for Industrial Products* and *Small- and Medium-Sized Enterprises. The Professions in the European Community* are covered in an edition of *European Perspectives* (another Commission publications series!) and there is a Catalogue of *Community Legal Acts and Other Texts Relating to the Elimination of Technical Barriers to Trade*. Industrial innovation is the subject of *A Guide to Community Action, Services and Funding* and various information packs are available on programmes such as *Brite, Esprit*, etc., either from the Commission or a source such as your own trade association. In addition to the above there is wide ranging literature on the environment, transport policy, company law, worker participation in companies, energy, youth, education and so on.

Statistical information about Europe is covered in various *Eurostat Publications*, produced by the Community's publishing office based in Luxemburg. There are both a *Eurostat News*, published quarterly, and an annual *Eurostat Review* which brings together the main statistics of the Community in considerable detail.

EC databases

Much time-sensitive (and general) information is best gained through use of online access to computerised databanks. Such systems originated in America, with large general databases such as Dialog, but more European databases are now coming online. They rejoice in a variety of acronyms such as *Eurolex* (European Legislation) or TED (Tenders Electronic Daily) and are available to subscribers, usually via one of the host systems such as Pergamon's Infoline or Reuters. These organisations and others provide a service of connection to more than one database (Dialog has over one hundred), and access is usually via a standard desk-top terminal which is connected through a modem to the telephone line, and then to the computerised database. When connected to the database and the information file of his choice, the user searches the database for the required information by using 'key words' (e.g. pollution). The system then comes up with the number of references to the subject, which can be printed on- or off-line. The references are to already published information and the database is pointing out the source.

Online searching is a complex subject and the service is offered by some libraries and other bodies who will handle a search on the exporter's behalf, for a fee. If the exporter decides to install his or her own terminal, the costs are quite low and usually on a pay-as-you-use basis without advance subscriptions. A first stop for someone new to online searching is an annual online conference and exhibition held in London in the autumn, where most of the database providers demonstrate their services.

If you feel the need to make direct contact with the Commission in Brussels, the *Directory of the Commission of the European Communities* lists principal officials from the President down to the staff of the twenty-two Directorates. Names are cross-referenced so that you find out where an official works if you only have his name and initials. Lists of European MEPs are published periodically and can be obtained from Commission and Parliament offices. As noted elsewhere direct contact with the Commission is preferably made via an interest group (such as a trade association) or through an MEP, and in any event the exporter is advised to first consult the office of the United Kingdom Permanent Representative in Brussels (details of personnel to be found in some guides, or from the Foreign Office).

Small Firms Services

In the interest of small- and medium-sized companies, the Commission set up a *Small Firms Task Force*, which is now incorporated into a new Directorate General. The small firms service offers a number of services aimed at helping small businesses find partners within the Community. This is done either through the Brussels-based Business Cooperation Centre or more recently through BC-Net. BC-Net was launched in 1987 on an experimental basis. Its object is to link 'business advisers' throughout the Community via a computerised network, so that offers and requests for cooperation can be fed into a centralised computer. There the computer searches for matches between offers and requests, and the results are sent to the business adviser who then passes them on to the client.

Business advisers or intermediaries range from regional development associations and Chambers of Commerce to small private management consultancies. In its early days the Small Firms Task Force appeared to be bogged down in the detail of the system's mechanics but advisers report that it is up and running with some good results. The system has led to the development of more informal links between British consultancies (including my own) and their opposite numbers in Europe.

As can be seen, making the most of the Community's information resources is not easy. A study of guides such as the Hopkins book already referred to will help the exporter to understand something about what is available, but much access is likely to be via third parties, such as Trade Associations (for example about technical standards), Chambers of Commerce (export opportunities) and regional business associations (in the case of grants and loans). Considerable help is also available from Britain's Department of Industry and other bodies which are considered next.

United Kingdom official sources of help to exporters

Understanding the wealth of information and assistance available to exporters from Britain's DTI and BOTB and other bodies is almost as complicated as dealing with the Commission. However, in an attempt to try and illustrate most of what is available it is convenient to divide the range of services into three broad groups:

- official publications
- libraries and information sources
- special support services

The DTI has also published its own guide to resources (*DTI: A Guide for Business*) which is a comprehensive guide to the national (Victoria Street, London SW 1) and regional offices, with the list of services broken down by functions (Research and Technology, Relocation, Export, etc.) and including the name and telephone number of the appropriate person to contact.

In a further section headed 'Market Contacts', the guide lists available services and contacts under industry sectors, from Aviation to Vehicles. A final section covering 'Policies, functions and support services' describes the main official services from Business Statistics to Weights and Measures. Telephone numbers and personal contacts are given throughout, and the user can return a reply-paid card to ensure receipt of future updates.

The British Government's 1992 initiative, although somewhat late in the day compared with her European competitors, has helped to increase awareness of Europe's export potential and the impact of the Single European Act. If he has not already done so, the exporter should ensure that a copy of the DTI's *Europe Open for Business* is acquired. Over 300,000 people have already received their information pack. This consists of two publications – *The Single Market: The Facts* and *An Action Checklist for Business*. A copy of the newspaper *Single Market News* is also usually sent with the information pack.

The *Facts* publication, in 32 sections, outlines the Single Market programme and its effects on the various sectors of industry, from technical standards to consumer protection. Advice is given on what to do about research and development, consumer protection, training, acquiring language skills, together with details of what further information and help can be obtained. Much of this is by reference to the DTI's own services for business. The *Action Checklist* is a virtual blueprint for company actions, and suggests practical steps to be taken in terms of marketing, sales, distribution, production, product development, purchasing, finance, training and information technology, and again backed by sources of help and further information inside and outside the DTI. *Single Market News*, the third part of the package, contains an update on progress towards 1992, information about regional seminars and courses, and cases studies of export success in Europe.

The DTI's European services are brought together under their Exports to Europe Branch, which is located in Westminster, and from them a wide range of country-by-country publications can be obtained. These include *Country Profiles*, which are available covering virtually all countries. Compiled with the assistance of overseas Embassy staff, the country profiles follow a similar format: a presentation of basic facts about population, geography, politics and government, industries, import/export trade, export conditions, marketing methods, investment, work and residence, travel and transport, and sources of further information. Some of them contain quite detailed information about export opportunities for specific products and services. Each country profile is about 50–70 pages long and available free from the DTI and regional offices.

Some of the major European markets are also covered by more specific publications, such as *Selling Consumer Goods* or *Mail-Order Houses*, and fact sheets on subjects such as *Licensing, Setting up a Branch Office, Agency Contracts* and *Language Requirements*. They can be obtained from the appropriate Country Desk within the DTI or from regional offices.

The Statistics and Market Intelligence Library/other libraries

Located in the basement of the DTI's main building in Victoria Street, Westminster, the Statistics and Market Intelligence Library is a valuable and essential information resource for the exporter. A great deal of initial desk research can be done using the wide range of publications available. Arranged in sections by country, they include ordinary and classified telephone directories and numerous general and specialised trade directories where names and addresses of companies and trade organisations can be found. Many overseas market reports are available, both from government and private sources, together with main statistics. There is also a product data store, which contains more product and market information. Limited assistance is given by the library staff and the exporter will have to do the research him or herself.

Similar services are offered by other specialist libraries throughout the United Kingdom. In London they include the British Library's Science Reference Library in Holborn, and the City Business Library in the City of London. There are also major commercial reference libraries in Aberdeen, Belfast, Birmingham, Glasgow, Liverpool, Manchester, Newcastle, Nottingham, Portsmouth and Sheffield.

The British Library publishes its own *Guide to Business Information* and it is a useful guide to the resources available in the Library (and other main libraries) as the following extracts indicate:

- **Trade directories** include *Directory of Directories*, trade associations, general UK and European trade directories, individual country directories, directories by trade/individual countries; *Current European Directories; Trade Directories of the World*.
- **Business journals** – current and past issues of General UK business journals, trade journals, general European business journals, specific trade journals by country/trade.
- **Company information** – *Directory of British Companies* (quarterly, with weekly updates), dissolutions, changes of name, annual reports; *Extel* cards for UK and European companies. Other similar card/looseleaf services for UK and Europe, including McCarthy's European Publications such as *Who Owns Whom?* for

UK and Europe. ICC Business Ratio Reports on leading companies and their performance.

- **Trade Literature** – the Science Reference Library has current literature from 20,000 mainly UK companies, house journals, stockbroker reports, exhibition catalogues. Also further information on microfiche.
- **Official Statistics** – including main statistics for United Kingdom; *Eurostat Index for EEC; Statistics Europe; Business Monitors* produced by the Business Statistics Office. Guides to Unofficial Statistics.
- **Market Research Reports** – include publications from *The Economist, Euromonitor, ICC Information, Jordans, Infotech, Market Assessments, National Economic Development Office, Mintel,* etc. (some of these sources are discussed below under Published Reports).

The resources of libraries will vary in each location, and in addition to public municipal libraries, libraries are maintained by organisations such as the CBI and Institute of Directors, trade associations and Chambers of Commerce as part of their services to members.

In addition the DTI operates an online database called *Spearhead* which can be accessed via a number of services such as Telecom Gold, Mercurylink and similar networks. This is primarily concerned with updates of EEC legislation. (See also below).

Special services for exporters

As previously noted the Department of Industry operates a number of 'Country Desks' within its Exports to Europe Branch and there are separate contacts for Belgium/Luxemburg, Denmark, France, West Germany, Greece, Ireland, Italy, The Netherlands, Portugal and Spain, as well as a multi-country contact point. Staff will either provide an immediate answer and/or point the enquirer towards other information and assistance sources.

Help with *technical standards* can be obtained from the Technical Help to Exporters Division of the British Standards Institution, based at Linford Wood, Milton Keynes. They can give assistance with technical information about standards and certification in European countries, and progress towards a common European standard.

Exhibitions, special promotions and outward missions (joint sales visits) are handled by the BOTB's Fairs & Promotions Branch, located in Westminster. They can assist with information about overseas events, including those in which joint participation is possible with BOTB assistance.

Export documentation and the programme to simplify it are handled by SITPRO, the Simplification of International Trade Procedures Board, located in King Street, London SW 1. They offer advice and assistance on the subject of export forms.

Export insurance is handled by the Export Credits Guarantee Department (ECGD) from its London and regional offices (Cardiff, City of London, Croydon, Belfast, Birmingham, Bristol, Cambridge, Glasgow, Leeds and Manchester).

Small firms can approach any of the above services through the special network of Small Firms Service offices throughout the UK.

Published reports

A number of market surveys, industry reports and directories are available from commercial publishers, banks and other organisations, either for purchase (sometimes free) or consultation at any of the libraries listed above. They can save the exporter a great deal of time and money, as it is clearly wasteful to commission general research that may have already been undertaken and is immediately available.

The exporter should endeavour to find out what published research is available, and there are a number of guides to help you to do just this. They include *Marketing Surveys Index* (updated monthly), *Market Research: Guide to British Library Holdings, Findex* and *Marketsearch*. The last-named is published by BOTB and Arlington Publications, and lists published surveys by industry, with details of where they can be obtained. Other useful publications are *A Guide to Official Statistics* (guide to all government produced statistics) and *Statistics-Europe* published by CBD Research, Beckenham, Kent (a guide to what is available in most European countries). Euromonitor's

European Directory of Marketing Information Sources lists more than 2500 sources of market and business information.

If you are searching online or have access to someone who can undertake this for you, there are a number of useful files such as *Industry Data Sources* on the Dialog system which will search for published research on almost any industry and list what is available, price and when and by whom it was published.

Some of the principal European information publishers should be noted. *Euromonitor*, as its name implies, specialises in a wide range of publications to do with Europe and covers virtually all industry sectors. Recent (1989) titles include:

Market: *Market Research Europe* (monthly update journal);
European Marketing Data and Statistics (over 100,000 statistics, estimates, trends, comparisons);
Consumer Europe (key parameters relating to over 500 products in 16 European countries);
European Consumer Expenditure Trends and Forecasts

Food: *The European Food Marketing Directory, Grocery Distribution in Western Europe, Snack Foods in France, Fast Food in The International Market* (includes Europe)

Drink: *European Drinks Marketing Directory, European Alcoholic Drinks, Spanish Alcoholic Drinks, Soft Drinks in West Germany*

Home: *European Household Chemicals Directory, European Cosmetics & Toiletries Marketing Directory*

Retail: *Hypermarkets and Superstores in Europe, Home Shopping in Europe, European Directory of Retailers and Wholesalers, Europe's Major Retailers, Franchising in Europe, White Goods in Europe, European Consumer Electronics*

The company also publishes a *European Directory of Consumer Goods Manufacturers* which is not only invaluable for studying competitors, but also as a reference for buyers seeking new sources for consumer products.

Dun & Bradstreet are well known for their company information services and in the European context they include listings of major companies in Belgium (15,000); France (30,000); Netherlands (9,000), Ireland (7,550), Italy (10,000 largest; 8,000 medium-sized;

80,000 complete lists of all registered companies); Spain (15,000); Portugal (3,500). Information on companies in Denmark and West Germany is included in *Principal International Businesses*; while *Who Owns Whom: Continental Europe* lists 8,000 parent companies and 90,000 subsidiaries.

More detailed industry sector reports may be published by Frost & Sullivan Ltd, London SW1. This company has a comprehensive, ongoing programme of research and publication, and lists can be obtained by main industry sectors of current and recent research reports. Because their prices tend to be on the high side (around £1500 to £2000 for an average report) F & S reports are not often available in libraries. However, the shorter *Key Note* publications usually are. They are concise surveys of key industry sectors, showing the main companies involved, market shares and so, and around 100 industries are covered.

General booklets on exporting and individual country guides are available from head offices of most of the major High Street banks.

A useful updating service about current European issues is provided by the Local Government International Bureau, London SW1. It publishes a monthly bulletin and although, as its title implies, the Bureau's main concern is with local authorities, the information contained in the bulletins is of wide general interest. A typical issue will cover recent Community events in agriculture, the budget, community reform, consumers, the environment, health and safety, industry, information technology, the internal market, regional policy, research, social policy, technology and transport. Each section is easily located, and recent relevant publications are listed.

A useful and inexpensive general survey of Europe's main manufacturing and service sectors is the *Panorama of EC Industry* published by the Commission (available through HMSO in Britain). This very up-to-date guide covers all the main industry sectors under Energy, Mining, Processing, Construction Materials, Glassware, Ceramics, Chemicals, Pharmaceuticals, Manmade Fibres, Metal Articles, Mechanical Engineering, Electrical and Electronic Equipment, Motor Vehicles, Transport, Food & Drink, Textiles, Clothing, Timber, Pulp & Paper, Printing & Publishing, Rubber & Plastics, Building & Civil Engineering, Distribution & Retailing, Transport & Communications, Banking & Finance, Professional Services,

Marketing & Other Business Services, Recreation. In all nearly 140 detailed European industry surveys are presented under the above broad headings.

Chambers of Commerce, trade and professional associations

Most of the major United Kingdom Chambers of Commerce are involved in some activities connected with exporting, and many have developed European initiatives with 1992 in view. Exporters will have access to a wide range of information and support services by joining their local Chamber. Perhaps even more valuable is the personal contact with other exporters and an opportunity to discuss common problems. The exporter should enquire what services are available in his or her area, but we take two examples from Chambers in Britain's industrial areas of Birmingham and Manchester.

As part of a comprehensive range of member services the Birmingham Chamber of Industry and Commerce has a special Export Initiative Centre designed to help exporters 'find markets and customers, investigate regulations and tariffs, appoint agents or distributors, communicate with customers overseas, complete the correct documents, arrange shipment of orders and obtain payment'. The services include information and advice by mail and telephone (about 8000 queries a month are dealt with); face to face counselling with export specialists; briefing seminars and short courses. The Chamber can put exporters in touch with potential agents and distributors through its links with overseas Chambers of Commerce. It offers practical advice on visiting countries and organises participation in overseas trade missions and trade exhibitions in conjunction with the BOTB sponsored programmes. Practical services like fax, telex and translation are also available. The Chamber further provides a comprehensive training programme.

Similar services are offered by Manchester Chamber of Commerce and Industry and include: organising, promoting and accompanying trade missions; organising seminars and conferences; trade clinics – private interviews for member companies with an expert in a particular market or sector; information and advice, including an online database facility for exporters; and the issue of certificates of origin and other documents required by exporters. Membership comprises 'large multinational PLCs to small firms of one and two employees' say the Chamber.

In addition there are a number of international Chambers of Commerce that the exporter may consider joining. They are either UK based, where the Chamber serves principally as a British outpost of the foreign country – its membership is a mixture of foreign and British firms – or Chambers which are based overseas in a European capital. The membership of the latter again comprises both British and foreign firms, but the emphasis is rather more on providing services to the (British) exporter by way of contacts and facilities such as meeting rooms, desk space, libraries, etc., and assistance on the ground during a research or sales visit. They can be a useful way of meeting other established exporters and nationals of the country concerned. Several have a network of regional offices and have close links with the host country's Chambers of Commerce, as well as the British embassy staff in the capital and regions.

A typical example is the busy and active Franco-British Chamber of Commerce. Situated in the pleasant 16th arrondissement of Paris, the Chamber offers a wide range of business support services, including meeting rooms, offices for short and long term rental, secretarial and message facilities, as well as a programme of seminars and social events.

In many European countries, the regional Chamber of Commerce has a very important role as its status is different from the United Kingdom equivalent organisation. Membership is obligatory for all firms, and the Chamber frequently acts as a major instigator of regional development and training, providing offices and factories, and even operating facilities such as the local airport. Because of their major role in the local economy contact with the Chambers is often necessary and certainly important for meeting influential local business people. Introductions, as already noted, can be made either by the exporter's own home Chamber of Commerce or through one of the international Chambers.

Employers' organisations

Britain's two major employers' organisations, the CBI and the Institute of Directors, both have an extensive range of export services available to their members. The CBI has a corporate membership of around 250,000 private and public companies, of which half are smaller firms employing less than 200 people, and around 200 trade, employer and commercial associations. It has some 30 standing committees, 13 regional councils and a special Smaller Firms Council. The importance of Europe to the CBI is reflected in its permanent Brussels office, which acts as a listening post and centre of influence with the European Commission. The office can brief members on latest Community developments, organise introductions and appointments within the Commission offices, and advise on strategy. A major thrust of its 1992 promotion programme in Britain has been the launch of the CBI Initiative, which includes an information hotline, publications and a series of seminars held throughout the United Kingdom.

A much smaller organisation, the Institute of Directors has around 35,000 individual members worldwide and offices in London's Pall Mall, as well as 28 UK branches and seven overseas. Members can use a range of library and information services including an online database facility, and a comprehensive Business Centre in Pall Mall. The IOD also publishes books and reports, organises conferences and is increasingly active in promoting and providing services on a European level to its members.

Trade and professional organisations

'The trade and professional association movement is stronger and more extensive than ever. There can be no profession, industry or industry sector which is not now represented'. So writes Patricia Braun, editor of the comprehensive *Trade Associations and Professional Bodies in the United Kingdom* which lists nearly 3500 trade and professional associations and regional Chambers of Commerce. Accordingly, there is bound to be at least one group that covers the activities and interests of the exporter. Joining it can bring a number of advantages.

Trade Associations frequently publish their own research which can be highly specialised, giving an in-depth insight into market opportunities for the exporter's particular product or service. Many of these reports are compiled with assistance from the DTI and are thus sold to association members and non-members at highly competitive prices. They represent a very cheap way of conducting some initial research into often quite complex areas.

Many trade associations are also effective lobbyists both at national government and Commission levels, representing their members views and the concerns of their industry sector generally. They therefore not only offer another avenue of influence that the exporter can explore, but also an up to date source of information – again much of it quite detailed – that may have a bearing on the exporter's products. Other activities include outward sales missions and joint participation at overseas trade fairs, in conjunction with the BOTB. Membership of a trade or professional association will also bring the exporter into contact with fellow business people who are almost always willing to share their knowledge and experience on an informal basis with others.

Commercial departments of British Embassies in Europe

These are discussed more fully in the following chapter on Visiting the Market, but the exporter can make use of a number of their services before leaving the United Kingdom. The quality of the services available from commercial officers varies and depends to an extent upon the experience and personality of the officer(s) concerned. Unfortunately, the best people tend to get moved on, and it is a frequent complaint that just as they are getting to know their patch well, embassy staff are transferred to another territory to begin the process all over again.

Enquiries can be addressed to British embassies by letter, telex or facsimile before making an overseas trip. As well as participating in the excellent *BOTB Country Guides* already mentioned, some embassies produce their own guidance notes on an ad hoc basis, sometimes in response to particular or frequent requests from enquirers. These are based very much on their local knowledge, and it should be borne in mind that the United Kingdom is represented by a consulate in a number of major provincial towns in Europe in addition to the main Embassy in the capitals. Up-to-date addresses and telephone numbers can be found in the *BOTB Country Guides* or simply telephone the appropriate Country Desk at the DTI or your regional office.

Languages

As has already been noted Europeans are generally better linguists than the British, and although many business people in Europe speak and understand English, this should not always be relied upon. An attempt to speak the local language is always appreciated and adds considerably to the pleasure of doing business and visiting the country concerned. An understanding of the foreign language will also help the exporter to read foreign trade literature, catalogues, trade magazines and newspapers as well as find his way around away from the safety of airport lounges and international hotels.

There are many ways in which languages can be learned. Crash courses for business people now exist, either inside the company or elsewhere, individually or in groups, by distance learning and/or with instructors. They are organised locally by schools and colleges, Chambers of Commerce, Trade Associations and the many commercial language schools. Language cassettes can be purchased to play at home or in the car while travelling and there are numerous self-teaching packages available from good bookshops.

Companies serious about exporting to Europe will have on their staff at least one person who can speak each of the main European languages, French, German, Italian and Spanish, at least sufficiently well to understand incoming letters and telexes. Failing this, there are numerous translation services offered, with fast turn-around for such incoming messages. It is helpful if the company telephonist has a working knowledge of one or more foreign languages and can route incoming foreign calls to their correct destination.

A set of European dictionaries is also useful to help cope with incoming enquiries, but this self-help approach to European languages should never replace the use of native speakers when it comes to preparing foreign trade literature. This subject is discussed more fully in Chapter 6 on promoting your product or service in Europe.

Keeping up to date

Keeping up with the changes occurring within Europe can become an almost fulltime occupation. Companies large enough to maintain a library and information department will no doubt subscribe to the serious daily and Sunday newspapers, *The Economist, The Director*, the CBI's journal and other publications which regularly cover European topics. Regular updates are given in many Chamber of Commerce and trade association publications, which maintain European files and offer an information service to members.

The DTI has its own computerised database called SPEARHEAD which can be accessed from a standard computer terminal. The service covers new measures adopted by the Community, but not implemented in every member state; measures which have been proposed and are still under discussion; and all planned and projected measures. The information contained in SPEARHEAD is highly detailed and exporters unfamiliar with online information systems may prefer to consult their Chamber of Commerce or trade association which will (for a fee) access the system on their behalf. To use the system direct you require a suitable terminal and some familiarity with computerised information systems. Training is given by the company operating the database on behalf of the DTI. They are Profile Information, part of the Financial Times Group, and based in Sunbury on Thames, Middlesex. Profile Information also operate a number of other business and current affairs databases. Charges are based on a registration fee, and then a rate per minute on a pay-as-you-use basis.

4 Field research – visiting the market

No substitute for visiting the market

This chapter is all about visiting mainland Europe with a view to improving the exporter's knowledge of the market and researching the prospects for sale of his goods or services. As has been repeatedly stressed such visits should not be undertaken without prior preparation, in the form of desk research described in the previous chapter. In this section we look at how to go about research in the field, on the ground or however else you may wish to describe it.

It is possible to sell to European customers – as it to customers in the United Kingdom – without ever having come into personal contact with them. Many businessmen report long-standing relationships that have been built up over the telephone and by letter and result in years of successful trade without ever encountering the end customer. And it may be that your first entry into the European market is in response to a customer request which leads to a sale or series of sales, and without thinking about it, suddenly you are exporting to Europe. If an exporter succeeds in doing business this way, he is to be envied and congratulated. For most of us, however, a lot of hard work will be involved in visiting overseas contacts, potential customers, agents, trade exhibitions and generally undertaking all the operations needed to create and maintain lasting relationship with Continental customers.

So in ninety-nine cases out of a hundred a field trip will be necessary. How does the exporter plan for this? How does he ensure the best possible results? How can he plan his trip to achieve his objectives? When and how often should he visit the market? These and many other questions will be answered in this chapter.

Organising a field trip

The purpose of the field trip will immediately have a bearing on when and how it is planned. No exporter should rush across the Channel without a clear objective in mind. So before you go, a question that must be asked is: What is the purpose of my visit? There are four most common reasons why a field research visit is usually undertaken.

- **To visit a trade exhibition**. This is certainly a good method of getting a feel for an industry or consumer sector. Not only will home-based suppliers be exhibiting but also exporters, future competitors; and the exhibition catalogue – perhaps the most valuable part of the visit – will list these companies about whom further information can be sought. (Exhibitions as a promotion tool are discussed later).
- **To visit retail outlets**. This is not a substitute for opening relations with an import house or retail buying group (discussed later) but a valuable method of seeing just what is on the market in European department stores and supermarkets. Can be combined with a trade fair visit.
- **To visit an agent or distributor**. This assumes that some prior contact has already taken place, a short list drawn up and pre-liminary information exchanged about the product or service for sale, and the agent's willingness and competence to handle it.
- **To visit a potential European partner**. Similar to the above and again assumes that prior research and contact have taken place, and that the purpose of the visit is to take matters a stage further, possibly to a final conclusion.

It is also possible that the exporter may be travelling to Europe in response to a customer enquiry. In this instance he should apply all the criteria that he would to any other sales enquiry and not be thrown off balance by the prospect of an exciting foreign trip. Questions to ask include the usual status checks on the enquirer, what is known about him, does he fit into your usual type of customer, is this a genuine enquiry or a 'fishing expedition'. Com-panies who check incoming sales enquiries in this way will save themselves a great deal of unnecessary travel and expense in the long run. Stories abound of businessmen travelling to some far distant city to meet a 'major company' which turns out to be a one-man business operating from a rented office with clearly no assets to support him. Excercise therefore more than usual caution when responding to such enquiries. A good rule is the greater the distance, the more thorough the prior checks. Another is, if the enquirer is not already known to you – at least by name or reputation – check, and check again.

From all that has been said so far, it is clear that every overseas visit has a clear purpose and that this has been established by desk research at home. It assumes that the exporter already has some basic knowledge about the market he wishes to enter, the products and services he wishes to sell to it. If visiting an exhibition, he may already have a copy of the catalogue before leaving and has planned his route round the various halls. If visiting agents or potential partners, already a lot of groundwork will have been covered in prior exchanges of information by post and telephone. It all comes down to advance planning.

Making appointments ahead of your visit

The exporter undertaking a well planned European visit will already have spent a considerable amount of time on the telephone, telex and fax machine setting up appointments before he leaves. This is not always easy, especially if a number of visits are planned and it is sometimes a matter of luck if times, dates and locations all slot into place during the course of a round trip. A lot depends on how flexible your European correspondents are. Despite what the books on business etiquette say about punctual Germans and more laid-back Frenchmen, I find that most overseas business people are fairly accommodating. They generally will accept an approximate time of arrival, especially if you warn them in advance that you are making a number of visits and will telephone ahead if your schedule is seriously disrupted. Most business people are aware of the problems caused by airline delays or traffic holdups and will take a fairly relaxed attitude. (If they do not, I am personally wary of doing business with them.) That said, it is clearly unwise to overload your schedule so that you are invariably late, always in a hurry to reach the next appointment. A little slack in the timetable will allow promising meetings to overrun without jeopardising your route plan. And if you finish earlier than anticipated and have spare time in between meetings – and this happens even on the best planned trips – this time can, for instance, be used for informal research such as visiting department stores to look at consumer goods, or visiting a good bookshop or newsagent to check out the trade magazines relevant to your industry. You can visit a local museum or even an exhibition (although visits to potential customers at the time of a major trade show are normally to be avoided).

In planning a series of visits, a round trip, it is useful to have your European or country map in front of you and a good idea of the distances and times between your various appointments. European distances can be deceptive: France is twice the size of the United Kingdom, West Germany runs north to south in a comparatively narrow band (since the split into East and West), Spain has concentrations of population and vast open spaces in between. The selection of road, rail and air services is discussed below, but in spite of generally superior transport links, services invariably fan outwards from the capital and many routes run north to south. Crossing some European countries from west to east can be surprisingly time consuming. The author spent all day and evening driving from Stuttgart in southern Germany via Strasbourg and Lyon, to reach Limoges in south west France. On the map the distances seemed manageable but it was an extremely long day, even though the majority of the travel was on excellent and uncluttered motorways in early spring.

Armed with a European map, it is a good idea to draw up a chart or provisional schedule, showing where you ideally would like to be on each day, with some leeway between morning and afternoon. Then when you or your secretary start making appointments you try and schedule them into their ideal slots on the plan – again allowing some flexibility in time of arrival and time between appointments. A spare morning or afternoon that emerges can be usefully filled. To be really economical of time, you can try to have two appointments in roughly the same area each day (one morning, one afternoon). You can reach the first one by early to midmorning, then travel over the dead lunchtime period to the next. After that you use the late afternoon and early evening to move on to the general area of the following day's appointments, arriving at your hotel by mid-evening. This gives ample time for dinner, and planning the next day's precise route. You can normally skip lunch, unless pressed, and recent experience has made the author realise the need to pack sandwiches and a flask of coffee the moment you travel off the main motorways! Facilities for a quick snack simply do not exist.

Once your appointments are scheduled it is a good idea to confirm them in writing. Letters have given way to telex, and now telex to fax. By keeping a precise, typewritten note on who you are seeing and at what time – in addition to the hastily scribbled entry in your pocket diary! – you will avoid potential disasters. It is a good idea to have more than one copy of your route plan – one for the office, one at home for your family, and two or three to take with you in case they get mislaid – showing your diary for the duration of the visit with appointments. Information can include date, time, location, directions to get there, contact, telephone number in case of delay; your hotel for each evening, with location, telephone. Armed with such a detailed plan you can proceed calmly to your appointments, telephone ahead if you are delayed, and leave contact numbers for anyone needing to get hold of you during the course of the trip.

Time differences in Europe are an annoyance in business. During the times that Britain is out of step with most of the rest of the Continent by one hour or more, business people can lose effectively four hours a day chasing colleagues in offices or factories who have arrived to work earlier, gone to lunch, returned from lunch just when Britons are going, and departed for the night by 4.00 pm British time. These time differences need to be borne in mind both when trying to telephone people in Europe and when scheduling appointments that depend on (local) arrival times by air or rail.

When to go, when not to go

In addition to the time differences, European working habits differ slightly from those in Britain. These can include an earlier start for many managers, particularly those working in industry, where 8.00 is not uncommon. A later start (around 9.00 am) is more common in the capitals, and big cities, largely due to the length of time spent commuting to work. Lunch may be taken early, around midday in the northern part of Europe, later in the large cities (1.00 pm) and the south. In Spain and Portugal, and in southern Italy but not the more industrial north, there may be a late lunch (2.00 pm) followed by a break until 5.00 pm when some offices reopen until 7.00 or 8.00 pm. Some Italian Government offices may close at 2.00 and not re-open, although some senior officials may be at work later in the day and can sometimes be seen by appointment. In Germany and most northern European countries, business ends promptly at 5.00 pm and no appointments would be expected after that time. There are wide variations in business habits, and clearly the exporter should enquire when making appointments just when people will be available.

Invitations to lunch may be offered or not. In some northern European countries, and particularly in large firms, lunch may be taken in the firm's dining room and the visitor may be invited to stay. Further south lunch is more of a leisurely, social affair and can take up much of the working day. As a result some executives are following the American or British habit of a shorter working lunch. Again customs vary and the visitor should not be put off if he is not invited to lunch during the early stages of a business relationship.

Europeans take their leisure and non-working time seriously, with more public holidays than in Britain. Enquiries should be made when setting up a series of appointments, particularly as in some countries there is a habit of lengthening the weekend when a public holiday falls on a Thursday. The Friday also is 'bridged', to take advantage of a four day break. Lists of public holidays are given in the *DTI Country Guides* and other manuals for travellers.

In addition to public holidays the business traveller should avoid the main holiday seasons, when many of his potential contacts will not be available anyway. The main periods to avoid are:

- the weeks immediately before and after Christmas
- around Easter,
- above all the months of July and August.

Although there are exceptions, European businessmen tend to take their main holiday – usually four weeks uninterrupted – during the months of July and August, with the result that many factories and to a lesser extent offices formally close down for a set holiday period.

Clearly this period is no use for business travel, and in any event the height of the holiday season is not the best time for European travel by any form of transport. The airports, trains and roads are all congested as holidaymakers head south to the sun, millions of them choosing to do it at the same time. The best times, therefore, for business travel are from February to June (but avoiding Easter and Whitsun breaks) and from September to the end of November.

The weather may be extremely hot in the southern parts of Europe during summer, which accounts for the shorter business hours and longer holidays. Lighter weight clothing may be required. At the opposite extreme, the winters can be long and cold in northern Europe, particularly Denmark, giving rise to an earlier start to business and prompt closing at the end of the working day.

In addition to the above, Europe hosts a number of major trade exhibitions when executives in the exporter's line of business will not be available in their offices, as they are visiting or exhibiting at such events. The importance of exhibitions cannot be stressed too much (see following section) and the exporter should familiarise himself with the main events in Europe, as means for research, as possible promotion vehicles for his products or services, and as an indicator of which industries or cities are best avoided at exhibition times. Cities such as Hanover, Dusseldorf and Cologne which host major events throughout the year attract many thousands of visitors during exhibition times, putting pressure on transport facilities and hotel accommodation. This makes it very difficult for the business traveller, who may find that flights are simply booked-up many weeks in advance.

Trade exhibitions

Europe has many more large purpose-built fair sites than the United Kingdom, many of them the same size or larger than Birmingham's National Exhibition Centre. For this reason, and of course ease of transport, many more international exhibitions are held in mainland Europe than in the United Kingdom. Full lists, together with details of assistance schemes, are available from the BOTB's Fairs & Promotions Branch (whose assistance in compiling this section is ledged). The main European events, which do not occur every year, are as follows. The months given are approximate and may vary from year to year.

General Trade Fairs
Frankfurt – International Spring Fair (February)
Hanover – Hanover International Trade Fair (April)
Frankfurt – International Autumn Trade Fair (August)

Agriculture, Fisheries, Horticulture, Machinery, etc.
Paris – SIMA (March)
Paris – International Agriculture/Poultry Exhibition (March)
Copenhagen – International World Fishing Exhibition (June)
Hanover – International Exhibition of Pig & Poultry Production (June)
Cologne – International Garden Trade Fair (September)
Nantes – International Fisheries Exhibition (September)
Paris – Garden Trade Fair (September)
Paris – Garden Furniture & Exterior Design (September)
Barcelona – Expo Avoga Poultry/Livestock Exhibition (November)
Frankfurt – International Technology Fair for Farm Production (November/December)
Zaragoza – FIMA International Agricultural Technology (March)
Amsterdam – European Fishing Tackle Exhibition (June)
Vigo – Vigo Fishing (September)
Paris – International Exhibition of Technology for Animal Based Products (November)

Aircraft, Aerospace
Paris – International Aeronautic & Space Exhibition (June)
Frankfurt – International Exhibition of Airport Construction Terminal Facilities Ground Equipment & Air Cargo Facilities (October)

Audio-visual Products and Services
Hamburg – Audio Engineering Society Exhibition/Convention (March)

Montreux – International TV Symposium & Technical Exhibition (June)

Geneva – World Electronic Media Symposium & Exhibition (October)

Stockholm – Satellite Exhibition (October)

Stockholm – Audio Engineering Society Exhibition/Convention (March)

Stuttgart – Viewdata, Cable TV & Microcomputers (June)

Building and Construction Industries

Utrecht – International Building Exhibition (January/February)

Munich – International Construction Machinery Fair (April)

Barcelona – Construmat (April)

Bologna – Building Industrialisation (October)

Oslo – Building Exhibition Reis Bygg (October)

Paris – International Building Exhibition (October)

Barcelona – World Fair of Concrete (November)

Paris – International Market for Subcontractors (November)

Hanover – International Building Trade Exhibition (February)

Munich – Building Materials and Systems (January)

Chemical Industries

Bologna – Perfumery & Cosmetics (April)

Amsterdam – Biotech (June)

Clothing and Fashion

Numerous events in Paris, Florence, Frankfurt, Stockholm, Madrid, Cologne, Milan, Dusseldorf, Munich, Amsterdam, Barcelona etc about which further information can be obtained from the British Knitting & Clothing Export Council

Computer Hardware and Software

Hanover – CEBIT (March)

Paris – Data Communication, Office Automation (April)

Brussels – Office of the Future (April)

Frankfurt – International Database Exhibition/Convention (May)
Utrecht – European Software Exhibition (May)
Zurich – Technology for Banking and Finance (May/June)
Stuttgart – Computer Aided Technology (June)
Paris – INFODIAL Information Technology (September)
Milan – EIMU Office Furniture (September)
Munich – Computer Systems and Applications (October)
Madrid – SIMO Office Equipment (November)
Paris – SICOB (April)
Cologne – Office Furniture Trade Fair (October)

Display and Shop Equipment

Dusseldorf – European Fair for Modern Shopfitting Equipment (February)

Education & Training

Stuttgart – International Exhibition for Education and Training (February/March)
Basle – International Trade Exhibition for Schools (May)

Electronics

Munich – International Trade Fair for Electronic Production (November)
Paris – COMPONIC Exhibition of Electronic Components (November)

Engineering

Hanover – Woodworking Machinery (May)
Dusseldorf – Foundry Trade Fair (May)
Hanover – International Machine Tool Trades Show (September)
Essen – Welding & Cutting Fair (September)
Paris – Woodworking Machinery (February)
Dusseldorf – International Wire & Tube Exhibition (April)
Milan – Shoe & Leathergoods Machinery Exhibition (May)
Milan – Woodworking Machinery Exhibition (May)
Stockholm – SPCI Paper Making Machinery Exhibition (May)
Bilbao – Machine Tool Trade Show (October)
Gothenburg – Hydraulics, Pneumatics, Automotive (November)

Essen – Sheet Metal Working (November)
Milan – Power Transmission, Drive & Control (November)

Food & Drink, Machinery, Catering

Cologne – International Sweets & Biscuit Fair (February)
Hamburg – Hotel & Bakery Trades (March)
Dusseldorf – International Bakery Exhibition (April)
Frankfurt – Meat Trades Fair (May/June)
Munich – World Fair for Beverage Technology
  (August/September)
Cologne – World Food Market (October)
Genoa – Hotel, Restaurant & Catering Equipment (October)
Paris – Hotel, Restaurant & Catering Equipment (October)
Gothenburg – Hotel & Restaurant Exhibition (October)
Barcelona – International Catering/Hotel Equipment (October)
Milan – Food Sample Show (November)
Amsterdam – International Hotel/Catering Industries Fair
  (January)
Paris – Contract Furniture Show (February)
Barcelona – International Food Fair (March)
Hamburg – Hotel & Bakery Trades Fair (March)
Utrecht – International Food Fair (May)
Paris – International Food Exhibition (October)
Dusseldorf – Trade Fair for Food and Catering (November)
Paris – International Food Machinery Exhibition (November)

Furniture, Furnishings, Lighting, Household Equipment, etc.

Cologne – International Furniture Fair (January)
Cologne – Trade Fair for Large Household Appliances (February)
Cologne – International Hardware Fair (March)
Frankfurt – Flooring Design Fair (April)
Lyon – International Furniture Exhibition (May)
Milan – Crystalware, Silverware, Gift Items etc. (September)
Valencia – International Furniture Fair (September)
Brussels – International Furniture Fair (November)
Paris – International Furniture Fair (January)
Frankfurt – Home and Household Textiles Trade Fair (January)
Stockholm – International Furniture Fair (February)

Milan – International Furniture Fair (September)
See also General Trade Fairs listed above

Heating, Ventilation, Plumbing

Frankfurt – International Trade Fair ISH (March)
Milan – International Trade Fair (February)
Brussels – EXPOCLIMA Heating, Ventilation, Air Conditioning
(November)

Hospital, Medical, Surgical Equipment

Stuttgart – International Dental Show (April)
Milan – International Optical Exhibition (May)
Hanover – International Hospital Exhibition (June)
Barcelona – TECHNOCLINIC (October)

Mining Engineering, Offshore

Dusseldorf – International Mining Exhibition & Congress (May)
Nice – Liquified Natural Gas Exhibition (October)
Amsterdam – Petroleum Technology (March)
Stavanger – Offshore Technology (August)
Amsterdam – Holland Offshore (November)

Motor Vehicles, Components, Accessories, Cycles, Motorcycle

Geneva – International Motor Show (March)
Gothenburg – Auto Show (March)
Barcelona – Motor Show (May)
Frankfurt – International Motor Show (May)
Paris – Car Components & Spares, Garage Equipment (October)
Milan – Cycle & Motorcycle Show (November)
Turin – Motor Vehicles Components Spares (May)
Barcelona – Expomovil (May)
Geneva – International Exhibition for Suppliers to Vehicle
Industry (May)
Cologne – International Trade Fair for Motorcycle & Cycles
(September)
Frankfurt – International Exhibition of Workshop & Garage
Equipment (September)

Printing, Packaging, Paper Making, Converting
Milan – Trade Fair for Packaging Technologies (November)
Dusseldorf – INTERPACK (June)
Paris – International Packaging Exhibition (December)
Barcelona – Packaging for Food Processing (February)
Dusseldorf – DRUPA (April/May)

Safety, Fire, Security
Dusseldorf – Industrial Safety & Occupational Health Exhibition
    & Congress (June)
Utrecht – International Security Exhibition (September)
Paris – International Exhibition of Police, Defence, Military
    Equipment (November)
Madrid – International Security, Fire & Safety (February)
Paris – International Exhibition of Safety & Security Equipment
    (November)

Ships, Shipbuilding, Ports, Marine Equipment
Dusseldorf – International Boat Show (January)
Amsterdam – MARICHEM (October)
Amsterdam – International Exhibition Shipbuilding etc.
    (November)
Paris – International Pleasure Boat Exhibition (December)
Piraeus – International Shipping Exhibition (June)
Hamburg – ITF for Shipping & Marine Technology (October)

Sports Goods and Equipment, Leisure
Munich – International Sports Equipment Fair (February,
    September)
Stockholm – Leisure Fair (April)
Essen – International Exhibition for Horse Sports & Leisure
    (April)
Amsterdam – European Fishing Tackle Exhibition (June)
Cologne – International Sports Goods/Leisure Show (September)
Paris – Sports & Camping Goods (September)

Water Treatment, Environment
Dusseldorf – International Fair & Congress (April)

Bilbao – International Environmental Protection (November)
Amsterdam – International Cleaning & Maintenance (May)
Munich – International Exhibition for Waste Disposal etc. (May)

The above list should not be taken as exhaustive, and further information should be obtained either from the BOTB Exhibitions and Fairs Branch, or from the exporter's relevant trade association. We shall return to the subject of exhibitions in Chapter 8 when discussing their potential for promoting your goods and services in Europe. But already it can be seen from this list that visiting major international events such as these in Europe is an excellent means of undertaking research into the market potential for your proposed product. At many such trade shows exhibitors frequently advertise their need for agents and distributors and again reciprocal business may result simply from visiting a few major European exhibitions.

Visiting British Embassy trade counsellors and overseas Chambers of Commerce

British Embassies and Consulates are established throughout Europe, in the capitals as well as some of the major provincial cities. Because they are close to the territory in which they serve they can be a valuable source of advice and information to the exporter, as well as local contacts. Many of the embassies and consulates produce detailed notes about special aspects of their local territory which are available for the asking – sometimes through the BOTB in London and the regions. Embassy staff are also usually involved in preparing the *Country Profile* booklets already mentioned, so their contribution to the exporter's market intelligence is both up to date and relevant.

However, it must be realised that embassy and consular staff are extremely busy and while they are invariably knowledgeable and helpful, they should not be used as a substitute for the exporter's own research. In preparing this book I contacted a number of British embassies in Europe to try and get a feel for the sort of advice they are most frequently asked for and what in general is the state of preparedness of the typical business visitor to the embassy or consulate. Here are some of their replies.

'The majority of companies who call on us at the Embassy are small and medium-sized manufacturing and service companies: we see fewer distribution companies. Some of those we see are new to exporting, and will not always have done their homework. But if as should be the case they have been in touch with the DTI in London or the regions, they should have a reasonable idea how to go about the task of exporting. The representatives that we see here sometimes by no means always speak French: we make clear that the ability to communicate in French and to produce literature in French is essential, and that if they do not have the skills themselves they will need to employ someone who does (e.g. a translation service). The demands of companies vary, but include requests for help in finding agents or distributors for their products, alongside more general information about how to go about tackling the market. Increasingly, against the background of 1992, we are now also receiving questions about industrial collaboration and mergers and acquisitions.' (*Counsellor, British Embassy, Paris*).

'It is difficult to tell you what types of British business we get involved with. It tends to be a complete cross section, though large international or multi-national companies tend not to need our help, unless perhaps a major problem looms that requires some interpretation of the Italian political system or official intervention with an Italian Ministry or the Minister himself. Many of our British visitors are looking at the Italian market for the first time, either to decide whether they should move into it, or to seek an agent to represent their interests. We are consequently asked mainly for market information and names of potential agents. Our experience has been that very few of our British visitors have little more than 'survival Italian' nor do they tend to come armed with trade literature translated into Italian.

'Our general advice to business visitors from the UK is that if they are serious about coming into this market they need to involve a local company or individual, whether this takes the form of an agent, a distributor, joint venture partner or manufacturer under licence. It is essential to have someone on the ground who understands the Italian way of doing business, Italian politics (which are all pervasive) and who can guide one through the

Byzantine bureaucracy. In the approach to 1992 we find that both British and Italian companies are actively seeking partners, so we are also refining a system of 'marriage broking' whereby we hope to bring together suitable companies for commercial or industrial collaboration.

'Once British companies are in the market, we can assist them in a positive way by making our presentation facility here at the Embassy available to them. They are then able, usually with the assistance of their agent, to give a professional commercial promotion in the Embassy to a selected audience. This is a successful formula and is a facility which we actively promote.' (*First Secretary Commercial, British Embassy, Rome*).

'At this Embassy we see visitors from all sorts of companies, large and small, in both the manufacturing and service sectors. At current rates, we see around 400 – 500 British visitors annually and a similar number of local business visitors. Moreover, we receive approximately 1500 telephone enquiries annually, either from British visitors already in Spain or direct from companies in the UK.

'The advice sought covers all areas – namely help in finding agents, general market information and introductions. Additionally, in the run-up to 1992, UK companies are increasingly investigating possibilities for industrial collaboration, joint ventures, mergers and acquisitions.

'Obviously we are not qualified to answer all the technical and other detailed questions which come our way and we believe that advice on appropriate contacts for the visitor is one of the most effective ways in which we can help. Many visitors come well briefed, but there are still some who have not "done their homework". Indeed this aspect is stressed in a recent DTI publication about the re-packaged services. Similarly many British companies do attach importance to their representatives having a knowledge of the Spanish language and to providing trade literature in Spanish. But it has to be said that many do not and that mailshots in English have only a limited chance of success. It is important for serious exporters to surmount this language barrier.' (*First Secretary Commercial, British Embassy, Madrid*).

From the comments of Embassy staff it is clear that some British exporters still arrive in the foreign country without adequate preparation, and as a result do not make the best use of their visit. In using the services of the British Embassies, as with all other sources of information and advice, the exporter should be clear about precisely what he is seeking. At this stage he can make a prior telephone call and if the subject is detailed or complicated send a written agenda ahead to the Embassy commercial department, either by post or telefax. This will help commercial counsellors to locate the relevant information, possibly even initiate some personal introductions, so enhancing the usefulness of the exporter's visit. It is clearly both helpful and polite to send ahead background literature about the exporter's company so that Embassy staff have an idea whom they are dealing with.

Addresses and telephone numbers of British Embassies and Consulates in Europe are given in the Department of Industry *Country Profiles* and *Hints to Businessmen* booklets, and can be obtained by telephoning the Department of Trade in London and regional offices. A telephone call to the Embassy will then establish the names of individual commercial counsellors, and facilitate later introductions.

Like all European offices, Embassies and Consulates – particularly the Commercial Sections dealing with less urgent matters than personal difficulties of British citizens abroad – have their opening and closing times, and are generally not available during the lunchtime period and may be short-staffed during holiday periods. A telephone call to the Embassy or Consultate will clarify these matters.

Mention has already been made of the links between British-based Chambers of Commerce and the various international Chambers located in the major European cities. They can offer a wide range of services such as library and research facilities, temporary offices and meeting rooms, and arrange personal introductions and informal contacts. The use of these facilities is generally on a membership basis and an exporter doing regular business with a particular country may find that belonging to the relevant international Chamber brings a number of advantages.

Travel in Europe

Europe's major markets are readily accessible from the United Kingdom by air, sea, rail and road. The choice of transport will depend to a certain extent on the destination: few exporters will want to drive overland direct to Denmark, Italy, Greece, Spain or Portugal simply because of the time/distances involved. In such instances a more natural choice would be that of air, followed by local travel by road or rail. This section is not intended as a visitors travelogue, but indicates the principal services available to reach and travel around the major European markets. The section is divided into countries but clearly most parts of Western Europe can be regarded as a composite whole, as national borders become progressively less relevant. However, it remains a convenient way of dealing with the subject.

France

France lies at the centre of most north/south European communications by road. It is a large country, but with an excellent motorway network which is being continually improved in an accelerated programme that should be completed by 1997. One of the aims of the programme is to alter the emphasis of the present system, which tends to offer the best links outwards from the capital Paris. The result is that most journeys involve passing through Paris, by way of the well-known *peripherique* (ring road). Motorway schemes are under way to improve cross country links that will avoid going through Paris.

The present motorway network is just under 5,400 kilometres, of which 4,800 are covered by tolls. This figure will almost double by the year 2000, with the emphasis on new international direct routes from Italy via Lyon, towards Nantes in the north west; from southern Germany via Lyon, towards Nantes and Le Havre. An outer orbital route is being constructed around Paris, some 60 kilometres from the *peripherique*, together with a second inner ring road some 7–10 kilometres from the *peripherique*. The outer ring is due for completion during the 1990s and will link the main north/south and east/west motorways. The inner ring is designed mainly to aid access to the long distance motorways and to assist local traffic moving around Greater Paris.

French motorways are subject to tolls, at a rate of around FF65 per 100 kilometres. These can make motorway driving expensive but fast and France's roads attract 90% of personal travellers and 50% of freight. However, apart from peak holiday times, there is considerably less congestion than on British roads and the French network provides rapid access by road directly with Belgium, West Germany, Italy, and Spain, and the United Kingdom via the Channel Ports. The motorway from Calais is now extremely fast and connects with the main A1 coming south from Belgium to Paris.

France's rail network is also one of the most extensive in Europe at 36,000 kilometres. French Rail have established a number of high speed routes using special TGV trains which can travel up to 380 kms/hour – the world speed record. There are high speed links from Paris to Lyon (2 hours), Nantes (3 hours), Strasbourg (4 hours), Rouen (just over 1 hour) and other major French cities, as well as the Channel Ports for Britain (average 3 hours) and to Brussels (2 hours 30 minutes) and Geneva (3 hours 30 minutes). Similar to the motorway network, French rail services tend to fan out from the capital and a programme of improving cross country links is in hand, as well as the provision of more north/south links that will avoid Paris and more direct international links, including the high speed rail link that will eventually connect London and Paris.

Paris is easily accessible by air from the United Kingdom, with international flights arriving at the northern airport of Roissy/Charles de Gaulle. Direct flights are available from London (Heathrow, Gatwick, London City Airport) and Britain's regional airports to Paris, and to major cities in France (Lyon, Marseille, Nice etc.). Internal flights within France are handled by Air Inter but one of the drawbacks for international travellers is changing flights in Paris, between Charles de Gaulle and Orly Airport, the latter handling mostly internal flights. However, increasing competition is opening up new routes between France's provincial airports and destinations in other European countries, for both passengers and freight. An agent specialising in business travel will keep the exporter informed of new services.

West Germany

As already noted there are a number of direct road links with Germany including those via the international motorways from Belgium and France. From Belgium the motorist can enter Germany at Aachen, and head towards Bonn, Cologne and Dusseldorf, and the industrial areas grouped around Essen. Further south entry is via Saarbrucken, having followed the French autoroute from Reims and Metz (for Frankfurt, Wiesbaden going north, and Mainheim, Heidelberg, Karlsruhe to the south). Via Strasburg the route is towards southern Germany (Stuttgart, Augsburg, Munich).

Within Germany, as a result of partition from the East, the main autobahn routes are from north to south, and sometimes the roads run in parallel either side of the river Rhine where traffic is heaviest. Motorway driving in Germany is not for the faint hearted. Roads are fast and reasonably well signposted, but a wrong turning can cause considerable delay and frustration in trying to get back onto the main road. It is possible to travel from the industrial Ruhr region to Munich in the south comfortably within the working day.

The German rail network is fast and efficient. It comprises international services connecting with other European countries, intercity services, and ordinary fast and stopping services. Within the larger conurbations of Hamburg, the Ruhr, Frankfurt, Stuttgart and Munich there are special *S-Bahn* services offering fast local connections. Direct rail services from the United Kingdom are via Dover to Ostend (Belgium) and Harwich to the Hook of Holland.

By air there are direct flights to the main German cities from London and also some services from Belfast, Birmingham, Manchester, Glasgow and Edinburgh. Within West Germany there are linking flights between Berlin, Hamburg, Dusseldorf, Cologne/Bonn, Munich, Nuremberg, Stuttgart, etc. Over the longer distances, such as Frankfurt to Munich, and Frankfurt to Hamburg, there are around 20 flights per day. Frankfurt is the hub of both the national and international networks, and readily accessible by *autobahn* from both north and south.

Belgium, Netherlands, Luxemburg

Belgium is easily accessible by road from the Channel Ports and from its European neighbours France, Germany, Luxemburg and Holland. The network of motorways and main roads is excellent, with numerous cross-border links where progress into a neighbouring country will scarcely be noticed. The capital can be bypassed using the well signposted Brussels Ring. Place names can appear in both French and Flemish so it is as well to be familiar with both. Motorways are prefixed by the letter 'A' and/or the more recent European (E) numbering system.

Rail services tend to radiate outwards from Brussels with important national and international links to Ostend and via Lille to Calais, north to Antwerp and onwards to Amsterdam, to Luxemburg, and onwards to Switzerland and Italy; and the express trains to Paris and to Germany.

London, Birmingham and Manchester are among the main airports offering direct air services to Brussels, and there are also direct flights from London to Antwerp, and London to Liege. There are additional services to Brussels from East Midlands, Luton, Southend and Stansted airports. Brussels Airport is about 10 kms from the city centre.

Luxemburg is served by the principal road and rail networks of Europe, and by direct air routes from London and other European cities.

The Netherlands is reached by road from Belgium and West Germany, and has an excellent internal motorway network linking the main centres of population between Rotterdam and Amsterdam, eastwards towards Utrecht and Arnhem, and north to Groningen. From Britain there are Cross Channel ferry links to Hook of Holland, and via the Belgian ports of Ostend and Zeebrugge.

Rail services are both international connecting with Hook of Holland for Britain and West Europe, and national covering all major cities.

By air, Amsterdam's Schiphol airport is a busy hub for international and domestic flights, and there are direct flights from London and other major European cities. Rotterdam is also well served by air and there are domestic airports at some other Dutch cities.

Spain and Portugal

By road Spain can be entered from France, using direct motorway links. To the north west they are via Biarritz to Santander, Bilbao and Spain's northern industrial coastline. To the south east, the main French autoroutes from Toulouse and from Nimes/Montpellier join together just north of Perpignan and enter Spain, continuing along the Mediterranean coast towards Barcelona. Within Spain there are motorways connecting Barcelona with Bilbao in the north, further south along the Mediterranean coast, and to the capital Madrid. Some motorways are subject to tolls. There are few major roads into Portugal, from the direction of Madrid, and from Sevilla in the south. Northern Portugal (Porto) can be reached via the Atlantic coast road from Vigo and La Coruna in Spain. Motorways are prefixed 'A' for *autopista*, and major National roads with the letter 'N'.

There are rail links to Spain mainly starting from Paris, but some journeys can take more than a full day. Rail services, operated by Spain's RENFE, reach the major cities of Spain and Portugal, and trains are modern and comfortable, although not as fast as in some other European countries. Sleeper services can be used overnight, for example, Barcelona to Bilbao and Barcelona to Madrid. Fast train services include those known as *Talgo* and Trans European Express, while *Expreso* and *Rapido* will be less fast.

Spain is well served by air from London, with regular flights to Barcelona, Madrid, Bilbao and Malaga. There are also some direct services to Alicante, Almeria, Gerona, Santiago and Valencia. There are additional flights to Spain from Britain's provincial airports during the summer, when the business traveller must take account of the seasonal holiday traffic. Internal flights by Iberia and Aviaco connect Madrid with some of Spain's major cities, and there are also direct links from Barcelona and elsewhere to other main towns. Air services to Portugal include flights to Lisbon and Porto. Services may be congested during the peak holiday season.

Italy

Italy can be reached by road from France and Switzerland, as well as from Austria and Yugoslavia. The roads from France and Switzerland leading towards northern Italy (for Turin, Milan) pass through mountainous regions but are generally open throughout the year, including the Mont Blanc road tunnel. Furthermore, the Mediterranean coastal autoroute linking Marseille, Aix-en-Provence, Cannes, Nice and Monaco continues into northern Italy at Ventimiglia. It can then be followed northwards to Milan and the northern industrial belt, or south towards Florence, Rome and southern Italy. Italy's internal road network includes motorway links with all the principal cities with coastal routes along the Mediterranean (west) side of the country and along the east (Adriatic) coast in a north/south direction. There are a number of cross routes linking Rome and further south Naples on the west, with the Adriatic. Motorways or *autostrade* are prefixed with a letter 'A' and usually attract tolls. National highways are prefixed with 'S S' for *strade statali*.

The Italian rail system is extensive and part-electrified. Main services include express links with the major cities, overnight sleepers and motorail services. Its international links include car sleeper services from Boulogne to Milan, Paris to Milan and Brussels to Milan. Within Italy fast and frequent services connect Milan to Rome and include Motorail and sleeper facilities.

The main air routes to Italy are by Alitalia and British Airways and include numerous direct services from London to Milan and Rome, Manchester to Milan and Rome, and Birmingham or Glasgow to Milan. Additional services are available, and may be extended during peak holiday times. Domestic flights within Italy include links between Rome and Milan, Turin, etc.

Greece

Because of its distance from the United Kingdom and indeed the rest of the European Community, Greece is best reached by air by the business traveller. Road links mean passing through Albania or Bulgaria and will probably not be permitted. Regular scheduled air services fly to Athens from the United Kingdom.

Denmark

As a result of its distance and complex geography Denmark is most likely to be reached by air. Scheduled services fly to Copenhagen, and may call first at Arhus on Denmark's Jutland Peninsula. With the majority of the population living in and around Copenhagen, travel to the other islands will probably not be required initially. Jutland is sparsely populated but because of its land border with Germany it is of growing industrial importance and can be be reached by road links north of Hamburg.

European road travel: an overview

The growing acceptance of the 'E' symbol to designate Europe's major trunk roads is an indication of the strategic nature of the network, with roads no longer regarded as ending at a country's national borders. It is now or will shortly be possible to drive to all the European capitals and principal cities using the motorway net-work, although the proposed Euro Tunnel rail link is a disappointing compromise. Distances are greater than the British motorist may be used to, but it is perfectly possible to reach almost all of northern Europe within a day of leaving the United Kingdom. The growth of high speed train services and increasing competition among airlines, leading hopefully to a reduction in fares, will also gradually make Europe easier and quicker to reach from Britain. This should make travel to Europe as matter-of fact as travel within the British Isles.

As well as the new 'E' symbols motorists will find that European roads are measured in kilometres. If it can be remembered that each mile represents 1.6 kilometres, the traveller will recognise speed limits – 100 kilometres is about 75 mph – and gradually judge distances without the need to convert. Most vehicle instruments are calibrated in both miles and kilometres making the process easier. Eight hundred kilometres can seem much more manageable when translated into just under 500 miles.

Throughout Europe traffic drives on the right but again it is relatively easy to adjust to his, even when driving a right-hand vehicle. Traffic regulations vary slightly between countries, and include restrictions on the use of the horn (surprisingly, in Italy), urban speed limits and so on, but an international system of road symbols makes these readily understandable. Whatever the precise regulations it is as well to be prepared for journeys in Europe by carrying appropriate items such as a first aid kit, an accident warning triangle and membership of one of the motoring organisations. Insurance packages include return of your vehicle to Britain, accident cover, third-party claims etc., in addition to the obligatory Green Card which offers minimal insurance protection.

All the major companies (such as Avis, Hertz, Europcar, Budget) offer car hire services, enabling the traveller to take a car from Britain or to hire one at his destination.

Services on European motorways are generally excellent, with frequent petrol/diesel stations and rest stops, as well as facilities ranging from simple snack bars to cafés, self-service restaurants and overnight accommodation. Off the motorways services are less readily available, particularly outside the summer holiday season. It can save time and frustration to carry a flask of coffee and something to keep you going.

Finally, it should be remembered that penalties for traffic offences in Europe can be severe, partly as a reaction to the appalling accident rates in some countries. Drinking and driving is a severely punishable offence virtually everywhere.

All that said, driving in Europe can be pleasant and efficient, less congested generally than in Britain – even at so-called peak times in July and August – and certainly at other times of the year when the business traveller will normally be on the road. It is quite possible to drive for several hours in parts of France and encounter only a handful of vehicles.

There are a number of excellent travel guides which list, among other information, details of hotels in major European cities. These are ideal for locating a city centre or airport hotel, and reservations can be made from the United Kingdom by telephone and telex. Reservation staff invariably speak English.

Away from the main centres it is more difficult, although there are a number of European chains such as Mercure and Novotel which provide basic standard accommodation at strategic points on the motorways. These are ideal for overnight stops while driving, as they avoid the need to drive into the centres of strange towns trying to locate a hotel. Some motorway guides list these out-of-town hotels, as well as giving details of rest facilities, petrol stations, etc., en route.

It is possible to trust to luck rather than book in advance, outside the holiday seasons, but the wise traveller will at least phone ahead to his next destination – a free service provided by the hotel chains – before setting off.

5 How can I do business with Europe?

Having carried out his desk research and possibly a field visit to the market, the exporter should now consider the different methods of selling his goods or services to Europe. There are a number of alternatives, not all of them suitable to every type of product, and this chapter and those that follow consider the possible options. Briefly they are:

- Selling direct to Europe from the United Kingdom
- Selling to UK based representative offices
- Selling through import houses
- Using a representative or agent
- Selling through a distributor or wholesaler
- Selling through your own branch office
- Setting up your own subsidiary in Europe
- Selling through a licensing agreement
- Joint venture with a European partner

Each of these options to some extent represents an increasing level of commitment to the European market. Although, as will be discussed later, it is possible to sell large volumes of goods direct to Europe from the United Kingdom, this generally involves less investment in 'sales infrastructure' than, say, setting up a European subsidiary or going into business with a European partner. However, these methods are not mutually exclusive and the exporter may start with one form of selling and convert to another, or indeed use a variety of methods in different markets. The various possibilities are considered in the following sections, and some are explored in greater depth in Chapter 7 'Selling consumer goods to Europe' and in Chapter 8 'Selling services to Europe'. The fiscal implications of the various European strategies are generally covered in Chapter 10.

Selling direct to Europe

This method of selling is the simplest to initiate and reflects the exporter's determination to treat Europe as an extension of his home market. It can be used both for capital goods and business-to-business goods and services which can be sold direct to European end users, and for consumer goods, thanks to the concentrations of buying power in the hands of supermarket and store chains, voluntary chains (symbol groups), as well as the establishment in the United Kingdom of agents and buying offices working on behalf of retailers (and some capital goods purchasers).

Direct selling can be used to test-market a product or service that is already selling in the home market. Some basic market research will have indicated that the item is as likely to sell in Europe as in Britain and as a result tentative steps can be taken to market the same or slightly modified product in Europe. The direct sale may simply result from the exporter's presence at an international exhibition, where his research/marketing effort has paid off in the form of an order placed by a European purchaser on the British company. Little or no further active marketing may be undertaken beyond this stage.

Some goods and services lend themselves particularly well to direct selling from the United Kingdom. They include:

- **Specialised capital goods** Where a United Kingdom based company has an international reputation for specialising in a particular field, then sales to Europe (as to other parts of the world) may be handled in much the same way as domestic sales. Typical specialisations are equipment for the process industries where detailed knowledge and expertise are regarded as part of the package and may command a premium. Examples from the author's own experience include a Hertfordshire based company selling high value (average 1 million pounds) coating systems for the manufacture of audio and video tapes, credit cards and other high-technology applications. Worldwide sales are conducted from the home base as the company is currently the world leader in this particular sector.
- **Goods for which there is a known customer base** Again following on from specialisation, some capital goods are sold only in known markets, for example, to the oil exploration industry, to

television broadcasting companies, or to paper manufacturers. Such industries are small and specialised even on a worldwide basis, and generally benefit from international trade directories where the potential customer base can be readily identified. Direct mail to the companies listed, backed by presence at international exhibitions, may result in European enquiries which can be converted into sales. Another example is that of a Yorkshire based company making specialised dryer equipment – using an air flotation principle. It knows that its markets are within the industries concerned with paper making and the processing of paper, films, foils, non woven materials. Potential users can be identified from international trade directories and at major exhibitions. The most important of these is held every four years in Dusseldorf and attracts over 250,000 visitors from all over the world. By exhibiting at this event the company can be fairly certain of exposing itself to its entire potential customer base. Local agents are of course used to generate and follow up sales enquiries.

- **Goods requiring a high level of service** My own consultancy has recently advised some firms that they are more in the field of problem-solving than manufacturing. Along with the machinery or equipment they sell, they offer high levels of knowledge and expertise, often unique to the company and as a result not easily transferable. This means that although local representatives can be used at the initial enquiry stage, company executives have to travel widely to deal personally with the customer to assess his precise requirements, propose a solution or decide on the detailed design of a one-off solution because they possess the necessary expert knowledge. The eventual sales process will frequently include on-site installation and commissioning, supervision of field trials, and ongoing service backup. Examples include businesses such as those providing warehousing and handling systems, where a high level of expert knowledge is required to assess the customer's requirements and prepare a detailed specification. Such operations border on consultancy, and indeed this may be provided either as a separate operation by the manufacturer or by independent professionals. In the above example, they might be design engineers or handling-systems consultants.

- **High value capital goods** Some capital installations are so expensive that they constitute occasional or one-off purchases. Examples include steel rolling mills or complete vehicle manufacturing plants. Although some initial selling may occur on the ground due to the efforts of a local agent, the agent's role is generally more that of intelligence gathering and performing the initial introductions for his United Kingdom principal. The United Kingdom based supplier is involved in complex and lengthy negotiation with the European customer, and for major projects is probably part of a consortium of suppliers coming together from all over the world. Selling is at the highest level, involving main board directors and uniquely qualified specialists from the home based company. A local office may in fact be required eventually, after the sale has been made, to supervise the completion of the contract.

In the examples cited above and other instances, the main requirements are usually for regular sales visits to Europe by representatives of the United Kingdom based company. They may be sales engineers or higher level executives. They basically respond to enquiries received at company headquarters, as a result of promotion (exhibitions, direct mail, etc.) instigated on a worldwide or European basis from the home office, and/or from local representatives on the ground. Technical literature has to be available in the languages of the markets to be covered, and fluency in foreign languages is clearly an asset for the salesman. Other promotional methods are high-level technical seminars for invited potential customers, held either at the home factory or in the field. (See Chapters 7 and 8).

Consumer Goods

Discussed in more detail under Retailing, many types of consumer goods can also be sold direct to Europe. This is because the main European retailers have centralised many of their buying functions. These can take the form of a head office buying unit, located in a European city; and/or a United Kingdom based buying office. Approaching the market is therefore relatively easy and may not require local presence in the market, other than regular sales visits from the United Kingdom.

Services

Some services (see also Chapter 7) can be sold direct to Europe. Again they follow many of the principles enumerated above of a known customer base that can be approached through direct mail and other means, and a high degree of specialisation and an expertise that is in demand by a worldwide customer base. Although some professional and business services may require a local presence (architecture, legal services) because of the need for frequent contact with the client, others can be sold from the United Kingdom (management consultancy, environmental services). For example, the author's London-based market and research consultancy has as many clients in Europe as in the United Kingdom.

Selling through import houses

This is a form of direct selling from the United Kingdom, where the exporter has limited or even no contact with the ultimate European customer. Many import houses handle a wide range of goods from raw materials and commodities, to both capital and consumer items. Others may specialise in certain areas and/or commodities. Importers buy and sell goods on their own account, and provide warehousing, storage and distribution facilities. In the case of industrial goods, many will undertake to hold spares and provide servicing facilities for their customers. Frequently such spare parts are supplied on consignment, and paid for as and when they are used by the end customer. Special arrangements may be required for servicing under warranty, which the importer may be unwilling to handle himself.

Not all importers will undertake to sell. Sales can be placed in the hands of agents, while the importer confines his activities to order fulfillment, warehousing and delivery.

Bulk commodities such as grains, rice, fruit, cotton, coal, oil and cake meal, fats, timber, wood, pulp, paper, fibres, rubber, synthetics, spices, herbs, wines and spirits etc., may be handled by importers, who buy, on their own account and provide storage, in bond if required. However, these commodities are often purchased direct by end users who bypass the entire importer/wholesale network.

Agents and representatives

By far the largest number of exporters will be concerned at some stage in their European sales operation with local agents or representatives. The following sections therefore deal at some length with what agents do, how they can be located, how to select them, how to get the best out of them. The use of agents is governed by, in some countries, very strict laws and although these are summarised in the text exporters considering appointing agents will need to take advice from the sources that will be suggested.

A good agent will in the long run save the exporter a great deal of time and effort in the market. He will open doors, perform introductions, keep his eye on competitor activities, suggest new markets and new products, and generally make life easier for you. Such paragons are not, however, easily found, and care is needed both in the selection and subsequent support of your European agent. Among the commonest mistakes made by companies is lack of care in the initial selection, and consistently neglecting the agent by not attending promptly to his demands. Invariably markets cannot be abandoned to the agent, however diligent he may be, and time spent in visiting and supporting him will be well spent.

Another common error is to imagine that a single agent will be sufficient to look after your interests inside a whole country. As noted elsewhere European markets are large and sophisticated. As a guide to the level of representation required in say France or West Germany, the exporter should ask himself how many sales people he has covering an area of equivalent size in the United Kingdom. All too often companies employing five or ten sales people to cover Britain feel that adequate representation in an important market like Germany involves using the part-time services of a single agent. Such an approach simply will not work.

How do agents operate?

Agents are normally self-employed individuals or firms who sell goods (and occasionally services) on the basis of a percentage of the value of the sales (a commission). Agents may work, and usually do, for a number of principals and as well as being individuals, agents may in fact be partnerships or companies of several people. When selling to their end customers, they may or may not disclose the name(s) of their principals. For example, an agent might represent a number of textile suppliers and his sources of supply are not of primary interest to his end customers.

Some agents may in fact stock some goods, either purchased from their principals or supplied on consignment, and in this respect almost become stockist/distributors.

Most commonly in the capital goods sector, an agent is used to represent the exporter's interests inside a given territory. The agent will normally expect exclusive coverage within a defined area and to be remunerated by commission, usually on all sales within this agreed territory. In some cases, as will be seen, the country's laws are quite specific about this type of remuneration, including the rights of an agent after termination of his contract.

Agents will naturally wish to enhance their chance of earning a living by asking for as large a territory as possible, and sometimes exclusive rights to a whole European country. This may be acceptable if the agent is in fact a firm, with perhaps a number of offices in key centres and sufficient staff that will ensure that the country is adequately covered from the exporter's point of view. Some agents operate through a network of associates, so that when approached by the exporter they may wish to consult their associates before taking on a new agency. No agent will sensibly take on a product that is not going to make money for him in the form of sales and commission, and some agents may wish to research the market before agreeing to handle the exporter's business.

How many agents do you need?

The exporter should have a clear idea about the size of territories that he feels can be adequately covered by an agent. A country's size may not be the only criterion. The size, importance and location of particular industries where the exporter knows from his research that sales can be made, can be more decisive. Geographically, a country can be split into a number of sales territories, in a similar way that the United Kingdom is usually divided up between members of the home sales force. The smaller European markets of Denmark,

Netherlands, Belgium and Luxemburg, Portugal and Greece may conceivably be handled from one location and indeed by a one-man agency.

France, however, may require separate representation for the north, perhaps based on Lille, the Paris region, the south west (Bordeaux), the south east (Lyon) and the Mediterranean (Marseille). Italy invariably requires separate representation in Milan and the north, as well as Rome and perhaps further south. In Spain, Barcelona and Madrid are usually the subject of separate agency agreements, with possibly a third to cover the northern coastal areas (Bilbao). West Germany has been described as a country of many capitals, and indeed from the point of view of representation one can justify separate coverage of the north (Hamburg, Bremen), the Rhine/Ruhr region (based on Dusseldorf), the Frankfurt region, and the far south east (Munich). High-technology products may have to be marketed from Stuttgart, where there is a British Government Advanced Technology Marketing Office, and separate arrangements may be required for West Berlin.

Dividing the larger European countries into geographic sub-regions is sometimes necessary in view of the travelling distances involved, particularly if fairly frequent contact is needed with customers and potential customers on the ground. Another way of dividing responsibilities can be according to product or market category. One agent might, for example, only call on supermarkets, another department stores, a third symbol groups. In the industrial sector, one agent might call on construction companies, another on local authority specifiers. These arrangements are similar to those frequently employed in the home territory.

In weighing up the possible permutations the exporter will want to ensure that he is neither under-represented nor over-represented. In the first situation, he may lose sales to competitors who are more active in the market and more widely represented. In the second case, sales may be lost because the agent cannot make a living from selling the exporter's goods and so concentrates on more profitable business for his other principals.

How to find an agent?

As already noted, unless the agent is a direct employed representative of the exporting company, he will be a self-employed person or firm working for more than one principal. In selecting an agent the exporter will want to ensure that the agent is not already too committed to do justice to the new representation, and normally that he is operating in a complementary but not competing sector. Clearly, an agent specialising in confectionery is of no value to an exporter of engineering products.

There are a number of possible ways and they include visits to trade fairs, advertising and using the services of British Embassies in Europe and other official sources.

A common sight on many trade exhibition stands are signs announcing 'agents required', sometimes spelling out the territories that need to be covered. A British exporter using a trade show to launch a new product or service in Europe can use the same method. Enquirers will approach him, and the process of selection can begin. Agents offering their services sometimes advertise in trade journals or the exporter can place an advertisement himself stating that he is seeking representation and outlining the territories. In addition many trade directories list agents in different countries, together with the companies they represent. Studying these the exporter may decide to approach one or more agents who seem to be carrying complementary lines to his own, and ask if they are willing to take on his products.

The exporter can also make informal enquiries through his trade association, Chamber of Commerce and personal contacts in the trade. Good agents are hard to find and jealously guarded by their principals, but an alliance of interest may result where the exporter's products do not conflict with, and may indeed enhance the prospects of, those already carried by an agent.

A number of more formal approaches can be made and one of the most useful sources of information and help are the Commercial Sections of British Embassies. Their services are comprehensive as the following note from the British Embassy in Bonn illustrates:

'The British Embassy and Consular Posts in Germany in the course of many years of processing agency enquiries and of visiting German agents, have built up a great deal of knowledge, experience and a large number of contacts across wide fields of commerce and industry in Germany on which they draw in their work of seeking agents for UK firms. The British commercial services also seek the assistance of the local branches of the Agents Federation, as well as of Chambers of Commerce and commercial and industrial associations.'

Agency enquiries are normally circulated from the Embassy to regional Consular offices within the country of interest. Commercial Counsellors suggest that preliminary information can be sent to them in English, with copies in the local language for potential agents: a single sheet describing the company and its products is regarded as sufficient at this stage. Before or at the same time as this information is being circulated to potential agents, the Counsellor can also offer a rapid assessment based on his knowledge of local conditions of the potential of the new product or service for the market. While no substitute for in-depth market research, this informal market appraisal undoubtedly has its value.

If the prospects look good, the Embassy will then request up to 50 or more sets of trade literature, approximate prices etc., together with samples where appropriate, and these are circulated to potential agents within each Consular area. In the case of foodstuffs, the Embassies point out that sufficient samples should be provided to enable fairly comprehensive tasting. In all cases prices should be in the local currency, to enable reasonable comparisons to be made with the local alternative products. At this stage the exporter must furthermore ensure that his intended product complies with the various European and national safety norms and engineering standards.

Any additional information about which markets the product is destined for should also be supplied. Embassy Counsellors are at pains to point out that they are not necessarily specialists in all types of industry and the more information supplied at this stage the more likely they are to be able to approach an appropriate group of potential agents.

The European Embassies estimate that these processes will take about eight weeks from receipt of the initial enquiry. During the summer holiday months this timescale could be extended, as many offices close or are only partially operational during July and August. Once a potential agent has been located, either by the Embassy or as a result of other means already described, status reports can often be provided by the BOTB (Exports to Europe Branch) or can be obtained within a few weeks. A small fee is charged for this service. In addition banks and credit agencies can assist.

How to select an agent

Whichever means has been used to shortlist a group of potential agents it is at this stage that the exporter must set aside sufficient time to visit the potential agents for preliminary discussions. A meeting at the agent's office (or home, as many one-man businesses operate in this way) will give an indication of the style of operation and whether the exporter feels confident in entrusting his product to the agent. Clearly a knowledge of the agent's own language will be of great benefit, but fortunately agents are among those Europeans who speak good English, particularly if they already represent companies in the United Kingdom. The visits should not be rushed and an initial visit will take half a day or a day if the product is complex and the relationship appears to have potential for both parties. A serious exporter would perhaps consider a minimum of three to five potential agents in this way.

At this stage or when an agent has been officially appointed, it is useful in most cases to invite him to visit your home office and factory. This will give the agent an opportunity to see the product during manufacture, so that he improves his level of understanding of what it is you are asking him to sell on your behalf. The better he is briefed the better he is able to perform. The agent will also have an opportunity to meet other members of your staff with whom he will be in frequent contact. 'Putting a face to the name' when subsequent contacts will be mostly by the telephone and telex will undoubtedly help future relationships.

A number of general conventions need to be agreed and clarified at the outset between principal and agent. While remuneration is in the form of a percentage commission on sales, the agent may require some up-front payment – in the form of advance commission. This, he would argue, is to enable him to print literature, undertake some advertising, and generally cover the cost of introducing the exporter's product into the market. Some form of retainer may also be paid, together with other contributions towards expenses.

Alternatively, some sales on the territory may be 'reserved' by the exporter. These may be existing clients already being serviced direct from the United Kingdom, and the agent is not normally entitled to (full) commission on these as he was not instrumental in obtaining the original order. If these accounts are subsequently handed over to the agent for regular servicing then some form of commission would be paid, perhaps at a reduced level.

There must be clear agreement between the agent and his principal about what authority the agent has during the course of negotiations with the end customer. Normally the principal will reserve the right to accept or not accept orders passed to him by the agent, and the exporter's general sales conditions usually include a clause stating that obligations entered into by agents are not binding until confirmed by the principal. The agent's discretion to offer discounts or other special terms will also have to be clearly spelled out.

In practice, agents can not normally be held accountable if the end customer does not pay for the goods or services supplied by the exporter. The agent may not be entitled to his commission and in the general course of his duties he will have ascertained that the customer is a reasonable credit risk. But it is the responsibility of the exporter to satisfy himself that the ultimate customer is able to pay for supplies and he should carry out the usual credit checks if in any doubt. Attempting to extract compensation from the agent is unlikely to succeed and it is doubtful if the agent would have sufficient resources in such an eventuality to pay damages to the principal.

Another contentious area can be advertising and promotion. Some exporters feel that the agent should pay for such advertising in his own territory, while others agree to share the cost of advertisements, where they indicate that enquiries should be addressed to the agent. The agent can also be helpful in translating sales literature and other documents but it should not be assumed that he will always have time available or will donate these services free of charge. He has other principals to serve.

The agent has a general duty towards his principal of 'using his best endeavours' on his principal's behalf, not to disclose commercially sensitive information, to account accurately for sales and not to receive bribes or inducements or generate secret profits.

If after all the the preliminary negotiations both parties are satisfied, then an agency agreement can be drawn up. The whole process from initial enquiry to contract is unlikely to take less than six months, where the exporter is new to the market.

Formal agency legislation varies from one country to another and in addition the European Commission has introduced a number of directives on the subject with a view to harmonising continental practice overall. The main provisions at both national and Community level concern the termination of agency contracts in circumstances other than dismissal for misconduct. There is normally provision for an adequate period of notice, and this increases in proportion to the length of time that the agent has been acting for the principal. Some continuing remuneration on sales is normally paid, particularly where it can be shown that the agent was responsible for gaining the business. However this cannot be continued indefinitely and the courts have been used in a number of cases to determine what is a reasonable period during which commission on sales within the territory are paid to the agent. The law in Germany is fairly strict on such points, while that in France goes into some detail defining the different types of agent recognised under the law.

There are also provisions in some countries for initial trial or probationary periods, and the obligations of the principal to supply reasonable amounts of supporting sales literature, information about customer leads etc. within the agent's territory.

A booklet on export agency agreements is available from some Chambers of Commerce and the Institute of Export, and the various British Embassies offer guidance notes for each country. These are available from the BOTB.

Although selling through agents is only one method of doing business in Europe, its importance should be recognised. Because agents possess local knowledge and contacts, they can create and maintain interest among buyers in the exporter's products. In West Germany as many as 70% of transactions pass through agents, according to the Embassy who note than some 70,000 commercial agents are members of the official German Federation (CDH). Agents tend to represent between five and eight principals (the higher figure being for food and drink) but their role is invaluable in regularly bringing the exporter's product to the attention of buyers who are sophisticated, price conscious and faced with a wide range of goods from which to make their selection.

French Embassy sources point out that 75% of purchasing power lies outside the capital Paris, and of France's 56 million population more than half live in towns and villages of less than 3000 inhabitants. So, although there are many supermarkets and central buying groups, there are still overall some 570,000 retail outlets and a hierarchy of 86,000 wholesalers. These and other aspects of the retail sector are discussed more fully in Chapter 6.

Selling through distributors and wholesalers

As already mentioned the complexities of the retail sector in Europe will be discussed later, but a brief look at the use of distributors is appropriate at this stage. They are in a sense an extension of agency activities, in that some agents may also import goods on their own account, in addition to selling on commission. Some importers also act as distributors, with exclusive rights to a particular territory. They offer warehousing and distribution services. The exporter can supply goods to them on consignment or direct sale, and in either case his trading relationships are with the importer and not the final customer.

Distributors can relieve the exporter of a number of headaches. The exporter's products are promoted and sold along with other competing or complementary lines, and many of the costs of launching the new products are borne by the distributor. However, each stage in the selling/distribution chain attracts a mark-up in the price of the goods handled, and the exporter may find himself being squeezed by the distributor once the latter has a hold on the market. The distributor may demand lower prices from the exporter, against the threat that without this they are not competitive in the market. There may be instances where it is more satisfactory for the exporter to go direct to the ultimate purchaser, and the growth of central buying organisations makes this increasingly possible. This may involve setting up your own branch office or subsidiary in Europe.

Selling through your own branch office or subsidiary

Once products have been established in a European market, it might be a logical next step to consider setting up a supply depot from which stocks can be drawn more quickly. This can be arranged through the agent who would receive goods on consignment, the goods remaining the property of the exporter until sold. An extension of this, as already noted, is when the agent imports on his own account or takes over the establishment and running of the depot on behalf of the exporter. The cost of this is either by means of a direct payment (rental or service charge), a higher commission or a charge per square metre inside shared premises. Anything more complicated than this brings the exporter into the area of foreign establishment in Europe which is the subject of the following section.

Branch offices of British companies are relatively easy to set up in any West European country. Although the local laws may vary slightly and professional advice should be obtained, the operation of a branch office generally implies that:

- the office is wholly under the control of the UK-based parent company and retains the same name;
- profits from the branch may be taxed locally;
- it may not always be a simple procedure to remit profits of the branch office to the United Kingdom;
- the branch may not be able to own property in the foreign country(although it can of course rent or lease business premises);
- registration with the local Commercial Registry is invariably required, including depositing copies of the parent company's statutes (UK Memorandum and Articles of Association);
- local staff may require authorisation confirming their professional /business activities;
- local staff employed are subject to the country's taxation and social security provisions, employee benefits, etc., which may be more onerous for the exporter than in the United Kingdom.

In light of the above it should be reiterated that Common Market policy clearly emphasises 'right of establishment' of foreign companies and individuals in Member States. In principle, as noted elsewhere, this means that a business or professional activity that has been carried on in one Member State can automatically be carried on in another. This extends of course to the opening of a branch office and the formation of a local company, as a separate and distinct entity from the parent company, and broadly known as a subsidiary.

A subsidiary can be set up in a Community country, with or without local partners participating in the 'joint venture'. All the forms of trading, from sole proprietor and partnership through to private and public companies have their equivalents in Europe. It is likely that the exporter will choose one of the forms of private or public company, all of which have roughly similar rules to the British LTD company or PLC. Detailed fact sheets are available from the BOTB and in booklets like the Ernst & Whinney series. Dennis Evans' *An Accountant's Guide to Europe* is a useful summary of company law in most European countries. Professional advice should eventually be sought and British Embassies offer lists of local lawyers and accountants who can assist.

The equivalent of the private limited company – such as the SARL in France, ApS in Denmark, GmbH in Germany, SrL in Italy – exists in all Community Member States. Formation and registration procedures are rapid and simple. There is generally a requirement for a minimum of two subscribers, although some countries are already adopting the new Community formula of the 'single person company' which extends the concept of limited liability to the one-person business. There are varying but similar rules concerning the amount of capital required to set up a private company, and procedures for registration and issuing of the certificate of incorporation. This document is required before the company can start trading and for social security, taxation and other formalities. There are invariably restrictions on trading-in or transfer of shares.

The public limited company or PLC also has its counterparts in Europe, in the SA of France and Belgium, AS of Denmark, AG of West Germany, SpA of Italy. The number of subscribers is greater than for the private company, the amount of capital larger and transfer of shares is freer. Registration procedures are more complex and may take longer. Public limited companies can generally raise capital on the stock exchange.

The main European differences in company legislation are in accounting procedures, inter-company pricing and trading, levels of personal and corporate taxation, employee pay and benefits, social security legislation, holidays and (in the case of larger companies) employee representation. There are also increasing trends towards the tightening-up of legislation on directors' competence and responsibilities in the event of company failure. Some countries' concept of a 'manager' (in France 'gerant') is that of the company's official representative. He will authorise and sign documents and is generally responsible for the company's conduct. He is in some ways equivalent to the British company secretary.

Costs of company formation vary between individual countries, and in some cases there are rules about nominal capital, all or part of which may have to be subscribed in cash at the time of formation. The capital has to be deposited with the bank (to demonstrate that the subscribers have sufficient resources with which to start trading) and is then withdrawn for use by the company once the formalities of registration have been completed. In general the rules concerning company formation are stricter in Europe than the United Kingdom and the procedures may be slower.

Arrangements for joint ventures with a finite life are also recognised at both country and Community levels, giving the exporter a variety of means whereby he can form permanent or temporary associations with European partners.

Subsidiaries can of course acquire local property either by purchase or rental (lease) and professional advice should again be sought locally.

The setting-up of a local branch office or subsidiary confirms a company's commitment to the European market and becomes a visible sign of its presence. This is good both for internal company morale and also an indication to the market that you are here to stay. It enables furthermore the direct employment of local managers and salesmen, as opposed to relying on the part-time services of an agent. Head office decisions can be more easily communicated and implemented, enabling tighter control of budgets, marketing and promotion policies.

The local office can be staffed by English or foreign nationals, and it is likely that there will be a mixture of the two, with a preference for local personnel who speak the language and know the local market. Finding the right people to manage and run the local operation is not easy. It is impossible to expect to run a subsidiary company with local management, like a branch office, and a clear framework within which independent actions can be taken will have to be agreed at the outset. Complicated head office reporting proced- ures should not get in the way of the subsidiary's job of managing and extending the local market.

Good two-way communication at the time of setting-up the local sales office and subsequently will ensure the smooth running of the operation. The UK sales manager will need to strike a delicate balance between constructive support in the form of regular visits and contact by letter and telephone, and what might be seen by the local office as unwarranted interference in their day to day affairs.

Manufacture under licence and other joint ventures

Manufacture under licence and other forms of joint venture involve seeking out and working with a European partner. The object of this approach is to secure a presence in the local European market, at reasonable cost, probably quite quickly, and without unduly stretch- ing the resources of the exporting company. A licensing agreement can extend to both the manufacture of goods and the provision of services (almost in this case operating like a franchise). Local manu- facture under such an agreement is suitable where costs can be reduced resulting from the use of local facilities (ready made factor- ies, available workforce etc.) and where it is impracticable to trans- port finished items economically from the exporter's home factory. An example is a British based company supplying heating systems who use local manufacturers to fabricate the large amounts of duct- ing required. As the managing director succinctly points out 'there is little point in exporting large volumes of fresh air from England' given the bulky nature of the finished product.

Where a product or process is unique the licensing agreement may involve an element of technology transfer. Intellectual property rights may also be transferred in the form of patents, know-how and brand names. Payments are usually in the form of royalties, with possibly an advance payment on signature of the agreement.

Franchising is a form of licensing agreement. Here the franchisor transfers a total unique concept to the franchisee against royalties and usually an agreement to purchase supplies from the franchisor. Examples of franchises are common and include concepts in fast food, hotel chains, instant print shops, etc. The franchisee benefits from a complete package of product and management expertise, assistance with site location, staff selection and training. The franchisor gains from having an extended visible presence in Europe at relatively low cost.

Other forms of joint venture may have a finite length. They are common in the construction industries, where different groups of people come together to bid for and manage a major project. The concept can be extended to other sectors where partners bring complementary skills which strengthen the resulting consortium.

The European Commission has expressed its intention of assisting cross frontier co-operation which it regards as one of the Community's most powerful economic weapons in the face of challenges from the United States and Japan. At the highest levels they have promoted programmes of co-operative research into areas such as semiconductors or advanced optics, with resulting collaboration between universities and higher education institutes. Some of the advanced programmes such as ESPRIT, BRITE, etc., attract large scale funding but are generally directed towards major companies in sectors such as electronics or pharmaceuticals. Directorate-General XII 'Science, Research & Development' is concerned primarily with initiating and co-ordinating such major programmes, covering nuclear safety, the environment, and biology, through to advanced manufacturing. It operates the Joint Research Centres in Brussels, Geel (Belgium), Karlsruhe and Petten (Netherlands). Another Directorate-General (DG-XIII) has similar responsibilities within telecommunications, information industries and innovation. Information about these programmes, including funding, can be obtained from the Commission or from the Department of Industry.

At the level of the small and medium enterprise the Commission continues to recognise the importance of their role in joint cooperation. The new DG-XXIII is concerned with small and medium enterprises. Among its institutions are the Brussels-based Business Cooperation centre and, of practical benefit to the exporter, the computerised BC-Net system. BC-Net is designed to act as a clearing house of offers and requests for cooperation among firms in different member states. Offers and requests can include proposals for joint manufacture or marketing to simple requests for agency representation. At the time of writing the scheme was still at an experimental stage, with access to the central database via local intermediaries. These include some Chambers of Commerce who can access the system on the exporter's behalf.

One of the results of setting-up BC-Net enjoyed by users, including the author's own consultancy, has been the forging of closer personal links between management consultants and regional business advisers all over Europe. It is through this informal network that the exporter can try and locate potential European partners. Other methods include British Embassies in Europe, trade associations and making direct contacts with potential companies encountered through personal visits to exhibitions.

Negotiation of co-operation agreements will require the assistance and advice of professionals, including lawyers and possibly patents experts, but generally there are few problems about remitting fees and profits. With the advent of 1992 what difficulties there may have been in the past are gradually disappearing. The British Embassies in Europe offer notes and guidance leaflets on the current situation. There is a Commission Document covering policy towards small and medium enterprises which covers grants and subsidies, loans, research and innovation, the internal market and cooperation, and Community policies towards external markets – all from the viewpoint of the smaller firm.

Some special situations: public purchasing

Another of the Commission's wide-ranging proposals for 1992 is the total opening-up of public purchasing by central and local government and public bodies in all the Member States. The object of these policies is to encourage and if necessary oblige public bodies to invite tenders for the supply of goods and services (above an agreed value) from potential suppliers anywhere in Europe, regardless of their country of origin. The proposed rules are quite strict, and for example, prevent the breaking-up of large contracts into smaller segments as a way of bringing them below the agreed value at which they must be put out to public tender. The object of the policy is to prevent governments from favouring national suppliers in a market which – according to the Cecchini report – is worth between 7% and 10% of the Community's gross domestic product (or around 500 billion pounds annually). Of this, Cecchini says, a minute fraction under current procedures is let to non-national suppliers. Increased competition among suppliers would, he argues, reduce public expenditure significantly.

Clearly the Commission directives will enhance the prospects of British exporters to supply public bodies with goods and services. The question is: Will it work in practice? Already tenders are advertised in the Commission's Official Journal, and trade associations, the Department of Industry and the Brussels Office of the UK Permanent Representative are among the bodies who are at the forefront of intelligence gathering on behalf of British companies. There is also a computerised service 'Tenders Electronic Daily' (TED) listing major contracts which can be accessed by potential suppliers. TED is operated by ECHO – the European Community Host Organisation – based in Luxemburg. In addition, public bodies are being obliged to publish advance notice of their purchasing requirements so that potential suppliers can plan ahead and target their market research with some degree of accuracy. Currently, the lower limits are around £134,000 for supplies (goods and services) and £3.3 million for construction contracts, and as already noted public bodies cannot artificially divide these into smaller units. Complaints of unfair awarding of contracts can be addressed to the Commission, who may oblige the public body to justify its purchasing policies and pay substantial fines if the Commission rules have been broken.

The new rules and the increasing levels of market research apply to all Community countries, so that the supply of goods and services – like so much activity after 1992 – will become increasingly competitive. But even without the Commission's initiative there is a considerable amount of public purchasing taking place within Europe, where direct supply from the United Kingdom is possible. Examples include supplies to British and American forces in West Germany, which can be negotiated through the NAAFI organisation in Britain or the government's Property Services Agency (PSA), part of the

Department of the Environment, whose responsibilities include government-owned properties abroad (embassies, forces married quarters.) The American Forces have their own PX organisation, the Army and Air Forces Exchange, and there are similar bodies for Canadian and French forces stationed in West Germany.

A booklet issued by the French government organisation UGAP (French Government Procurement Agency) spells out its procurement policies on behalf of more than 50,000 'clients' (hospitals, schools, armed services, social services, etc.) with an annual turnover around 4 billion francs. Clear guidelines are given in the booklet, which is available in translation from the Department of Industry (French Desk). The DTI state that British exporters should not be deterred from trying to supply goods and services to French public bodies, and cite the French navy, army, railways and electricity supply industries as clients of British companies. Direct approaches can be made to these bodies, initially by letter in French, after which submissions may be invited.

The Commission Document on SMEs referred to above has a helpful section on public procurement within the Community, including principal addresses.

6 Selling consumer goods to Europe

Background

The retailing boom, so long a British phenomenon, is also apparent in several of the other Community countries also. During the 1980s there has been almost continual growth in the retail sector in Britain, France, Germany, Italy and Denmark, where wages have risen ahead of inflation. Some slowing down was apparent in Britain and elsewhere at the end of 1988 and early in 1989 as some economies tended to over-heat. In a bid to restrain spending, Britain introduced higher interest rates (which also had the additional effect of reducing some companies' capital investment).

Nevertheless, retail spending accounts for between 40% and 75% of all consumer spending within the Community, with a European average of a little over 50%. Spending patterns vary considerably, but as noted in earlier sections there is evidence of a decline in spending on foods and other essentials in northern states, in favour of luxury items, holidays, leisure, cars and travel. Although total retail spending is roughly equivalent in France and Germany, per capita spending is highest in Luxemburg, followed by France, Denmark and Belgium with West Germany slightly below the Community average.

To accommodate the consumer boom retailers have reacted swiftly and decisively. Because of the power of the retailers such as the major supermarket groups, there is increasingly close and direct contact between them and the manufacturers – to the detriment of traditional wholesale networks. The latter are surviving, however, in sectors such as fresh fruit, vegetables and flowers, and meat and fish. The large wholesale markets such as Covent Garden in London and Rungis near Paris are a tribute to the resilience of the wholesale sectors.

However, large retailers are increasingly buying direct from manufacturers and nowhere is this more evident than in the fast moving consumer goods (FMCG) sectors. Largely thanks to uniform product coding systems and machine readable marking of packages (including both outers and retail packs), scanning systems have been introduced at the supermarket checkout. These obviate the need to key-in the product code and all the cashier has to do is pass the product/package over a low intensity laser light source which reads the bar code and identifies the product. The computerised till automatically looks-up and displays the retail price. These systems avoid the need to price-mark individual items, using conventional price ticketing machines. Prices need only be displayed on the shelf-edge, although there is still some consumer resistance to non-marking of individual items.

It is only a short step from scanning at the checkout to incorporating automated stock control systems: as an item is recorded as 'sold' at the checkout an in-store computer can deduct it from a stock list. The system can then be programmed to re-order when stocks fall below a certain level. The next stage is a direct computer link to the supplier's own computer for the automatic transmission of orders from the supermarket. It is by automating time-consuming procedures such as these that supermarkets have been able to grow, reduce costs and dominate so much of the retail sector. Faced with such power the independents have reacted by banding together, for example in symbol groups like Spar or Vivo, to take advantage of centralised purchasing and co-operative marketing.

At the consumer end electronic payment systems have grown to keep pace with credit cards, and again the large retailers have reacted by installing transaction terminals which will machine-read the customer's credit card and automatially debit his or her account within seconds. This does away with the need for multipart credit card slips and, save in exceptional cases above the store's accepted credit limit, telephoning through to the credit card company for authorisation of the customer's purchase. The wider use of charge cards which are automatically settled by direct debit at the end of each month will gradually take over from cash and cheques supported by a bank guarantee card. Credit cards will continue to be used mainly for larger purchases.

The greatest advances in retailing occur in the more developed of the European countries (Portugal still has only a couple of hypermarkets in the whole country) and reflect changing lifestyles. With more women working fulltime, there is less time for shopping for the essentials such as food. Much shopping is done in the evening, with a major excursion to the supermarket or hypermarket once a week or less. Large shopping centres are now located on the outskirts of towns, catering primarily for the motorised shopper. The power of television advertising should not be overlooked: many FMCG products are available all over Europe, and the overall contents of a supermarket in Brussels are much the same as one in Barcelona.

The number of retail outlets varies widely between individual countries, the highest being in Italy where retailing is highly fragmented. The following table lists the total numbers of outlets per country:

	Total Retail Outlets	Population
Belgium	122,000	9,858,000
Denmark	51,000	5,114,000
West Germany	413,000	61,024,000
Greece	160,600	9,935,000
Spain	392,000	38,602,000
France	661,000	55,170,000
Ireland	32,000	3,540,000
Italy	1,000,000+	57,141,000
Luxemburg	3,900	367,000
Netherlands	158,000	14,492,000
Portugal	81,000	10,157,000
United Kingdom	342,000	56,618,000

Table 6.1 Number of retail outlets per country
(*Source – adapted from Euromonitor, Eurostat*)

Types of retail outlet

Hypermarkets and supermarkets are a feature of all West European countries, with the exception of Italy which has only around 20 hypermarkets in the whole country. At this top end outlets are usually over 2,500 square metres with at least one third of the sales area given over to food, although some countries restrict these definitions to stores over 5,000 square metres, and class those between 2,500 and 5,000 as *superstores*. Superstores include non-food outlets, such as those selling DIY or electrical products, furniture and household goods. The development of the hypermarket and super-store sectors appears to be limited only by the availability of suitable sites, and recent concern about the erosion of inner city shopping centres as trade moves out of town.

Up to an area of 2,500 square metres a large (food) store is classified as a *supermarket*, and below 400 square metres as a *superette*. Supermarkets of this size usually sell around 70% food items, the balance being household goods. Supermarkets are almost always part of a chain, except in the Netherlands and Greece, where, similar to many smaller superettes, they are family owned and managed, and usually belong to a co-operative buying group. Superettes are increasing in importance in Belgium and Italy. Elsewhere food purchasing is dominated by the supermarkets and hypermarkets as shown in the following table.

	Hypermarket	Supermarket	Total (all%)
Denmark	10	47	57
Luxemburg	31	25	56
France	25	21	46
United Kingdom	12	33	45
Netherlands	10	33	43
Spain	15	20	35
Italy	1	9	10

Table 6.2 Food shopping in Europe – % by type of outlet
(*Source – adapted from Euromonitor*)

Department stores are familiar sights in the capitals and large cities of Europe, although less prominent in Portugal, Greece and Italy. They comprise several departments, one of which may include food, and are usually located on several floors of a building. As a percentage of total retail sales, department stores are strongest in the

United Kingdom (over 13%), Denmark and Ireland; followed by Germany, Belgium, Netherlands, France and Spain. A down-market and usually similar version of the department store is the *variety store*, often used to sell cheaper goods and most commonly seen in France. Large store groups or *multiples* are a feature of the more developed European countries, and these groups usually have interests in all sectors of retailing – supermarkets, hypermarkets and department stores, sometimes also in mail order. Department stores are often part of a chain or group, with centralised buying offices and considerable purchasing power. For the exporter of consumer goods they represent an important point of entry into the European market.

The **Cooperative** movement has generally been declining in Europe, apart from in Denmark where cooperatives account for 37% of total food sales (but only 24% of food outlets). Overall their influence is small – in France as low as 3% market share – but through centralised buying and some rationalisation they are hanging onto market share.

Independent retailers continue to survive alongside the larger supermarkets and store groups. In Belgium, as already noted, one third of the hypermarkets and half of all supermarkets are independently owned, and independents account for 70% of retail sales. In France the figure for independent retailing is even higher, well over 90%, but accounts for only 70% of sales – still a very high figure. Within the FMCG sector independents are frequently linked to symbol groups such as Spar, Vivo, VG, etc., for the purposes of central buying and some joint promotion.

These figures disguise the fact that many non-essential items continue to be sold through independent retailers who specialise in areas such as fashion clothes (for both men and women), leather goods, china and glass, lighting, stationery and office equipment etc. Specialist shops of this kind are an important feature of the main streets of prosperous cities across Europe. Much of their purchasing remains through the traditional distribution and wholesaler networks.

Although **franchise operations** have increased throughout Europe in both food and non-food sectors, much of their purchasing is centralised and they may present few opportunities for the exporter at the level of the retail outlet. However, the concept is growing, particularly in France, Germany and the United Kingdom, and already accounts for 4% of total retail sales.

	No. of Franchises	No. of Outlets
France	456	22,968
United Kingdom	300	20,000
West Germany	259	18,000
Netherlands	227	7,422
Spain	90	8,200
Italy	80	8,000
Belgium	70	2,800

Table 6.3 Franchises in Europe
(Source – adapted from EC Statistics)

Despite the growth in retailing, selling by **mail order** manages to survive although not achieving more than 5% share in any European country. The strongest markets are West Germany, France and the United Kingdom. The size of companies varies enormously, with over 3,000 operating in Germany. Although goods are sold through the traditional mail order catalogue, computerised ordering systems (for example through the French Minitel), telephone ordering and the wide use of credit cards all help to sustain the mail order industry.

Finally, as noted above, the strength of the retailers and their central buying policies have eroded the activities of the **traditional wholesaler**. Wholesalers nevertheless continue to survive, largely as a result either of specialising by products handled or adding to their range of services. Many European wholesalers are independent, family-owned companies (or at least have their roots there) and specialise in commodities such as wines and spirits, fresh vegetables, meat and fish. To their range of services they are adding stock control, storage and warehousing, distribution, import documentation, telephone ordering and so on. Some even go as far as to offer marketing and market research services for their customers. Although the sector overall appears to be declining, the companies that survive are improving their services to customers and in that sense remain an important link in the selling chain. Cash and Carry

Warehouses supply many (independent) retailers and symbol group members.

(Wholesalers are also active in the sale and distribution of many industrial goods and commodities, including industrial consumables).

Opportunities in the consumer goods market

Food market

The European retail sector has a voracious appetite for new consumer goods. Within the food sector only 3% of new products launched actually survive, and less than half of those that survive have a life cycle of more than four years. Although this means that product development is concentrated among the major manufacturers, the food and other sectors still offer opportunities for innovative consumer products. Smaller firms are among the many suppliers of own-label items to large retailers, with this trend strongest in Britain and France. Speciality foods, with a strong national characteristic, and high added-value items are also commonly traded between EC Member States. Some 13% of the trade in biscuits is between different countries, and the British Christmas pudding is considered a comparatively rare luxury in France and shows that it is possible to introduce new ideas and products even into a seemingly overcrowded market.

The trade in alcoholic drinks offers further evidence of the export potential of distinctive commodities, frequently with a high added value. Examples include Scotch whisky and French brandies – for instance Cognac and Armagnac – where 80% are consumed outside their countries of origin. Exports to other community countries of these and other regional-based liquors account for 40% of trade. However, because of their greater bulk and low value, beers and lagers are less widely exported although even here there is a growing speciality market for some imported beers with a distinctive brand image. Examples include Italian Peroni beers or German Groltsch. Some manufacture of 'foreign' beers may in fact take place within the country of consumption, under licence. Soft drinks appear not to cross national frontiers, except within the Benelux countries.

Non-food household items

Within the sector of non-food household items, a glance at super-market shelves in any European country shows that many such items are routinely traded across national frontiers. Examples include dis-posable paper items such as nappies and tissues which may be manu-factured in Belgium or the United Kingdom and appear in German shops. Many small electrical appliances are similarly exported within the EEC, often to the detriment of British home manufacture, and it is not uncommon for Italian lighting to be sold in shops all over Europe, along with Dutch toasters and electric kettles, or German cookers. European companies such as Philips, Zanussi and Electro-lux are known throughout the Community in this sector.

The European tableware industry numbers some 400 mainly small and medium enterprises, although these industries are threatened by imports from third countries, notably Taiwan. The decline of young marriages within Europe has further affected this industry, although this is partly off-set by the rise in leisure and tourism for companies supplying to the hotel and catering sectors. Distinctive luxury table-ware is still in demand. The glass tableware industries also appear static, both in terms of exports outside the Community and intra-Community trade, with the best prospects again being in highly prized items such as Waterford crystal.

Europe's clothing industries are distinguished by the large num-bers of small firms. Of these 75% employ between 20 and 100 people, accounting for over 5% of total industrial production (in-cluding knitwear and textiles). In response to competition from cheaper Far Eastern imports of everyday clothing, the industry has generally moved up market into high quality fashion items and leisure and sports wear. Because of fragmentation the industry is able to innovate and respond rapidly to fashion trends. The British Knit-wear and Clothing Export Council are vigorous promoters of Brit-ish companies in this sector.

Selling to Europe's supermarkets

Britain's Department of Industry has prepared a number of excellent, detailed guides to selling consumer goods to selected European countries, and the following notes are extracted from them and typify the wealth of information available from this source alone. As noted in the chapters on market research and visiting the market, the intending exporter is strongly recommended to visit supermarkets and other retail outlets in the country selected in order to get a feel for the sort of products that are on sale and the prices charged. Forms of promotion such as 'British Weeks' and attendance at trade fairs and exhibitions are discussed in Chapter 8.

European supermarkets operate a system of centralised purchasing, sometimes combined with buying by store or by section managers at the local level. Centralised buying may involve placing the supplier on an 'approved list' with the selling still required to be done at store level. Terms of sale, discounts, packaging and the type and frequency of deliveries may be dictated by the central buying office, and should not be altered by the individual supermarket. 'Delivery' may in fact involve delivery to a central distribution warehouse, to regional warehouses and/or to individual stores. If the patterns of delivery expected are frequent or complex, the exporter may have to consider maintaining buffer stocks in the country either in his own warehouse or in shared premises.

The BOTB warns that European buyers are inundated with offers from would-be suppliers and simply sending trade literature is not enough; it will probably not get read. It is necessary to find and make appointments to visit buyers, armed with samples and trade literature (in the appropriate language). You should also have a clear idea of the prices and discounts you are prepared to offer, what supporting store promotion you will undertake, advertising schedules and other evidence that you are serious about supplying the market.

Because a lot of buying is centralised it makes doing business somewhat easier in the sense that a lot of ground can be covered quickly. The buying offices have enormous purchasing power and scope as the following examples illustrate. The following sections concentrate on the situations in France and West Germany, as typical of Europe's developed economies with populations and lifestyles most like those of the United Kingdom. More detailed information on retailing in these and other countries is obtainable from the BOTB, from notes prepared by British Embassies, and the specialist directories listed in Chapter 3.

France

Paridoc, with an annual turnover of F70 billion, are located in greater Paris and act as central buyers for over 500 outlets, including 112 hypermarkets and 470 supermarkets. These include the Mammoth hypermarket chain, and Suma and Nova supermarkets. It also operates through a group of 12 regional purchasing organisations, which have to be approached separately. They are:

Groupe Casino (St Etienne) – 39 hypermarkets, 187 supermarkets
Chareton (Brittany) – 2 hypermarkets, 6 supermarkets
Cofradel (Lyon) – 9 hypermarkets, 57 supermarkets
DOC-Francois (Tours) – 8 hypermarkets, 12 supermarkets
Docks de France (Tours) – 45 hypermarkets, 200 supermarkets
Economats du Centre (Clermont Ferrand) 7 hypermarkets, 52 supermarkets
Epargne (Toulouse) – 4 hypermarkets, 14 supermarkets
Guyenne et Gascogne (Bayonne) – 5 hypermarkets, 19 supermarkets
La Ruche Picarde (Amiens) – 11 hypermarkets, 31 supermarkets
S A S M (Strasbourg) – 9 hypermarkets, 49 supermarkets
SM DOC (Southern Paris) – 6 hypermarkets, 31 supermarkets
Somaga (Montrouge) – 1 hypermarket, 14 supermarkets

The SAMOD/Carrefour group is based at Evry near Paris and includes 67 hypermarkets, 3 supermarkets, and 14 garden centres (plus 36 hypermarkets outside France). Carrefour were the first hypermarkets in France and one of their strengths is in non-food items. Selling is still required at the store level, particularly for food and all deliveries are direct to the individual stores.

Galec are the operators of the Leclerc hypermarket (127) and supermarket (337) chain, and a further 50 clothing and shoe stores. The stores are in fact independent, and buying is handled through 15 regional purchasing offices.

Euromarché comprises around 70 hypermarkets and 60 non-food stores. Their rather down-market image is being improved.

The Promodes group acts for more than 1800 stores, including 300 supermarkets (Champion, Banco) and 35 hypermarkets under the 'Continent' name (including some of both in Spain and Germany), the group is strongest in northern France. Food and non-food buying are handled separately.

ITM comprises nearly 1000 supermarkets and 13 hypermarkets, all of them independently owned, and operating under the 'Intermarche' name. The accent is on food.

Other groups include CORA (48 hypermarkets), FNCC (representing cooperatives, including supermarkets and hypermarkets), CODEC-UNA (over 400 supermarkets and 1000 smaller food stores), Comptoirs Modernes (hyper and supermarkets in the Paris and Lyon areas), Systeme-U (nearly 800 supermarkets, 6 hypermarkets, 1300 smaller stores), Rallye (28 hypermarkets, 98 supermarkets), SODIM (60 supermarkets, 5 hypermarkets), Garco Disque Bleu (80 supermarkets, 8 hypermarkets and 8,000 independents), Genty Cathiard (21 hypermarkets, 224 supermarkets) etc.

As can be seen the number of central buying groups and their 'customers' is extensive. The image of each group varies, so that visiting a number of stores is an important part of market research. Some compete primarily on price, while others are interested in unusual or distinctive lines which set them apart from their competitors, including British made products.

West Germany

Germany has an estimated 80,000 grocery outlets, plus a further 2,000 stores carrying some foods and 550 food halls within department stores. Much of the strength of the retail chains and buying groups is regional and voluntary buying groups operate for the cooperatives and symbol groups such as Spar, as well as for directly owned supermarkets and hypermarkets. There are a number of important groups:

The Aldi Group is divided into north and south groups and has around 1,000 and 800 outlets respectively. Aldi Nord is based in Essen, and Aldi Sud in Mulheim. Another major group based in

Mulheim is Tengelmann. This company owns various interests including A & P Stores on American bases, Plus and Grosso supermarkets, and Kaiser drugstores. Rewe-Leibrand operate Toom supermarkets, Minimal hypermarkets, Idea drugstores and Penny discount stores. They are based in Bad Homburg.

Other mainly food groups include Metro (Dusseldorf) who operate Primus and Meister supermarkets, and several cash and carry stores; Schaper (Hanover) with 30 Realkauf hypermarkets in southern Germany; Asko (Saarbrucken) who own hypermarkets in north and south Germany; Lidl & Schwarz, mainly south Germany; Werhahn Group (Frankfurt, Mulheim) owning 350 supermarkets and 18 hypermarkets split into regional groups; Nanz & Gaissmaier (Stuttgart) with 25 hypermarkets.

The British company Associated British Foods owns a major group of supermarkets and hypermarkets in Germany, under the Deutsche Supermarket name (head office is in Saarbrucken). Included in the grouping are 2 Desuma hypermarkets and about 180 multiple stores.

The cooperatives benefit from a central purchasing organisation based in Frankfurt, responsible for nearly 2,000 stores (mainly supermarkets), 27 self-service department stores, 70 DIY stores, and other sports and leisure outlets. A special import division, located in Hamburg, deals with initial offers from overseas suppliers.

Among the voluntary symbol groups, Spar (Frankfurt) have around 5,500 retail members and operate 10 wholesale warehouses. Some food buying is also handled by regional offices. Einkaufskontor (Frankfurt) services around 750 members, purchasing both food and non-food lines.

Gedelfi (Cologne) have around 6,000 outlets and HKG (also Cologne) some 300 larger and 13,000 smaller retail shops.

The remaining EEC countries

In the Netherlands, there are several major cash and carry (wholesale) groups: De Kweker, who serve retail outlets; and ISPC which concentrates on the hotels and catering sector; Makro which serves both retail and catering outlets, and also carries non-food lines. Supermarket groups include Miro (12), Albert Heijn (420),

Edah (350), Maxis (7 hypermarkets) etc. There are a number of buying groups for food, clothing, household and DIY items.

Belgium has a number of hypermarkets and supermarkets, and smaller superettes; in Denmark the accent is on smaller in-town stores, due to planning restraints; Italy has few hypermarkets, and there are only a handful in Portugal. Spain has both hypermarkets and supermarkets. In all these countries, as noted above, central purchasing organisations operate for cooperatives, wholly owned store chains, symbol group members and independents.

Selling to department stores

France

Any visitor to France will be impressed by the splendour of the major Parisian department stores such as Printemps and Galeries Lafayette. The Paris stores and those of Nouvelles Galeries, La Samaritaine, BHV and Bon Marché are the flagships of major store groups, many of whom also have interests in supermarkets and hypermarkets elsewhere in France. The British have also made in-roads into France in the shape of C & A and Marks & Spencer, and latterly the Conran/Habitat group.

Printemps is a very up-market store, with the Paris outlet on Boulevard Haussmann accounting for one-third of the group's turn-over. There are a further 63 wholly-owned or affiliated stores, and buying is centralised (through SAPAC) but varies widely between stores. Frequent British promotions are undertaken. Close by, Galeries Lafayette have a major store (65% of turnover), and the group owns a further 20 stores (plus 9 Dames de France), plus a major share of Monoprix variety stores. Printemps and Galeries Lafayette have an image similar to that of Harrods and Selfridges respectively.

Bazaar de l'Hotel de Ville (BHV) own 8 department stores and 30 DIY outlets. The Paris store is large and popular with the main emphasis on household goods. La Samaritaine (3 stores) has a similar product mix. Nouvelles Galeries have nearly 300 stores in France, of which about one third bear their name, and account for 30% of total sales floor in this sector. In addition they own a further 75 specialised stores and 16 garden centres, BHV (above) and Uniprix supermarkets. Their central purchasing organisation SFNGR located in Paris is an important point of first contact, although some buying of food is handled through wholesalers.

The Anglo–Dutch group C & A have 28 stores in France, and Marks & Spencer have 6. The product mix is similar to their British stores, and much of Marks & Spencer's range is supplied through their London headquarters.

Variety stores are similar to department stores, but carry fewer lines – although these include food, clothing and household items, usually located on one or two floors only. The major operators are Monoprix and Uniprix (part of Galeries Lafayette) with 270 stores, and Prisunic (part of Printemps) with about 300 stores. Both groups have a high proportion of own-label items, alongside the well-known brands, but openings exist in both areas for British goods.

An important central purchasing group is GAGMI (Paris), which buys non-food items for 450 shops, including a hypermarket, department stores and variety stores/supermarkets. (Further information on French store groups is contained in *French Markets Review* by Peter Douglas.)

Germany

Germany has four major store groups – Karstadt, Kaufhof, Hertie and Horten, all of which have widespread and varied retailing interests. Buying is invariably centralised, including local offices in many supplier countries (including Britain), although some final decisions may be left to individual store or departmental managers. Karstadt (head office in Bremen) have around 160 stores, with some concentration in northern Germany; a mail order company, with some 75 stores (Neckermann Versand) and travel agencies. Overall there is heavy concentration on textiles and carpets, household goods and furniture, with about one-fifth food. Many fashion items are sold under the group's own brand names.

The Kaufhof group today own 80 Kaufhof and 115 Kaufhalle stores, the latter carrying the cheaper, more popular lines. They also have interests in travel and tourism, mail order (Friedrich Wenz, Reno) and are part-owned by the Metro cash and carry group. Some stores are tending to specialise or reducing the range of lines carried.

With their head office in Frankfurt, Hertie are the third largest group with 125 Hertie stores, including Europe's largest (in West Berlin) and about 50 Bilka stores catering for the cheaper end of the market. The group is privately owned and is best known for its own in-house credit card and extensive advertising of promotions and special offers.

The Horten group (Dusseldorf) is a mixed retailing organisation which includes around 60 Horten stores of varying sizes. Some are operated on the 'shop within a shop' or boutique format, with many own-label fashion items. Some stores also sell home computers, and the group has interests in mail order and travel.

Woolworth's are comparatively strong in West Germany (230 branches), with some emphasis on household goods and textiles. The head office is in Frankfurt.

Within the textiles and clothing sector a number of important groups should be noted; including C & A (120 stores), H Dyckhoff (30), Boecker (20), Gebr Hettlage (20). Sales can also be made through the major hypermarket and supermarket groups already noted; Asko (Saarbrucken) which operates Adler clothing stores and Pratiker DIY centres; Globus (St Wendel/Saar) which operates a dozen self-service outlets; Alfred Massa with hypermarkets and garden centres, etc. There are also central buying organisations for clothing, shoes and other items serving large numbers of independent retailers. (See also *German Market Survey* by Peter Douglas.)

The remaining EEC countries

Among the Netherlands' better known stores are Maison de Bonneterie who have a fairly up-market image (4 stores). Their Amsterdam store is hung with chandeliers and rivals London's Harrods. Other groups include Hema with 80 mixed outlets, Vroom en Dreesmann (66 outlets), Gebr Blokker (240) and Peek & Cloppenburg (West Germany) with 90 medium priced and specialist clothing shops. De Bijenkorf (large fashionable store in Amsterdam) own 6 department stores; and Confendex and its associates operate some 130 ladies and mens clothing outlets. In addition there are a number of buying groups for mens and womens clothing.

Italy's retail sector is more fragmented, although cooperatives and buying groups are emerging. There is at least one cash and carry chain (Metro). Department stores include Rinascente (visit their very up-market branch in Rome as a sample) and Coin (large attractive stores in Rome and Milan). A list of Italian central purchasing agencies in available from BOTB. Department stores are popular in Spain's principal cities including Barcelona (Corte Ingles, very fashionable) and Madrid, and markets are growing for DIY, sports and leisure goods, and high fashion clothes for both men and women. Illum and Magasin du Nord are large popular department stores in Denmark, with typical showcase outlets in Copenhagen.

Mail order

Despite the buoyancy of Europe's retail sectors mail order businesses flourish in Germany and France, and to a lesser extent in Italy where they aim to compensate to some degree for the lack of conventional sales outlets in the southern half of the country. Germany has more than 3000 mail order companies, many of them linked to the major department store groups while in France nearly 200 major companies are listed in a comprehensive guide available from BOTB. This covers firms supplying books and magazines, cameras, video and hifi equipment, clothing, DIY items, household goods, furniture, jewellery, office equipment – an indication that almost anything that can be sold can be sold by mail order.

Mail order is less strong in Portugal and Spain, and Belgium and Denmark's small populations ensure that operations are on a smaller scale.

Selling to mail order companies relies on a direct approach to the head office buying group, which as already noted may also be servicing other parts of the retail sector. Because catalogues are produced to a strict timetable and can include up to 50,000 items, buying and sampling periods are equally regulated. Most companies consider offers for their autumn and winter catalogue during the previous January and February, and the spring/summer catalogue the previous June and July. Deliveries of goods ordered will be expected to start arriving three months before the catalogue launch date (ie. June for the autumn/winter). Prices are guaranteed to the customer during the 6 months life of the catalogue and suppliers are expected to adhere to the same rules.   Many mail order items are sold under the operator's own brand name and there are opportunities to supply goods on this basis if they fit within the mail order company's desired image. Some deliveries may be requested direct from the manufacturer or supplier to the end customer.

Analogous to mail order are various forms of home based selling, where representatives of the manufacturers call personally on customers or groups (i.e. party plan). Products that lend themselves to this type of selling include those where an element of demonstration (e.g. vacuum cleaners) or trial (cosmetics, books) are important elements in the decision to purchase.

Studies of direct selling operations reveal that although the industry is quite large it accounts for only 0.3% of retail sales. Direct sales representatives are mainly women, most of whom work part time.

One of the interesting effects of the removal of barriers after 1992 may be on mail order or distance selling operations. Theoretically European customers could be served from any country within the EEC, and we may witness growing cooperation between mail-order houses, for example in the exchange of valuable customer lists. A United Kingdom store group which retains records of purchases by its European customers, for example, could use this as a basis for mailing a catalogue of selective items for direct purchase. Certainly the Post Office and other organisations are already gearing-up for this kind of distribution operation.

The removal of customs barriers is likely to give a boost to mail order after 1992. The present value of parcels that can be sent without raising a customs charge is around £7, so inhibiting most mail order transactions. Removal of restrictions will open up the market for mail order, although by harmonising other tax rates such as VAT within the Community, any trend towards buying goods in another country simply to save VAT will be discouraged.

Among Europe's largest mail order companies are Otto Versand and Quelle in West Germany, and *La Redoute*, *Les Trois Suisses*, *Camif* and *Quelle* (run independently of the German operation) in France. Some of the companies maintain buying offices or agents in the United Kingdom. Further information is given in the BOTB guides cited.

Breaking into Europe's retail sectors

As can be seen from earlier paragraphs Europe's retail sectors are prosperous and undoubtedly offer opportunities for selling British consumer goods. The practice of central buying means that fewer individuals have to be contacted and cultivated. Delivery problems are also reduced as a result of centralised warehousing and distribution. However, as so often reported, many British companies making excellent products fail to make an impact in European markets as a result of inadequate preparation and incorrect approach.

European buyers, it has been stressed, are able and used to demanding high standards both of goods and service. It should go without saying that all correspondence and meetings will be conducted in the foreign language, and the exporter who can speak French, German or Italian will make considerably greater headway in those markets than he would using an interpreter. Delivery dates should be quoted on the basis of arrival time at the buyer's premises and not when the goods are expected to leave the British factory. Late deliveries can result in cancellation of orders and will certainly discourage future business. Prices should be quoted including delivery to the customer, and weights and measures stated using the metric system. Product literature should of course be in the appropriate language.

In addition to the information sources listed in this section and elsewhere in this book, exporters of retail goods will find the services of British Embassies and Consulates particularly useful. Staff are in constant touch with buyers – the British Embassy in Bonn and its Consulates call on some 6,000 firms in any one year, for example. Visits to trade fairs such as the large general and specialised events will acquaint the exporter with the market, put him in touch with potential agents and distributors, and enable him to assess whether he should exhibit his products at a future event. Consumer exhibitions are also useful as a means of examining competing products, as are visits to shops and supermarkets as part of the exporter's programme of field research.

There is a range of services that the exporter can use to help launch and sell his products. Although much buying is centralised, some deliveries may have to be direct to regional warehouses or even to individual stores. There are companies that can store goods, break bulk and deliver, collect payments, operate a VAT account and control stocks.

Commission agents are still widely used for the purchase of many imported items. The agents are in regular contact with group buyers, understand their requirements, and are always seeking new products that they can offer. They may be able to approach buyers, by being on an 'approved list', where the exporter may not succeed through a direct approach. As described in earlier sections, agents are found through Embassy contacts, through trade exhibitions, their own trade associations and by consulting directories.

Technical and safety standards are gradually being harmonised at the European level, through mutual acceptance of individual Member State regulations. This generally means that a product which is sold in one country will be permitted in another. However, this relaxation does not take account of the need to adapt some products to suit local market conditions. Among some of the more obvious examples are different electrical voltages in Europe, the difference between bayonet-type and screw-in light fittings, different television standards, variations in spare parts for cars and so on. Packaging and containers vary from one country to another and at the very least will have to be worded in the language of the individual country. This is particularly important – and in some cases a legal requirement – where directions or instructions for use are an essential part of the product.

The process from initial examination of a European retail market and making the initial sale can last anything from one to three years. Certainly perseverance and a willingness to support the selling effort are required, through frequent visits to the market, continuing support for agents and calls on important buyers. Sales may be slow at first while the product and the exporter are both 'on trial' but the results are invariably worthwhile.

7 Selling services to Europe

Introduction

As was discussed in Chapter 1, one of the most important acts of the Brussels Commission has been the opening-up of Europe to providers of services and members of the professions. The language used in the various documents is unequivocal and the definitions have been widely drawn. Based on the principal of mutual recognition of national qualifications, the new laws allow both the 'right of establishment' in any Community State, together with the freedom to follow one's chosen profession or vocation in any part of the Community. The laws apply equally to self-employed and employed people, and clearly offer wider opportunities for companies and individuals to expand their activities in Europe.

Many individuals and firms have been doing this already for some considerable time, in situations where few barriers to international trade existed. In many areas of counselling and consulting, the provision of business services, firms involved in export selling and distribution services, some practical restrictions may have existed in the past. Any remaining ones will be swept away by the end of 1992.

The Cecchini Report looking at business services estimated that they provided some 4% of the Community's Gross Domestic Product or around 124 billion ECUs value – the figures excluding 'operational' services such as catering, hotels, etc. The principal barriers noted were in different taxation levels, financial and other barriers to establishment, illiberal public procurement procedures and different product regulations. Different product standards were found to affect professionals such as computer consultants; and the providers of on-line information systems were hampered by varying technical standards and national regulations about the provision of cross-border telecommunications links. This has affected French companies wishing to offer direct computer access to potential clients in Britain or vice versa, for example.

At the fiscal level, West Germany has restricted the activities of advertising and PR firms by limiting their access to additional funds by means of publicly quoted shares. This has not helped the growth of major British groups in advertising (such as Saatchi & Saatchi) and public relations (Shandwick Group). Differing advertising regulations, particularly on television, are also seen as hampering the development of services in film and video production, media buying and placement.

Engineers in all disciplines have complained about public procurement policies which favour national firms, and architects have traditionally been barred from following their profession due to complex licensing procedures and other restrictions on establishment. Bias in government procurement was also noted by research institutes and some computing services.

Summarising the effect of these barriers, Cecchini describes them as unfair, restrictive, and leading to higher prices both in the promotion of business and professional services in Europe, and also for the purchasers of such services. In light of all this, the Commission then formulated its wide ranging proposals.

In considering the range of 'liberal and intellectual professions' the parameters have been widely drawn and include (a selection only) the following professions: actuary, agronomist, analyst, architect, archivist, artist, auditor, author, composer, computer scientist, consultant (all disciplines), designer, engineer (all disciplines), estate manager, journalist, landscape gardener, lawyer, photographer, publicist, sociologist, veterinary surgeon, writer. All these are in addition to the full list of medical and health professionals and operational services such as catering, transport, warehousing, distribution, travel agencies, tour operators etc. and specialist areas such as banking, insurance and financial services which will all be similarly liberalised. The lists indicate the wide range of occupations that can be followed anywhere within the Community.

Before considering a number of these occupations in greater detail, a number of general observations can be made.

Well before the Commission's programme of liberalisation many of the professions have got together at the European level, usually by means of a federation which links a group of national associations. Examples abound and include bodies such as FEACO (The European Association of Management Consultants), CERP (for PR Consultants) and CEBI (European Committee of Consulting Firms). These and other bodies have met for many years to discuss points of common interest to their members and more recently to assist in the Commission's programme of harmonisation and acceptance of national standards. Participation by professionals in their national association and at the European level contributes to the wider dissemination of information and policy formulation for the benefit of all members and their clients.

The adoption of a common approach to the professions may result in more (self) regulation in some areas where United Kingdom law is fairly liberal. Examples include unregulated activities such as estate agency when practised by unqualified individuals, which is a cause of concern to members of the various Chartered bodies such as auctioneers and valuers. Any tightening-up of regulations will have undoubted benefits for the consumer and bring British practices into line with those of the rest of Europe.

Because of the personal and complex nature of many business and professional services, the removal of barriers will not automatically open up the market for firms and individuals wishing to practise in another Member State. Clearly some knowledge crosses frontiers: medicine and dentistry are the same whether practised in Bournemouth or Barcelona. To a certain extent also services such as management consultancy, engineering, design or sales promotion use the same principles when dealing with clients in any part of Europe. However, where an intimate knowledge of local markets, local regulations, culture and, of course, language are required, these will obviously continue to act as natural barriers – which the foreign firm or individual can attempt to overcome if he so wishes. As one EC Commissioner stated when promoting the idea of mutual recognition 'no one will hire a lawyer in Germany who is ignorant of German law'. However, the option remains for the foreign national to acquaint himself with Member States' laws and compete on equal terms with local practitioners.

Methods of promoting services and professions in Europe will be discussed in a later section. But from the outset it should be recognised that – due again to the personal nature of many services – it is unlikely that many of the methods available to sell goods will be available to the service provider. Generally, a third party such as an agent or sales representative would not be used, and promotion will involve some form of establishment within the market and at very least continuing personal contact with potential customers will be required. How this can be undertaken, including from the United Kingdom base, will be covered later.

Some occupations cross frontiers

The level of service activity is expected to continue to rise within Europe. Examining the effects on seven EC countries, for whom full information is available (Belgium, Denmark, Germany, France, Italy, Netherlands and UK) the share of market (productive) services shows continual growth from 1980 as the following tables indicate.

% Share of Economic Activity	1980	1983	1986
Manufacturing activity	27.6	25.8	26.3
Non-market services (eg. education, welfare)	15.6	16.1	15.7
Market services	44.1	46.0	47.7

% Share of Employment	1980	1983	1986
Agriculture	9.4	8.9	8.1
Industry	36.9	34.3	32.5
All Services	53.6	56.8	59.5

Numbers employed (1000s)	1980	1987
Agriculture	11,959	9,886
Industries	46,729	40,630
Services	67,910	75,905

Table 7.1 The rise in service activity
(Source – adapted from Eurostat)

As can be seen, the total share of services is now almost two-thirds of Community added value. This figure includes non-market services such as education, health and welfare, which alone have not grown significantly between 1980 and 1986. However, they account for a smaller share of employment (21%) than market services at 40.6%. Market services contribute a higher added value both in relation to non-market services and to industry, set against the numbers employed.

The increase in numbers employed within services of 8 million between 1980 and 1987 almost exactly reflects the decline in manu-facturing and agricultural employment over the same period. (Un-employment results from the growth of the potentially active work-force over the same period.)

Over a similar period, the services sector has demonstrated im-pressive rates of growth. Between 1980 and 1986, financial and insurance services grew by 91% and other market services by 65%. Statisticians argue that there is not in fact a progression towards a service economy, so much as a transfer from internal to external sources of supply of services. By reducing internal staffs, companies (and public sector organisations) find that while they retain flexibility and achieve certain economies, they have to rely increasingly on external suppliers. This is good news for providers of the broad range of business to business services. One of the 'hidden' growth areas noted by the Commission is in office cleaning services, which currently employ over 2 million people. Above average growth is also noted in management consultancy, consultant engineering, technical consulting, construction economics, market research, and security and express delivery services. Another service, temporary employment, has grown by 20% across Europe.

At the level of consumer services, similar growth can be noted: hotels and restaurants have grown by 84% and retail and repair services by 59% over the same period (1980–86).

A lot of the growth documented arises from the increasing pre-sence in Europe of non-EEC based companies, such as American management consultants or Australian express courier services. In-creased turnover can also result from activities of Community based companies working outside Europe. Consultant engineers in Britain, France and Germany derive 30% of their turnover from Third World projects; the Italians manage 50% , the Netherlands 25%. There will be increasing scope for cooperation between engineering firms in different Member States in third-country projects, particularly as intra-Community export accounts for only 4% overall.

Consultants in computers and management

Britain has for some time been considered a leader in the design and supply of computer software and numbers Scicon, Thorn EMI and Logica among the top ten suppliers in Europe. The industry is, however, dominated by smaller companies, an estimated 15,000 each employing an average of 20 people. Sales of standard and customised software products account for 58% of the market and other services 28%. Training is an important element, and is growing at an annual rate of over 20% (and accounts for 12% of turnover).

Although many of the products offered are of American origin, they require installation and implementation at national levels. English is widely understood in computing services, but a knowledge of languages is clearly an advantage particularly for training users. Software consultancy accounts for some 7% of business and independent software supply a further 18.5%. There is increasing competition from hardware suppliers offering packaged solutions and from major systems houses, but smaller firms have the advantage of proximity to their customers and a flexibility and willingness to respond: their average growth rate is around 23% per annum.

Management consultants have never felt held back by European regulations and apart from having to overcome differences of language and some detailed regulations, they can and do offer their services widely throughout Europe. Again the industry includes major companies, either American (Arthur Andersen, Arthur Young), Anglo-American (MacKinsey) or European (Atkins Planning, Bossard). They tend to attract the major national and international contracts, but a third of all consultancy firms comprise fewer than ten consultants, and a further one-third between 11 and 50 consultants per firm. Competition has also come in recent years from accountancy firms and traditionally non-profit making organisations such as universities who offer consultancy services in addition to their main activities.

The larger consultancy firms tend to belong to national organisations such as the Management Consultants Association in the United

Kingdom, whose 30-odd member companies attract two-thirds of consultancy business in Britain. Bodies such as the MCA are in turn affiliated at the European level to a Federation of Organisations representing management consultants, but their overall membership accounts for less than half of all business. The total number of firms is estimated to be around 3,000, grouping some 40,000 consultants. Many small firms and even one-man consultancies survive either by specialisation (geographically and/or by sector) or by grouping informally with other consultants in joint venture arrangements or permanent associations.

A fairly high proportion of consultancy business is exported – up to one-third by Belgian firms – within and outside the Community, as techniques are readily transferable from one national situation to another. Overall the level of business is expected to increase at a rate of about 15% per year but the effects of 1992 are difficult to gauge. One expert put it to the author that consulting services overall might gain as little as 5% of new business. Management consulting is fairly unregulated, as the less than 50% membership of national bodies confirms, but this is also accounted for by the fact that the range of services offered now includes marketing, research, personnel, computer and technical services whose practitioners may find membership of FEACO affiliated bodies inappropriate to their areas of activity. The right of establishment confirmed by the Commission should encourage even more firms and individuals to try their luck alongside the major consultancies anywhere in Europe.

Consultants in marketing and public relations

Other consultancy activities that travel well are marketing and public relations. Public relations consultants were among the earliest groups to form European affiliations around the time of Britain's entry into the Common Market, in an effort to offer their clients a pan-European level of service. Unlike advertising agencies, PR consultants find that operating in a foreign European country presents few complications other than those of language. The PR culture certainly varies, with the industry's American/Anglo Saxon approach slightly alien to Mediterranean Europeans, but similar techniques and principles apply throughout the Community although the degree of sophistication may vary.

There are several representative bodies, comprising either corporate membership (such as Britain's Public Relations Consultants Association) or individual membership (Institute of Public Relations, which includes in-house PR practitioners). There is a European co-ordinating body (CERP) which includes both corporate and individual members.

The PR industry ranges from one-man (or woman) consultancies to major firms, which are sometimes affiliated to advertising agencies. Out of the top dozen European firms, ten are British and they have increased their representation in Europe largely by acquisition or association. But because the industry is relatively easy to enter, new firms are continually being born – often as breakaways from other consultancies. The level of capital investment is also comparatively low.

At the small firm level, there is considerable scope for specialisation in one or more of the industry's growth areas. These include consultancy in corporate affairs, government relations, EEC information and monitoring services, crisis management and international relations. Consultancies with a reputation in these areas are in demand, regardless of their size.

Marketing advice may be provided either by PR firms or advertising agencies as part of their portfolio of services, or by specialist marketing consultants. Market research is more clearly defined, and documented, and is generally undertaken by specialist companies or individuals. Services are usually divided between consumer and industrial research, although some firms may offer both. The industry includes some large American companies such as A C Nielsen, British companies like AGB and Mori, and at least two major West German firms.

A number of bodies represent research firms, particularly those involved in wide scale sampling, and there is a European coordinating body (ESOMAR).

It is consumer research with its emphasis on mass opinion polls and large scale sampling that attracts many of the headlines, and a fairly large company infrastructure is required for this area of market research activity. Qualitative research involves use of smaller groups of people and is used to analyse opinions and attitudes. Market and product research can be undertaken by small firms and individuals even on a European-wide basis, and many firms survive by specialisation in particular industry sectors and/or countries. With the increased competition resulting from 1992, all forms of market research and marketing consultancy will increase as firms are obliged to re-assess their place in Europe.

Creative services

Many creative talents are readily transferable and in the New Europe there will be increased opportunities for those involved in writing, photography, design (graphic, corporate, product) and specialist services such as creating audio visuals, films and conference presentation. Indeed, many specialist companies already work throughout Europe where their unique talents and creative flair are in demand. British design groups such as Conran, Pentagram and others are well known in Europe (and elsewhere) and Britain's reputation in creative services is strong.

The creative services industries are highly fragmented, largely unregulated and therefore not well documented. By specialising in a single sector such as graphic design or producing TV commercials, small firms can survive largely on the reputation of one or more partners whose personal involvement in the creative process is crucial – and largely what the customer is buying. Good design is recognised and appreciated throughout Europe, for products, company literature, building interiors and fashion goods such as textiles and wallcoverings. Much of this draws on the talents of individual writers, illustrators, photographers and artists.

The gradual deregulation of television and the increase in the number of channels bring with them demands both for new programmes and commercials. Through fear of domination of channels by programmes imported from America, the Commission has proposed quotas that will ensure a proportion of home-based or European material. Not only will this ensure that European culture is not obliterated from TV screens, but it will increase opportunities for programme production – much of which is already undertaken by small independent companies. With the availability of all the production equipment needed on hire from a single day upwards, small teams can be assembled rapidly on a project by project basis. Indeed, many production companies consist of little more than a single executive who comes up with the ideas for a documentary film and prepares a script before selling the package to a television network who will finance the entire operation.

Britain also has an excellent reputation for producing television commercials. With the standardisation of markets and products across Europe there will be some rationalisation of advertising. However, experts are at pains to point out that national and regional cultural differences are ignored by advertisers at their peril, and it will not always be sufficient to add a new foreign-language soundtrack to a basic TV commercial. The demand for more commercials will keep pace with the increase in television channels. Although TV advertising is planned by (large) advertising agencies on behalf of major clients, production is usually handled by smaller, independent companies.

Sophisticated presentation services are already widely used to launch new products and services, for example to a company's sales force or distributors. These may involve film and audio visual techniques, music, slides and live presentations – all of them requiring the services of specialist companies with expertise in these areas. Demand for these services is clearly likely to grow.

Business and group conferences are also increasing. Conference organisers, again frequently small firms, can take over the organisation and management of such events, arranging travel, accommodation, translation and interpreting services, hospitality, registration and reception. A British based company can easily organise such events anywhere in Europe without the need for major capital investment or even local representation.

Construction industry services

Another area of consultancy activity that continues to enjoy sustained growth is that connected with construction. The wide range of associated professional services includes architects, building designers, interior designers, consultant engineers, planners, surveyors, site managers, specialists in building and estate management,

construction economists, environmental planners, geologists, carto-
graphers. All these professions will benefit from:

- increased construction activities including house building, provision of leisure and entertainment services, retail complexes,
  hotels;
- the construction of more science, technology and business parks;
- major infrastructure projects such as improved rail and road links
  across Europe, major expansions at airports and seaports
- EEC funded projects aimed at improving the infrastructure –
  some of these are aimed at the Southern European states, others
  are intended to regenerate some of the former coal and steel areas
  of the north;
- third-country projects where construction companies and professionals from different Member States will come together in joint
  ventures.

One of the effects of the Single European Act has been to give greater
prominence to the European Regional Development Fund, which
will continue to direct aid towards the poorer regions of the Community on the basis of a quota system, as well as to Europe's former
industrial regions. Some of the aid packages are so large that some
experts say several of the regions are having some difficulty absorb-
ing the available funds; they simply do not have the expertise and
manpower necessary to propose and coordinate large scale projects.
It is likely, therefore, that British companies will find increased
opportunities for cooperation with local firms in helping to exploit
European aid.

Outside the Community, aid to Third World countries will continue, under such arrangements as the Lome Conventions for the 66
African, Caribbean and Pacific (ACP) states. Now that Spain and
Portugal are Members of the Community, the same experts argue
that British companies will benefit by associations with firms from
these countries which have access to their former colonies and overseas dependencies.

Opportunities for architects to practise in Europe are further en-
hanced by the shortfalls in qualified and experienced practitioners

that are noted in some Member States, including France and to some extent in the United Kingdom. Vacancies are being filled by architects from other countries. The numbers of registered architects vary considerably between Member States. For example, Italy has around 65,000 (and a further 66,000 students) against Britain's 28,000 (7,000 students), France has only 20,000 architects but Germany has three times that number. The differences are partially accounted for by the variation in the type and extent of work carried out (not all Italian architects work inside the profession). Overall, increasing specialisation is seen as eroding some of the activities of the general architect which may today be handled by other building specialists.

Due to the increasing complexity of large scale projects construction economists (or quantity surveyors, as they are sometimes known) are now widely recognised as a separate profession. Their numbers are highest in the United Kingdom (20,500) and Spain (16,000) against only 6,000 in France, reflecting the uneven development of this separate profession. Firms are usually small – up to 20 partners in a typical British practice, but between 2 and 5 in several other Member States. Up to 10% of their professional activities are exported, and the profession is expanding into areas such as civil engineering and construction engineering. The opportunities for collaboration both within and outside the Community appear to be at least as strong as for architects.

Consultant engineers and other specialists are widely employed in the preparation of economic and environmental studies, property management and project administration. The United Kingdom is particularly strong in this sector, accounting for 20% of consulting firms and one-third of Community turnover, much of which (33%) is exported. However, Italian firms perform even better, with 50% export of their services. Exports are largely (33%) carried on outside the Community, in markets such as the Middle and Far East, Eastern Europe and Africa. Firms vary in size, the largest on average being British practices with up to 50 members, ahead of the Community average of only 11 staff per firm. Similar opportunities for collaboration on both intra-Community and Third Country projects exist across all consultant engineering disciplines.

Legal and accountancy services

Within this sector it is unlikely that Community harmonisation policies will directly result in large numbers of individuals or firms setting up practices in Member States purely to compete with local firms to provide basic accounting and legal services. The complexities of local laws and practices and the need to build up a local connection all rule this out. It is at the international level, however, that professionals will find most growth as companies and government organisations come to terms with the effects of the Free Market. Increasingly they will require specialist information and advice from professionals versed in European laws and regulations.

Indeed the provision of legal advice by foreign firms not 'admitted' to local national courts is already common in Britain, France, Belgium and the Netherlands, where foreign companies have chosen to invest. There are around 300 such lawyers in France, 450 in the United Kingdom and 100 in Belgium. A smaller number are registered at the bars and law societies of Member States and their numbers may increase as a result of Community legislation after 1992.

Overall growth is forecast in the supply of legal services to business and among the areas of specialisation envisaged are patent and copyright law, product liability and consumer protection, and contract laws as more mergers and joint ventures become a feature of Europe in the 1990s.

With over a quarter of a million accountants already in Europe the profession would at first sight appear overcrowded. However, just under half work in private practices, the remainder being fulltime employees of private or public organisations. Their main areas of work include the accounting and auditing services required under company laws of Member States, taxation, insolvency and trustee and administration work. Again the growing complexity of corporate level activity in Europe is likely to maintain a steady demand for accountancy services, with smaller firms and individuals able to survive by specialisation. Already many major accountancy firms have overseas offices providing a full range of services to local clients. As already noted some practitioners are also involved in diverse activities such as management consultancy, for which there may be a requirement in some countries to set up a second organisation separate from the traditional accounting functions.

How to sell your services

As was noted earlier in this chapter, not all the methods used to sell goods to Europe can be adapted to the promotion of services. In particular it is doubtful that the use of a representative or agent will be of great value, although many professional and business services have active links with European 'associates' in different forms of joint venture arrangement. Methods of promotion range from the simplest – such as mailing your multi-lingual brochure to potential European clients, to working with European partners and setting up your own office. These are considered in the following sections.

Manufacturers of capital goods can also profit from much of the advice given in this section. They operate in the same business-to-business environment where the company's image and reputation are as powerful influences on sales as the products they are selling. Concepts such as past contracts fulfilled, innovation in design and performance, up to date manufacturing methods, after sales service – all these are the intangibles sold along with the final product. As the author has stressed many times to clients, capital goods manufacturers are essentially in the problem-solving business. While off-the-shelf solutions can be and are frequently provided, other intangibles are being sought by the intending purchasers. The manufacturer of capital goods is in reality offering a service.

These concepts have to be portrayed as benefits to the potential customer, and use must be made, as in services, of techniques such as a corporate brochure, films and audio visuals, lectures and technical seminars, corporate advertising and public relations, all designed to project a favourable image of the supplier to his target audiences.

Already some of the promotional tools available to the service-provider are becoming evident. However, it is only in recent years, with the relaxation of regulations (in the United Kingdom) governing the promotion of some professions, that service firms have started to adopt some of the means available to them. Previously – and it may still exist in some sectors – there was a feeling that it was

somehow undignified to advertise or solicit business. Beyond hanging up one's brass plate and discreetly putting the word out among
friends and business contacts, many professionals were restricted in
what they could do to attract new customers.

The need for promotion

A number of factors have made changes both necessary and desirable. They include increasing competition for work in both the
public and private sectors, where the supply of services is invariably
put out to tender. Although high-value tenders must now be openly
advertised, at the lower levels they will continue to be restricted in
practice, as organisations make use of a short list of candidates
invited to submit proposals. Firms wishing to bid for this type of
business must first get onto the short list and they do this by
self-promotion.

Another factor has been the extension of many professional firms
into associated services. Notable examples include accountancy practices who have moved into management consultancy and providing
additional services in such fields as data processing and high technology. These moves have obliged them to design attractive sales packages in order to impress clients, and some of this activity has spilled
over into their mainstream business. One large firm of accountants
explained to the author that their consultancy division frequently
finds itself bidding competitively alongside 'companies much more
expert in promotion, drawn perhaps from advertising and marketing
or new product development. Against them we have the old image
of the accountant as staid and unimaginative. As a result we have to
work twice as hard at presenting an up-to-date image that compares
well with competing firms coming from very different backgrounds
to our own'. As a result such firms are now among the best at
producing well-designed brochures and visual aids, and at self presentation when invited to reply to tenders.

It is likely then that the professional firm or service provider
eyeing Europe has already developed a number of basic promotional
tools for use in the home market. Whether this is the case or not, it is
as good a time as any for the firm to pause and take stock of itself
before mounting an all-out attack on Europe. In addition to asking
itself the basic 'What business are we in?' type of question, you can

use this opportunity to review your range of service 'offerings' and the implications of promoting them to a wider market with such considerations as:

- What are the main services that we offer? Do some dominate and provide the bulk of our income (the old 80/20 rule)? Are some of them in danger from new techniques, new service firms? Does this restrict development of new services? Are we happy with the present mix of services? If not, how can be alter the mix?
- The firm itself – how do we see ourselves five or ten years from now? Will the same senior partners and managers still be around? Is there a succession problem? Will we succeed in recruiting talented newcomers to the firm? What size of firm will we be, should we be? How will we achieve this growth?
- How can we broaden our markets? Can we extend the present range of services to our existing clients? Can we attract more clients to use the existing services? Can we offer new services to existing clients? Can we offer new services to new clients?
- What is our market? Is it local, regional, national or international?
- Are we specialists within a particular sector or industry group? Can we develop satisfactorily within the present framework? If not, can we offer new or existing services to groups outside the existing framework? What are the implications of this?
- Our image – how do others see us? What are we best known for? Are we known for services we do not wish to provide or expand? Is our image staid or progessive, reliable or fly-by-night? Does our image accord with the reality? What can be done to alter our image?
- What are our strengths and weaknesses? Is it our senior people, their track record, their acknowledged standing in the industry? Or is it our ability to adapt and recruit bright young brains, to be ahead in new technologies?
- What are the implications of going into Europe? Do we have the right kind of services to offer? Do they travel well? Do we have the financial and human resources to mount a sustained assault on the market? Have we enough linguists within the firm? Can we operate with European partners? Do we need a branch office?

The answers to these questions – and others, the list is not meant to be exhaustive – will help the professional firm to focus on itself and the range of services that it can and is willing to provide to the new European market. Implicit in this form of self-analysis is a realisation that the firm wishes to expand into new markets and has the human and financial resources necessary to promote and sustain such expansion. That said, this sort of exercise should not discourage the smaller, specialist organisation that has always got by and even prospered by attending to the needs of niche markets. These markets exist abroad in the wider context of Europe, and by self-promotion and possibly such means as linking with a foreign partner even the smallest firm can operate in Europe (the author's own consultancy manages to do just that!). The techniques described in this chapter can be used and adapted by firms of almost any size, the principles remain the same.

Reaching your market

In earlier chapters we have stressed the importance of market research required for companies engaged in selling both consumer and capital goods to Europe. In many ways, the service market is more closely defined and many business-to-business operations can be extended quite naturally and logically to a wider market in Europe. The more specialised the service, the more clearly defined the market. Indeed in some areas, specialist firms – say, in computer systems or software, hydrology or building design – already have to look upon the whole world as their marketplace, if only because there is not sufficient demand for their highly specialised skills within the home or neighbouring countries alone.

Because some specialist occupations are worldwide they tend to be well documented. This occurs through international 'world conferences', through trade and professional journals, and international business directories. As a result, if you are selling complex medical equipment or diagnostic know-how, it is almost as easy to locate potential customers in Wolverhampton as it is in Waltenhofen (southern Germany). It is by attending international conferences and exhibitions, studying the professional journals and looking through trade directories (the last two all available in the DTI libraries) that the service provider can start to get any idea of the potential market and whether there is a place in it for him.

If the market is comparatively small – say, in the case of our hydrologist it concerns the principal European water authorities – then a direct approach is possible. This is achieved by sending a 'capabilities brochure' to the target users, and backing this up perhaps with some PR or corporate advertising (these techniques are discussed later). If the potential market is wider and the firm has limited resources, then consideration might be given to third-party recommendations. For example, accountancy services could be sold to small businesses by recommendation from banks and businesss advisers who would be approached by the service provider, rather than attempting a direct approach which would be costly and time-consuming. Or the specialist firm may consider links with a European partner to jointly exploit a potential market. This is happening increasingly in management and construction services, where the idea of joint ventures and other forms of cooperation are well established.

There are also public supply contracts to be had throughout Europe, for the provision of both goods and services. As noted in earlier sections, the service provider will need to set up a system for monitoring opportunities to tender through study of official journals or using sources such as TED or other abstracting and information services. The aim will be to get onto prospective short lists (where they apply) and to prepare a submission that will lead to gaining at least a percentage of the contracts being awarded.

Whichever market approach is used – direct, through European partners, through competitive bidding – a number of promotional techniques can be used and adapted to help the service provider improve his chances of securing business in Europe. These are now considered.

Your capabilities brochure

This rather grand title is used to denote the basic document which describes the services offered by the professional firm or service provider. It can be more or less elaborate depending upon the requirements of the market and your available budget, but essentially it is a working document that should include the following information. The order of presentation will depend upon the format selected:

- Name, address, telephone numbers, etc., of the service company, with a brief outline of what it does;
- Short history of the company, from its foundation to the present, with notable events and successes;
- Profile of the founder, owners and senior partners (education, industry experience, areas of specialisation, published books and articles, professional affiliations);
- Clients of the firm, either listed by name if appropriate, or by sector e.g. small business, public authorities, to indicate in which markets the firm operates;
- Detailed listing of the services provided e.g. surveys, feasibility studies, project management, accounting, personnel recruitment, training all might be listed by a construction industry professional;
- Case studies and examples of work done – either by name, with full disclosure including illustrations as appropriate, or by sector worked in (e.g. banking, medical care, small firms, etc.);
- Recent assignments – similar to case studies, but describing the types of work recently undertaken, e.g. market reports, feasibility studies, projects managed, new products developed;
- Firm's code of practice (which may be linked to that of its professional association) and terms and conditions of business;
- Your next step? Final exhortation to the recipient of the brochure indicating what you want him to do (e.g. send for further detailed information, telephone for a preliminary consultation, etc.).

As can be seen there is a large amount of information that potentially can be included in a capabilities brochure, which results in it being a fairly lengthy and elaborate document. There are, however, ways of achieving the firm's needs without needless expense, as we shall see, by correct choice of format. However, the most common mistake made by firms is to confuse the capabilities brochure with what is more accurately described as a 'mailshot'. Both have distinct objects and both can be used during promotional programmes aimed at getting more business.

As already noted one of the methods of securing European business is by direct approach to the target audience(s) and/or through partners. In the early stages names may almost be picked at random (from professional directories, exhibition catalogues, bought-in mailing lists, etc.,) and it is clearly wasteful to send all of them the full company brochure. Further, the brochure is not meant to be used in this way; what is required is a mailshot.

Mailshots

Whereas the brochure is usually handed over or mailed after some initial contact has been made with a potential client, the mailshot is designed to open doors and refine the target list, reducing it to manageable numbers for follow-up and further work. Further, the mailshot is different from the brochure (which generally has a longer, more permanent life) in that it is often time-sensitive, designed to get the prospect to take some specific course of action – including sending for the full capabilities brochure. Mailshots are widely used to announce the holding of a seminar or conference; the opening of a new office or showroom; the publication of a new book, research report or brochure. In every case they are designed to encourage some action on the part of the recipient – to reserve his place at a seminar, to accept the invitation to the official opening ceremony, to send for your latest research report.

To encourage rapid response and positive action by the recipient, the mailshot is specially designed to encourage action. A mailshot will normally include a personal(ised) letter, so that properly targeted it has more than a fair chance of reaching a named person; it may have one or more enclosures such as a leaflet or prospectus outlining the offer and almost invariably a reply card or envelope to make replying easy. In the case of time-sensitive material, there may be further encouragement to reply quickly by offering incentives such as a price reduction.

Mailshots are widely used as part of a marketing programme and another of their distinctive features is that they may form part of a progressive campaign, with the target prospects being mailed more than once. It is quite common for two, three or even more different pieces to be sent before either the prospect reacts or the company writes him off, at least for the time being, as not worth further mailing. To illustrate the sort of mailshot programme described – and finally reinforce the differences between the mailshot and the capabilities brochure – we can cite a programme mounted by a company wishing to sell its catering management services to companies within a major European city.

The company, already well known for supplying fairly up-market beverage vending equipment, decided that the target group comprised no more than a few hundred top companies of a certain size and, where possible, identified as operating a staff restaurant (the market research phase). The catering or personnel manager was identified within each company and a four-stage mailing programme launched. This entailed sending an introductory letter containing a small pen-and-ink print of one of the city's old coffee houses – again linking the company both with provision of high class coffee service and the city. The offer went on to say that three other prints were available, and if the manager collected all four, he would be presented with a frame in which to display them on his office wall. Further letters followed to those who did not react immediately, offering the second, third and fourth prints. Careful management and good 'list cleaning' were essential at this stage, to ensure that those who responded were not again mailed.

The object of this exercise was to get the target group of catering and personnel managers to say 'Yes' to the offer of the picture frame, which the company's representatives naturally had to deliver personally (on the grounds that it was fragile and could not be posted). At this stage, they came armed with the company's brochure and were already well on the way to being invited cordially and receptively to make a formal presentation of the company's catering services.

This rather elaborate programme achieved its objectives, with a final high take-up of the catering management programme. Its success was due to good research, targetting the right people, persistance, good management and an attractive offer which people found hard to refuse.

Not every mailshot programme will be as elaborate as the example cited, but if this approach is used good results are rarely achieved by mailing a full capabilities brochure 'on spec' without some prior contact. The mailshot may contain much of the information contained in the full brochure, but as already noted has a specific purpose, to refine the target list and get worthwhile prospects to take some immediate, positive action. It may be a continuing process spread over months or even years, provided the prospect is still regarded as worthy of further effort.

Using printed media

In an interesting survey of how engineering and design professionals keep their names in front of the market (*Marketing for the Small Design Firm* by Jim Hogan, published by Whitney/Phaidon) most of the firms described regular programmes of mailings to prospects drawn from lists as varied as 'former clients, contacts, friends, unselected names from mailing lists and directories, leads from newspaper articles, results of cold calls'. A variety of materials was sent, mainly personal letters (asking for a preliminary meeting), sometimes accompanied by tear sheets of recent work, particularly where it referred to the prospect's own area of business. For example, a firm recently completing a major hospital project would mail information about this to other hospitals within their catchment area. The numbers involved were anything from 150 to 1,500 mailings a year depending on the size of the design firm.

What format should your printed materials adopt? This will depend upon a number of considerations including budget, but more important, on what is appropriate. By appropriateness is meant the size and standing of the firm, and the value of the services offered or contracts sought. Clearly, a major firm of international consultants seeking large public works contracts will require a more elaborate presentation than a smaller specialist consultancy seeking to secure contracts of much lower value. However, in addition to content discussed above, a few further points should be considered in helping to select the appropriate format for a printed brochure or mailshot:

- How long? How much needs to be said about the firm? Can it be said in two pages or twenty? What is the expected life of the brochure?
- Is the information likely to date quickly? If we need to provide updates does this mean preparing a completely new brochure or can we use a loose-leaf format and provide inserts?
- Does our service need describing with illustrations or diagrams? Do they need to be drawings or photographs? Black and white or full colour?

- Do we need to use full colour (for illustrations, as noted) to show off our company logo? Can we get by with single colour printing on a coloured stock?
- What size is appropriate? Is the brochure more likely to be mailed or handed over personally? Are special envelopes required?

Within these broad parameters a wide range of options exists. These include choice of colours (ink and paper), size, quality of paper, layout, design, typeface, etc. There are powerful arguments for using standard sizes of paper (A4 or its variations) as envelopes are available to fit these, and documents of this size are easily filed. Odd or awkward sizes invariably cost more money, due to the amount of paper wasted (which the customer pays for).

Although it is advisable to use a designer or at least a printer with a design department, with modern graphics software it is possible to use systems such as the Apple Mackintosh to design your own printed materials in-house. Loose leaf inserts can be prepared using a modern typewriter face on printed headed paper, perhaps in different colours to emphasise the various departments or activities of the firm. Looseleaf brochures can be made up using either comb-bound or glued systems, offering cost effectiveness and maximum flexibility to alter or update the text. A4 folders with pockets for inserts are another approach that is widely used by professional firms.

Copywriting is a specialist task and not everyone can write well about themselves. It may be advisable to use an outside specialist who will work from a brief given by you.

The question of foreign languages is of course paramount when preparing a series of brochures destined for the European market. As mentioned earlier the translation must be carried out by a national of the country concerned, and preferably someone who demonstrably has a grasp of your industry sector and any specialist terms used. How accurately these are translated will reflect on the professionalism of your approach. In considering foreign languages, one of the questions that must be addressed is whether to produce a series of separate brochures in each of the main Community languages (or according to the markets selected for targetting) or to combine several languages within one brochure.

The second method raises a number of problems, as languages are not of even length and you may require half as much space again to accommodate your German text alongside English. There is also less flexibility, as any change means scrapping the entire brochure. A more flexible approach is to prepare separate brochures, possibly using common printed 'shells' into which foreign text can be inserted, preserving a consistent house style throughout the range of brochures.

Whichever format is adopted, a crisp well designed brochure can be produced for moderate sums provided sufficient thought is given to its content, text, translation, design, typesetting and production.

Newsletters and reports

Because, as we have seen, many professionals and service providers know more or less accurately who their target customers are, it is logical to consider further means of keeping in regular touch by use of such promotional devices as newsletters and reports. These can be used, along with seminars and conferences which are also precisely targetted, in conjunction with wider ranging publicity activities, such as advertising and public relations, topics which are discussed in Chapter 8.

The newsletter or house journal is a popular device that enables a firm to write about itself in the manner of a newspaper or magazine. Although it emanates from the firm's own publicity department, the house newspaper seems to command respect among clients and potential clients – provided of course that its contents have some genuine intrinsic value and do not consist simply of re-cycled publicity material. While every direct mail campaign will eventually bore its audience or simply run out of steam, newsletters can be sent regularly to a target group. They are essentially 'soft sell', designed to keep one's name in front of prospects who may one day need your services.

Like brochures, newsletters can range from the simple to the elaborate, and the same considerations of appropriateness generally apply. They can be produced using a desk-top publishing system, incorporate illustrations and diagrams, and range from a basic 4-page document (i.e. A3 folded once), which is regarded as the minimum acceptable size, to publications of 8, 12, 16 or more pages. How often they are produced depends again on budget and the amount of potential news and information content, which again depend upon the size of your firm. Firms considering a house journal should think in terms of not less than two issues a year – otherwise the gap between issues is too great for the publication to remain topical – and not so frequently that after one or two issues you simply run out of things to say!

What goes into a house newspaper? The main decision is whether it is designed for internal or external consumption. It is difficult to write a house newspaper that appeals both to employees and to (potential) customers. While the former can help generate an *esprit de corps* by coverage of promotions, marriages, the apprenticeship scheme or the results of the annual darts match, such news is of little interest outside the narrow confines of the company. Some organisations, such as hotel chains or airlines and others with far–flung activities, may appear to straddle both formats in their news coverage, but basically such publications are designed for one type of audience alone. It is likely in any event that most service and professional firms have small staffs whose size does not merit an internal publication. (Other means of internal communication can of course be used which may include a simplified staff bulletin, notice boards and formal and informal briefings where news of the firm's activities is brought to the attention of all staff.)

Given that the format is external, what sort of information should such a house newspaper contain? As a PR man I was continually surprised at the number of firms who react to the suggestion of producing a house organ with the reaction that they do not have anything to tell! This comes about as a result of familiarity with what is going on – it's no longer news to them – and is a powerful argument for using an outsider to put together the editorial. Someone with a nose for a good story can turn the most mundane event into something interesting and readable.

Typical content can of course include:

- news of orders gained and contracts completed;
- staff appointments and promotions;
- availability of new brochures or other literature;
- 'think pieces' about industry topics;
- guest written articles.

Staff news should not become too parochial and a good general rule is only to write about those members of staff who are likely to be in contact with customers (i.e. the export manager, not the retirement of a sales clerk). Orders won and completed can be written up as full-length illustrated features, and within the bounds of client confidentiality can be referred to in subsequent issues. In the case of building contracts, these can be regularly covered from foundations to handing over to the customer, over several issues.

Think pieces are more or less in-depth discussions of topics likely to be of interest to customers, and while they must impart some useful information, preferably not published elsewhere, they are designed principally to project the firm's staff as experts in their particular field. An extension of this is to invite guest writers, for example from among past clients who would write about how you solved their problems.

Allied to house newspapers are regular or occasional special reports. These are lengthier documents covering a relevant topical subject on which you have a point of view. In Jim Morgan's book cited above, he describes a firm of accoustic engineers who issue authoritative technical reports on their specialist subject, as well as detailed case studies. A consultant who designed point of sale systems used to generate considerable interest among retailers (his target audience) by controversial but well researched statements about the failings of supermarkets. Another, involved in management training, writes about training problems in accountancy firms, the banking sector, public authorities and elsewhere where she has actual or potential clients she wishes to reach.

One way of generating information for a report is to undertake some research and then publish the findings. One company involved in designing electronic teaching aids researched the subject of youth education and produced a startling report highlighting the shortages of trained computer manpower that would be occurring during the 1990s. Clearly the subject chosen in the European context must have wider appeal, and of course the newsletter will require translation into the appropriate languages. The usual cautions apply.

Seminars and conferences
Another way of influencing target audiences is by means of seminars

and conferences – either by organising your own or by appearing as a speaker at those organised by other people. Either way they can generate considerable promotional mileage. This is not only through your impact on the audience, but in subsequent coverage in the trade and professional press. The text of your presentation can also be published as a special report and you can of course cover the event in your own house newspaper.

Being invited to speak at events organised by your trade or professional association, Chambers of Commerce and other such bodies should be the natural result of your standing within your profession. However, as this is often not the case and your own undoubted expertise is often passed over in preference for some less experienced speaker, you must do all you can to aid the process of being invited! This means being genuinely and fairly selflessly involved in your professional sector and its wider concerns, and being an acknowledged expert on current issues – through articles, books, reports, etc. You can of course volunteer your services, making it known that you are available as a speaker and offering a range of subjects in which you are expert. Lists of forthcoming seminars are published in trade journals, many of which include a section inviting submission of papers, usually at least six months ahead of the event.

Organising your own event is not difficult, even outside your home country. I helped two clients to do just this. They were involved in designing systems for coating and then drying paper and other materials used for packaging and the plastic films used to manufacture audio and video tapes. Because there is a high level of expertise involved and much of the technology was new, they particularly wished to target large companies in West Germany and France. Given their comparative lack of resources, including a very small sales force, and the need to move quickly, I suggested holding two one-day conferences. These duly took place in Frankfurt and Paris, to audiences of nearly two hundred and one hundred respectively.

Apart from visiting the hotels selected beforehand – and this is an essential piece of ground research – both events were organised from the United Kingdom. The package included issuing invitations in German and French, sending acknowledgements including an admission card and location map, preparing translation of the conference speeches into German and French (1.5 tonnes of printed paper!), organising simultaneous interpreting (all the presenters spoke in English), catering and overnight accommodation. Both events went without a hitch, largely due to the choice and use of top class hotels (Sheraton and Hilton International). The publicity gained included full length articles running to several pages in the main European trade publications.

Given a judicious choice of services – from the designer of the invitation to the technical interpreters – such events can be organised cost effectively and offer considerable impact for the newcomer to the market. The two clients mentioned were both fortunate in having first class sales agents in each territory who provided the initial lists of personal contacts to whom invitations were sent. And both companies were fairly well known within their particular field, both by existing customers and from regular appearances at major trade exhibitions. However the formula can work well for other companies selling services (and capital goods) where there is sufficient 'intellectual' content in what they do to be able to sustain four to six fairly in-depth presentations during the course of a one-day seminar.

For firms daunted by such a prospect, an alternative is to hold half-day sessions (two in one day can save costs). There are arguments for and against timing these to coincide with trade exhibitions. On the one hand while large numbers of potential customers will be present, competitors will also be using the event to promote their own seminars and teach-ins. There is also competition for available meeting rooms, most of which are booked up many years before the major European events. This factor alone may rule out use of an exhibition for this purpose.

Experts in their field are not necessarily natural-born presenters and any time spent rehearsing and refining ones speaking skills will pay dividends. There are numerous training courses available to help inexperienced speakers to improve their technique. Films, audiovisuals and other aids can be used to liven-up a presentation. These are discussed in Chapter 8. While it is clearly better to be able to speak in the foreign language, this should only be attempted if your proficiency is good. Otherwise simultaneous interpretation, backed up with a copy of the printed text contained within the seminar documentation package, will enable speakers to present their text in English.

Marketing professions and services can be time-consuming. Some studies estimate that firms spend between 10% and 15% of their gross income in practice promotion, and this may not include the true value of principals' time. New-business getting should be a continual process, and if a service provider intends to move into Europe even greater efforts may be required. Some of the particular techniques available have already been described, and other more general promotional tools such as PR and Advertising are covered in the following chapter.

8 Promoting your product or service in Europe

Introduction

As a sophisticated developed economy West Europe enjoys all the means of promotion that will be familiar to the user or observer of the publicity media in Britain. These include national and regional daily newspapers, radio and television, cinema advertising, posters and hoardings, point of sale promotion, direct mail and of course all the forms of public relations. Theoretically all these promotional avenues are open to the exporter, within the bounds of national regulation and custom which we will examine in due course, and some of which have been covered in Chapter 7.

However, in order to logically study a 'typical' promotional programme involving a new product or service about to be launched in Europe, this chapter will consider the available media in the order that they are most likely to be used for the launch of a product or service within a new European market. The chronological sequence would therefore be something like the following:

Trade or Consumer Exhibitions:	used for initial research (see Chapter 4) to view competing or existing products; to locate potential agents and distributors. Now to (test) launch product to trade and/or consumer markets.
Trade Literature:	required to support presence at exhibitions; to launch product or service to agents and end consumers.
Agent/Distributor Support:	activities needed to help your Agent introduce your product to the market – literature, information/training, audio visual, factory visit etc.
Point of Sale:	use of packaging and other promotional media

	at the point of purchase; in-store promotions, British Weeks etc.
Trade Press:	advertising or Public Relations in the relevant trade press to back up Agent/Distributor activities; to alert end consumers (business to business products) and trade buyers.
Regional and National Press:	(Consumer products) to heighten consumer awareness, support (local) promotions. Can involve advertising and/or PR.
Outdoor Advertising:	mainly, but not exclusively, consumer products. Directed primarily at end consumer, includes posters, semi-permanent hoardings. Can be regional or national.
Radio and Television; Cinema	Primarily consumer products. can be local, regional or national. Aimed at end consumer.

These methods of launching and promoting your product or service in West Europe are now considered in more detail in the following sections.

Trade and consumer exhibitions

As was noted in Chapter 4 under Research, there is an extremely wide range of trade and consumer exhibitions taking place virtually all the year round in Europe. Some of the major trade fairs are truly international and may occur only once every second or third year. If they are a critical factor in your European product launch then your marketing programme may have to be built around the fixed and immutable dates of one or more key trade fairs.

Already it can be seen that advance planning is required, not only to identify the relevant trade shows but also to arrange your firm's participation. Among your first calls should be one to the Fairs and Promotions Branch of the BOTB. This publication lists virtually all the trade and consumer fairs occurring in Europe for a period up to two years from date of publication. More importantly it indicates which fairs are supported by a BOTB subvention and to whom applications should be submitted. It should be noted even at this stage that cut-off dates for applications can be a year or more before the event, and that some events are over-subscribed. Again, early investigation and planning are essential.

The Fairs and Promotions Branch is divided into a number of sections. These cover Overseas Trade Fairs grouped by (European) country, as well as Store Promotions (discussed later) and Outward Missions. Outside London contact can be made with regional BOTB offices but you may find it quicker and easier to telephone the relevant person direct in London.

Many of the references to financial support from the BOTB are through trade associations who administer a joint scheme on behalf of the BOTB and their trade members. The normal procedure is for a British group stand, which offers a unified shell scheme within which companies can rent space, complete with other support services. Early application to your trade association is advisable, although due to pressure of demand for subsidised space some intending exhibitors are invariably too late. They can then try to go it alone by booking a stand direct with the fair organiser, but as noted most of the important trade exhibitions are oversubscribed and have waiting lists. All this in spite of continuing programmes of building and extension at many of the major fair sites in Europe.

Preparing for an exhibition

Exhibiting even within a joint British group is not without its problems and the key to success is thorough prior planning. This can be divided into three principal sectors – the exhibit itself, publicity before and during the exhibition, and management during the period of the exhibition. Let us look at each of these in turn.

Fairly soon after application has been made either to the coordinating group (BOTB or trade association) or direct to the fair organiser, a bulky package of documentation will arrive containing application forms, and demands for deposits of money up-front. Also included are what seems like a morass of companies offering ancillary services (from flowers to stand cleaning) and regulations detailing what you can and can not do within the confines of your expensive few square metres of stand space. Let there be no illusions about the cost of exhibiting in Europe. Faced with a quotation for building a fairly basic stand for a five-day event in Frankfurt, a German acquaintance of the author's exclaimed that for the money demanded he could have purchased a retirement bungalow in Bavaria. He was probably right.

Early on a decision will have been taken about what you propose to exhibit, as this will clearly have a bearing on the size and type of stand you require. If you are a manufacturer of machinery and plan to show equipment from your range – either static or working – then this calls for considerably more space and planning than if you intend to set up a simple information booth, where you would largely display photographs and distribute literature. BOTB schemes invariably allow for both approaches within the overall concept of a group shell scheme.

If you plan to go it alone and not accept a shell scheme (either within the BOTB group or direct from the organisers), then you will require a stand designer/erector. Such people invariably have to be 'approved' by the fair organisers, due to the protectionist policies of exhibition contractors, and cetainly the stand design will eventually have to be submitted for approval. It is as well to do this in advance, as objections can be made not only by the organisers but by other exhibitors. How competitors find out about your proposed scheme is something of a mystery, but it happens. Clients of the author had to radically modify, at a fairly late stage, a major two-storey stand destined for Dusseldorf following objections from a neighbouring exhibitor who complained it interfered with the view of their stand from one direction. The changes demanded entailed a total redesign at considerable extra cost. (In what must have seemed like a spirit of poetic justice the nearby competitor suffered a spate of embarrassing machine breakdowns throughout the run of the show to the barely concealed delight of the British contingent.)

Included in fair documentation will be lengthy and detailed regulations about the weight, size and operation of exhibits; requirements for safety guards, exhaust ducting, electrical safety standards; and equally complex rules about the stand itself – dimensions, height (particularly if you are deciding to build a two-storey effort), projection into gang-ways, signposting and so on. The application forms will ask you to state your requirements for electrical services, include 3-phase power if required, and special requirements such as compressed air, water, waste disposal and other services provided by the organisers' contractors. Among the many other suppliers wanting to know your requirements will be those for telephones, fax, signwriting, carpets, furniture, lighting, catering – all decisions that have to be taken many months in advance.

Even if you use the services of a stand designer/builder these official forms have to be completed and signed by an authorised member of your firm and must be submitted before the deadline demanded. This applies also to cash deposits. Exhibitors have been known to lose their stand, or some of their required services, as a result of not forwarding application forms and money deposits at the times requested. All this may seem harsh but fair organisers are generally operating in a seller's market and their terms are tough, and they stick to them rigidly.

A locally based stand contractor can sometimes save cost as the stand does not have to be transported from the United Kingdom. He also generally has local contacts, speaks the language and may therefore be better equipped to sort out the inevitable problems that will occur during the build-up period. An experienced shipper, possibly the one normally used to transport your goods abroad, should be consulted early on about the shipment of your machinery or other exhibits to the fair site. Again this has to be planned in advance to conform with the organiser's requirements and also allow sufficient time for customs clearance under any 'temporary import' regulations that may apply until after 1992.

As it is an expensive process to transport a piece of machinery to a fair site and back again, wise exhibitors try to ensure that it is sold prior to shipment, preferably to a customer within the country where the fair is being held. A newly appointed local agent may also be in a position to accept all or part of your exhibit as part of your promotional support programme. Many companies also hope that into their stand and support material will be designed an element of portability and re-use. Unfortunately, this rarely happens in practice, and the resulting wastage of design talent and materials is regrettable but seemingly inevitable.

Another early decision that has to be taken concerns the people you wish to have on your stand, ensuring that they are informed of this and above all that hotel accommodation is booked for them. This last point may be neglected by the first-time exhibitor, who should be warned that for major European events all the hotel accommodation is booked-up months or even years in advance. This is particularly the case in West Germany, where the main fair cities of Dusseldorf, Frankfurt and Cologne in particular still lack sufficient hotel accommodation. Deposits will be demanded with bookings. Failure to send them will result in rooms being re-allocated without notice. Faced with such a situation where clients had failed to secure nearby hotel rooms, the author endured a daily two-hour drive to and from his hotel during the course of a German trade fair in addition to eight hours spent on the stand.

There is also a tendency by some companies to assume that staff can be accommodated in 'friendly little pensions', share rooms between two, and generally make do with inferior facilities in a spirit of pioneering adventure. This is both insulting to your sales people and will also prevent them from being at their best during the demanding few days of the exhibition.

Promotion and trade literature

The purpose of attendance at a European exhibition is to put yourself in front of your intended public during the few days of the event. You can of course rely on chance – someone is bound to stop by your stand – or with a little prior planning you can ensure that the key people you want actually come to visit you. Given the extremely high costs in terms of time, manpower and direct expenses associated with exhibiting, it is folly to neglect the prior promotion that should be undertaken before the event.

This pre-planning should include direct invitations to customers and prospects, and active publicity and public relations.

If we assume that at this stage you have selected your local agent – and may even be exhibiting jointly with him on his stand – both you and he will hopefully have an idea, following your market research, of who your actual and potential customers are. They should, therefore, be informed of your presence at the exhibition and invited to come and visit you. Such prospects can be ranked in terms of priority, and personal letters and follow-up telephone calls made to the most important. The object here is to get them onto your stand at an appointed time, when your senior staff and your agent will be on hand and properly briefed to deal with them.

For the wider group of potentials, a printed notice or invitiation can be used. This can include some incentive, such as a prize draw. Methods such as these might seem hackneyed but they still seem to appeal. This wider publicity needs to be backed up with editorial coverage through PR and possibly some advertising. Among the forms supplied by the organisers will be a request for material for the exhibition catalogue; it is essential that this is submitted in time for inclusion, as trade fair catalogues have a life that extends long after the event when they are widely used as reference books. Not being included is a serious omission.

Some major fairs also publish an exhibition newspaper before and during the event. Copies are widely distributed as part of the organiser's own programme to attract visitors, and offer valuable opportunities for promoting your firm and its products through editorial and advertising.

Wider publicity can be undertaken in the trade press, again through advertising and public relations. If you are not at this stage a major or regular advertiser, a special insert in one or more trade magazines tends to have more impact as a one-off, and can make good use of promotional materials such as leaflets or a house journal that you will be preparing in any event for the show. The cost of insertion is usually more than a single or double page printed spread, and there may be weight limitations particularly where magazines are mailed to a controlled readership. However, aside from these considerations, there are cost savings in production and translation, and the impact of the insert is usually greater. The insert can be loose or bound-in and there are arguments for and against either. Loose inserts may be lost but on the other hand may be taken out and retained by interested parties. Bound-in they become associated with the life of the magazine.

Public relations will include regular announcements about your presence at the trade fair and what you intend showing. Photographs of people and machinery (where appropriate) will enhance such releases. As always such material has a better chance of being used by magazine editors if it is translated into the appropriate country language.

Publicity destined for use during an exhibition also requires careful planning. Clearly everthing that you intend to use should be in translation. Because publicity material is expensive to produce strict control should be exercised before it is handed out. Every exhibition attracts its share of brochure hunters, as well as wily competitors anxious to get hold of sensitive information about you and your products. It is therefore wise to leave out for public consumption only the most basic leaflet or house journal, and reserve expensively produced catalogues for selected recipients. Indeed, some firms refuse to hand out any literature at all during exhibitions and insist on taking the enquirer's name and address (and usually ask for an official business card as well) before they will send on brochures or leaflets in response to a specific enquiry. This may seem like a tough line to take but it does cut down on wastage and goes some way to ensuring that material does not fall into the wrong hands. The advantage to the enquirer, you can point out, is that he or she does not have the problem of carrying round a heavy pile of literature for the rest of the show.

Management of the exhibition stand

Stand management is the third area of exhibition planning. This should comprise sufficient levels of staffing, including during lunch breaks and peak times. Rotas should be drawn up and adhered to, and sales people not allowed to wander off without the appointed stand manager knowing where they have gone. Walkie-talkies and bleepers can be used to round-up personnel but they have a habit of being switched off by people really determined to disappear.

Stand security is an increasingly important consideration, not only from the point of view of acts of terrorism or sabotage against particular countries or companies for whatever reason. It includes the loss or theft of briefcases and other personal belongings; and completed client enquiry forms that would assist your competitors and whose loss effectively negates your presence at the show. It is therefore necessary to keep a watchful eye on bags and packages that are not accounted for, and once logged, enquiries should be detatched from the pad and placed in a secure file. Some companies take the added precuation of faxing them back to head office several times during the day.

Hospitality can be provided on the stand if your size and budget warrant it. Some stands turn into little more than open–all–hours licensed bars, which is hardly conducive to doing business, but many exhibitors are now limiting refreshments to tea, coffee and soft drinks. Such abstemiousness is quite acceptable in today's more realistic business climate. Overnight stand cleaning is generally pro-vided by contractors, but during the day care should be taken to ensure that waste bins and ashtrays are emptied and coffee cups removed regularly, as there is nothing more off-putting to a client than an untidy, cluttered stand. Good management and attention to detail invariably reflect well on your company.

It should go without saying that follow-up after the event is also essential. This can be a daunting task as major exhibitions can result in the logging of anything from a hundred to several thousand enquiries. Some system of priority needs to be exercised, during the initial conversation with the prospect and experienced sales people can usually tell who are the serious enquirers. They should be subject to special treatment while on the stand, and in subsequent follow-up. The priority order can range from a personal visit by the salesman or agent, detailed written submission, special or standard brochure, down to sending a routine literature pack – with the intention of later follow-up if at all justified.

Promotional support for your agent or distributor

Sales agents are a much maligned group and failure by companies to get the best out of them can frequently be put down to misunder-standings and poor communications between the two parties. How often after a morale boosting visit to the field does the hard working sales manager return to base, full of good intentions. Back at the office, however, his in-tray has grown by another few inches, and nothing that should have been done in his absence appears to have been accomplished. So is it surprising that his pledge to respond rapidly to the agent's request for new brochures or the urgent preparation of a sales quotation gets overwhelmed by the tide of other jobs to be done? The result is that the agent thinks his principal is not really interested, and after a few weeks he gradually puts the matter out of his mind and decides to concentrate his efforts into promoting your competitors.

Or take the opposite scenario as described to the author by an extremely conscientious Italian agent, talking about his principal. 'I cannot understand' he explained, 'why it is that when head office has a lead anywhere in Italy, I am supposed to drop everything and go rushing off to see this potential client. Even when I have established in a telephone call that the enquiry is not urgent and I have promised to call on them when I am next in the area. But when I have an urgent problem, like a sales quotation that is already weeks overdue and I am in danger of losing the business, no amount of phone calls or telexes to head office produce any response. It seems that business is not urgent when it originates from me, but it is when it originates from them!'

These two examples probably represent extremes, but they do indicate that often after spending time and effort to locate and appoint an overseas agent, British companies fail to get the best out of them as a result of incorrect handling. Responding rapidly to each others requests for prices or other information is just a matter of common courtesy, let alone common sense. But they should be seen as part of the wider process of educating and developing the agent so that he effectively becomes your partner in opening up and exploiting a new European market.

The question of agency agreements was discussed elsewhere, and these cover only the bare bones of the relationship. Success will depend on how the relationship develops into one of mutual trust and understanding. One of the first ways to do this is to sit down with the agent and together work out a plan for the new market and what support is required and how you intend to supply it. This will be a logical extension of the research that will have been undertaken by you and the agent at the earlier stage when you were investigating the market, and the agent was doing his own research before agreeing to become your representative.

It assumes also that very early on in the relationship the agent has been invited to spend a few days at your United Kingdom office or factory. The purpose of this visit is twofold: to get to know more about your products and processes, and also to enable the agent to meet other members of your staff with whom he will be in frequent contact by telephone and letter. Because the typical sales manager travels frequently, his deputy or secretary should know how to act in his absence. Knowing the firm's agents from face-to-face meetings will help both parties to understand each other's problems and requirements.

These personal visits will be succeeded in later years by regular gatherings of all the firm's agents at a sales meeting. They create opportunities to review markets and discuss successes in different countries. This sort of information is invaluable to agents, who frequently complain that while negotiating with a multinational company in one country, they are not informed that a successful sale has been concluded with the same multinational in another country. Such information would clearly help their chances.

Keeping the agent(s) informed through such sales meetings can be supplemented by regular bulletins from head office. If you produce a house journal (as discussed in the previous chapter) copies of this can be sent to the agents. Sufficient copies should be sent to cover the agent's staff if he has a large office or branches, and some agents may like additional quantities to send to their customers and prospects – possibly overprinted with their own name and address. In smaller organisations, a less formal method may be used. One engineering company known to the author writes a regular 'open letter' to its agents, with three or four pages of company news, signed pesonally by the managing director.

During the time they are in your care, agents should be looked after as you would any other guest of the company. Frequently, however, the British are lacking in hospitality and at least one group of agents has complained to the author that when head office sales people visit them in their country, the agent meets them at the airport, takes them to a hotel or invites them home to dinner, and generally makes their visits thoroughly enjoyable. In contrast, the British company would leave the agents to make their own way to their hotel, take a taxi to the factory, and depart for Europe without ever having invited them into the homes of senior managers in Britain.

More formal support of agents and their staffs will include product literature (in translation) and appropriate sales training where required. This can be at the British factory in the case of capital goods, where the product has to be demonstrated during manufacture and in use. For consumer (and again, some capital) goods, such training may involve field trips by the sales manager, during which he accompanies the agent on sales visits. Some in-store training of customer sales staff may also be required, particularly if the product is innovative or is sold by demonstration. Where such training needs are widespread you might consider using an audiovisual to get across the essential background history of your company, its range of products and how they should be sold.

Packaging

Retail products designed to be sold primarily in hypermarkets, supermarkets and large stores can benefit from the use of promotional materials at the point of sale. Promotional elements include the product pack itself, static or mobile display materials, and more concentrated merchandising efforts such as trials and tastings, store demonstrations and special offers. Some of these techniques such as packaging are applicable also to some business-to-business products and industrial consumables. They are considered in the following paragraphs.

The importance of packaging cannot be overlooked. Packaging typically represents up to 10% of the retail cost of an item and in the case of luxury goods, such as cosmetics and toiletries, this figure can be as high as 40%. With the need to produce packaging suitable for a wide European market, these costs may vary if several languages have to be incorporated or pack designs radically altered. However, there will inevitably be some economies of scale.

Packaging decisions are not to be taken lightly, and re-designing or re-vamping a pack can often breathe new life into a tired product. Multinational companies are adept at such techniques, and spend large sums of money on research and design in order to keep their popular brands looking fresh in the eyes of the consumer.

Design considerations

In designing his packaging, the manufacturer has to achieve a number of aims. They include *containment and protection* of the product from the place of manufacture until it reaches the point of sale, so that the product arrives at the shop or supermarket shelf in precisely the desired quantity and form. An outer protective package is frequently incorporated, which may also be used as a display at the point of sale.

Among the devices that can be used to *enhance sales appeal* are incorporating a dispenser in the pack, making the product oven-ready or self applicating, by dividing the contents into individual portions, or helping re-use or storage after purchase. Multiple pack sizes can help segment and at the same time extend the market to more groups of purchasers, who have a choice of 'family size' down to 'economy pack' according to their needs. All these elements can be seen as pluses by the consumer – and by the store buyer considering the initial stock purchase.

Although not all manufacturers can (at this stage) afford extensive consumer advertising in the new market, packaging can be used to *project and reinforce a strong brand identity*, acting as a reminder at the point of purchase and afterwards in the user's home. Even with a product new to the market, the colour, shape, design and feel of the pack reflect whatever image you wish to project – from economy to luxury. The pack can also directly enhance the appeal of your product. This is common with purchases such as perfumes and cosmetics, high quality confectionery and time-sensitive purchases such as Easter eggs or Christmas drinks.

The shelf appeal of your package must include *whatever demands are imposed by the retailer*, – increasingly a major supermarket chain. The mistake of designing a pack that will not fit supermarket shelves can rule out its purchase by the store buyer. He is also looking for a pack that is easy to handle, price-mark and store; accepts bar coding in many instances, and fits into existing shelves and displays. The pack should promote sales without encouraging damage or pilfering. There is also an increasing demand for tamper-evident packaging in these days when major manufacturers find themselves subject to threats resulting from contamination of their products once they have entered the distribution chain.

The outer pack must likewise *satisfy the requirements of shippers and handlers,* and be capable of storage and transportation, without causing extra work or inconvenience or damage to the content.

Another important element in the European context is *labelling or marking.* The UK manufacturer will have to sit down with his distributor and major retailers to discuss points of detail such as the placement, size and content of information, instructions, warnings, money–off coupons, bar codes and so on, not only to ensure compliance with national regulations (for example as to language) but also ensure that his product offers maximum buyer appeal.

In his market research the exporter will note that packaging can sometimes be a critical element in launching or re-vamping products. Established products and even commodities are often displaced by innovative packaging of the same or similar item. Milk bottles give way to cartons, shaving cream is now dispensed from an aerosol, obsolete razor blades now appear as integral disposable razors, shampoos are packaged in safe plastic bottles instead of glass, tea is in bags instead of loose leaves. By carefully examining his product and its packaging, the exporter may find an opening in what appeared to be a saturated market.

The manufacturer of retail products will be familiar with the problems of competition for shelf space. Supermarket and store owners argue that they must give prime position to nationally known brands which are heavily advertised on television and the other media. Because the UK exporter may not have this advantage, you and your agent/distributor will have to fight hard to secure proper display. This is why shelf appeal is so important, and this can be backed up where possible by judicious use of point of sale promotional devices.

Promotion at the point of sale

A lot of money is wasted every year on point of sale materials that are ill conceived and simply not appropriate to the market they were intended to serve. Some store groups simply will not accept them, and their proper use often depends upon the determination of the supplier or a specialist company to physically erect and maintain them on site. Many unsuitable materials end up gathering dust in the back stores of shops and supermarkets, and eventually go out of date and are discarded.

Thorough market research will have to be carried out to see what is and is not possible before any decision is taken to invest in the design and production of point of sale materials. Used correctly, they are extremely cost-effective compared with other forms of advertising. Greater success can be assured if the proposed device is simple – such as a cut-down outer frequently used as a dispenser for jars, bottles or cans – and saves time for the shop owner. Dump bins and other special dispensers come into this category, as they are clearly seen as having advantages for the retailer, whose acceptance is vital.

Clear instructions and diagrams as to their use, printed on the outer or the display item itself will assist in situations where it is not possible for the distibutor to physically enter the shop and do this himself. Where elaborate displays are to be used, perhaps for a special promotion, the distributors' normal sales team may have to be augmented temporarily by specialist merchandisers. They would be responsible for installing the POS displays, re-stocking as required, replacing damaged or worn out materials, and generally exercising considerable control over your whole operation. Without these elements, point of sale devices should be regarded as a possible bonus to the manufacturer if they get used and therefore the cost of their manufacture and supply should be kept to a minimum.

Moving displays can be neatly divided into two categories: those provided by machines and those by humans. Non-human intervention in the form of films or audiovisuals can be used to introduce new products or usage ideas, and are popular in such sectors as do-it-yourself and cookery. Short instructional films projected onto a television screen can offer an effective moving display, particularly if the content is 'educational' rather than simply a repeat of a television commercial. Even when projected to captive audiences, such as the queues in British post offices, such films can provoke as much resentment as impulse to buy if they are not extremely carefully produced.

Human demonstrators are a common sight in department stores and supermarkets. Their activities can range from offering samples of food and drink to demonstrating 'gadgets' and interesting new products. Such demonstrations are usually mounted for short periods of time, before being moved on to another store location, to avoid staleness among regular shoppers.

'British Weeks' are also popular devices set up by the BOTB in conjunction with groups of British manufacturers and important stores in Europe. These can either be built around a limited theme, such as food or clothing, or a broader based promotion encompassing all things British. They certainly have their place in a retail launch programme, particularly for the first time exporter who will benefit from the experience and marketing expertise of many of the supporting organisations.

Promotion using the trade and professional press

As was noted at the start of this chapter, the trade and professional press can be used – either through advertising and/or public relations – as a powerful promotional tool, particularly during the early stages of your European launch programme. Among its functions are to support the activities of your local agent or distributor, as he tries to promote your products among trade buyers, to alert trade buyers to the existence of your products, and to directly influence trade buyers of business to business products. The printed press discussed here includes both trade and professional publications, and those that can be similarly used to promote the launch of new services or professional activities in the European market.

All the Common Market countries benefit from a more or less established trade and professional press and many of its titles will already be known to the exporter. A large number of trade journals are European or international in their outlook, and there has been a recent tendency for some British-based publications to 'go European' even if it means little more than adding the word European to their title while they try to build up their circulations outside the United Kingdom. English language journals of British, American – and increasingly European – origin are already well established internationally in many sectors, including the newer technologies such as computing, engineering and the advanced sciences, as well as disciplines such as marketing, management consulting, international law, architecture and design. It is likely that the exporter of goods and services in such sectors is already using these magazines, either through advertising or editorial/PR, reflecting the international nature of his business sector.

Many trade and professional journals are distributed either on subscription or through controlled circulation, whereby they are mailed direct to the intended reader. Circulation figures are sometimes certified by the relevant controlling body (such as the Audit Bureau of Circulation – ABC – in Britain) but even so circulation figures have to be treated with some caution. The exporter himself or his firm doubtlessly receives several such controlled circulation publications, many of which may go largely un-read. At the other extreme some firms complain that they receive too few copies of journals important to their business, and by the time they have gone the rounds of the principal executives, the last recipient on the list is probably reading news that is already weeks or months out of date.

How to select appropriate publications

There are several ways in which the exporter can select appropriate European journals in addition to those known to him for the purposes of advertising or public relations. There are a number of directories and other information sources (discussed below) but among the less formal methods of research are: asking your agent or distributor, asking your end customers, and noting which journals are prominent at trade fairs and exhibitions.

Your local agent is bound to know the principal trade journals that are published and circulated within his territory, and by extension will have a good idea of what his customers (your potential customers) normally read to keep them abreast of events within their area of interest. Your agent may already enjoy contacts with editors and journalists locally, which will assist in the eventual placement of PR materials when you start to prepare them. He can also assist with local trade advertising, advising on the copy and layout and local requirements.

The more important journals are invariably present at the major European fairs and trade exhibitions, where they maintain a stand from which they distribute copies and solicit subscriptions and advertising. During his early market research, which includes visiting such fairs, the exporter should have picked up copies of these magazines both in order to get a flavour of his industry or service sector, but also to compare which journals are more likely to represent vehicles for advertising and PR later on. Trade journals frequently publish special bumper editions to coincide with major exhibitions, so the journal you pick up may not be truly representative of the rest of the year's issues. Special fair issues can be a valuable medium, however, for both PR and advertising as they tend to be retained for reference, particularly if they incorporate a fair guide or other useful information.

Back home there are a number of formal sources of information, some of which are contained in BOTB publications such as their series of European Country Guides. Useful media guides include the *Advertisers Annual* which has a section on European publications. In the DTI library in Victoria Street there are media guides from all the main European countries, written in their language of origin of course. They list titles by subject classification, and usually include circulation figures and possibly advertising rates (not always up to date).

If you do not already use an advertising agency, the Institute of Practitioners in Advertising (IPA) in London can help with publications, guidance notes, and lists of European 'media consultants' and more importantly UK representative offices of many European publications. These exist to sell advertising and will supply rates, circulation breakdowns, mechanical details and sample copies on request. Some of these UK offices represent many journals or groups, and can facilitate the placement of advertising in due course. They are not generally a good channel through which to funnel PR materials; here direct contact with the European editor is preferable, with all materials translated into the appropriate language of course.

The media guides list the main trade and professional publications which can be considered as international or European in their scope. They are defined as those which 'are intended for circulation in more than one continent or worldwide' and pan-European – those that circulate throughout West Europe. These are in addition to journals that are mainly national in their coverage and distribution.

International and pan-European journals as already noted are generally strongest within industries or subject areas where the body of knowledge is universal and spread among a fairly close-knit worldwide community of, say, immunologists or marine geologists and other such experts. If your product or service is important to such people then you have relatively easy access via these journals to project your expertise through advertising and editorial on a European-wide basis.

Some less esoteric English language titles can clearly be regarded as pan-European, and they include Britain's *Financial Times* and *The Economist* which are both widely circulated and respected throughout West Europe. There is not, at the time of writing, a truly European general business publication and circulations of several Euro-titles are in fact quite small. Within sectors such as construction, engineering, energy, environment, computing, clothing/fashion, design, and some areas of consulting there are major titles already circulating throughout Europe.

Straddling somewhat awkwardly the gap between European and international are the in-flight magazines issued by virtually all the world's major airlines. British Airways' *High Life* will be familiar to the traveller. This monthly glossy journal has a print run of around 215,000 copies. Other European flight journals include *Atlas* (Air France, 250,000 - 380,000), *Ronda* (Iberia 280,000), *Germany* (Lufthansa, 100,000), *Sphere* (Sabena, 140,000) and *Ulisse 2000* (Alitalia, 180,000). The mix of editorial and advertising can be studied by the exporter and a judgement made – perhaps in consultation with his advertising agents – about the value of these publications for your own purposes.

Coming down to the level of national country trade and professional journals, your agent and his customers are once more your most reliable guides to those which they themselves find useful. The editorial content will necessarily be more tighlty focussed on the country concerned, and invariably advertising and editorial matter will have to be translated into the local language. Engineering and technical journals are particularly well produced in Germany and Scandinavia, as well as in Britain.

All trade and professional journals are hungry for advertising, and in the case of free circulation publications, advertising is their sole source of revenue. They are sometimes produced by very small editorial staffs who are also looking for news items of interest to their readers. This does mean that they make use of a great deal of PR generated material, such as news releases, feature articles and photographs, which are supplied by manufacturers. It is foolish not to take advantage of this opportunity for free publicity. Sometimes there is accompanying pressure to advertise, but as a practitioner of some 25 years standing the author would always counsel against directly linking advertising and editorial (one detracts from the other) and above all against 'advertorials' – paid-for space which is filled with editorial matter prepared by the manufacturer.

How to get your news published

To have any relevance all PR releases, whether they are short announcements or full length feature articles, should contain information of intrinsic value to the journal concerned and its readers. If so, it should be worthy of inclusion (an editorial decision). If a publisher insists that he will only print your news story in return for some paid advertising, ask him if therefore your news is not of interest to him or his readers. This argument usually works.

It is essential that all PR material is sent to the editor translated into the foreign language. The only exception might be very short news items, as many trade journalists are willing to translate and include these. Experience shows that once a relationship develops with a particular editor, it is possible to send a longer feature article or outline in English for his consideration. If he agrees to publish it (in translation) the exporter can then arrange for the translation to be done, knowing that he has obtained a prior commitment from the journal to publish.

Good photographs will enhance any story and are always welcome. An editorial front cover – perhaps in colour – can sometimes be negotiated, where the exporter contributes something towards the cost of the colour production (separations, plates etc.).

The use of loose or bound-in inserts has already been mentioned, and their value is that they enable the exporter to make use of already printed leaflets and other promotional materials. These should be designed, of course, with this additional usage in mind, and fortunately many European journals adopt the popular A4 format which facilitates the use of inserts.

Where page advertising is bought, there will be the additional costs of 'production'. If you are advertising simultaneously in several markets, then a standard advertisement layout or 'shell' can be prepared, into which the appropriate foreign texts are inserted. This can save costs, particularly if full colour illustrations are used. However, such advertisements must be designed at the outset to take account of the additional space required by the foreign text (for example, German) if a direct translation of the original is contemplated. (This is not always advisable, see below.)

Although as noted there is some standardisation towards the A4 format, some journals may present odd or irregular sizes, which means that advertisements have to be re-shaped for particular markets. All this adds to the cost and as a general rule, the cost of producing the final advertisement is generally equivalent to the space cost. So that a typical full page will cost £1,000 for the space and a further £1,000 in studio and production costs. If you plan to alter the text frequently, each change attracts similar production charges for what is effectively a new advertisement.

Direct translation of the original English text is not always advisable, unless your advertisement is a practical, straightforward statement of say the principal features and benefits of your product or service. Clearly some concepts and allusions do not cross frontiers well, even in expert translation and the advertisement copy may in fact have to be re-written for each market. It is popularly believed that Germans require more bald statements of fact, backed up with solid references; whereas the French and the Italians will appreciate a more subtle approach. The best person to advise you is your local agent or distributor, but he should not be regarded as a copywriter. That function should be left to an expert, under your guidance.

National and regional consumer press

When we come to discuss Europe's consumer press, the numbers are somewhat mind-boggling. Taking daily newspapers alone, there are over 1,900 titles which print 74 million copies every day. Within these figures are wide variations – Germany has over ten times more daily newspapers (1,300) than Great Britain (around 100). France, Spain, Greece and Italy all have between 80 and 120 each, and Belgium, Denmark, the Netherlands and Portugal under 50 each.

To these figures should be added the weekly general newspapers, including free sheets, which circulate in every corner of Europe, and the weekly or monthly consumer magazines. These are either classified as 'general interest' – the equivalent of France's *Paris Match* or Italy's *Panorama* – or specialist consumer, covering every area of interest from angling to zoology. Among this latter group and of particular importance to manufacturers of consumer goods is the very wide range of home and women's interest magazines which circulate in all European countries. Some of these such as *Maison de Marie Claire* appear across Europe in different national editions, as do numerous versions of *Vogue* for both men and women.

In the countries with high levels of daily publications, there is no national press on the scale known in Great Britain. France and Germany have traditions of a very strong regional press. In West Germany, important dailies are published in Berlin, Bonn, Cologne, Dusseldorf, Frankfurt, Hamburg and Munich but circulations average under half a million copies. Although France has a number of national newspapers including *Le Figaro, France Soir* and *Le Monde* (all circulating below 500,000 copies each) there is a marked concentration of these titles on Paris; whereas in the regions there are important dailies such as *Ouest France, Voix du Nord, Midi Libre* whose titles give a clue to their centres of interest. France also has a number of business publications such as *L'Express, Le Point,* and *L'Expansion* (all under 500,000). Italy has about 80 daily newspapers, with small circulations (almost all well under 250,000) and although they may be perceived by outsiders as nationals, *Corriere della Sera* is in fact published in Milan, *La Stampa* in Turin and *La Republicca* in Rome.

Readership across all publications appear to be generally higher in southern Europe compared to the north, but is down overall particularly among young people who tend to buy fewer daily newspapers. Not unnaturally, this has had an effect upon advertising, which has lost out to television and other media. Spain has a very low adult readership, with fewer than 10% of the population buying a daily newspaper although Sunday papers are popular. The Netherlands has no Sunday newspapers but has nearly 50 daily papers. As a share of total advertising expenditure, newspaper advertising has declined in Belgium, Netherlands, Germany and Portugal, where it represents between 30% and 40% of the total spent – similar to the position in the United Kingdom.

Language problems occur in Belgium, with the split between Flemish in the northern part of the country, and French in the south. Brussels is officially both French and Flemish speaking.

Until VAT is harmonised under EEC regulations, advertising rates vary considerably between different Member States and are levied on the space costs in publications and on the production costs of the advertisement.

The wide diversity of press media can be used by the exporter for both advertising and public relations. The use of daily newspapers means that advertising decisions can be implemented quickly, whereas the regional and local papers can be used for test marketing and concentrations of promotional effort in selected parts of the country. A recent survey by the European association of newspaper editors also points out that the press is fighting back against competition from other media through the increased use of colour in editorial and advertising, strengthening their editorial coverage (the number of journalists employed is rising) and using readership surveys to keep abreast of their readers' changing tastes and requirements.

As a medium for public relations, the daily and weekly papers can be targetted with specific information about new products and services, addressed to the appropriate section editors (business, home page, leisure, travel, fashion and so on), in much the same way as you would in the United Kingdom.

The increased consumption of coated printing papers bears testimony to the popularity of glossy consumer magazines and colour supplements which are a common feature throughout Europe. By using magazines devoted to his areas of interest, such as gardening or do-it-yourself, the British exporter can again target advertising and editorial promotion this time by sector, but with national coverage. The more general interest glossies are used for much corporate advertising and promoting luxury items such as holidays, travel, hotels and airlines, as a glance at any one of them will confirm.

Outdoor advertising

Various forms of outdoor advertising media are available including semi permanent poster sites and hoardings, bus and metro cards and will be familiar to the traveller in Europe. They can be used locally or regionally to support a special promotion (e.g. shop or store launch, a British Week) or nationally as part of an overall sustained advertising campaign. They need to be used strategically and among the best sites are those on main routes into town from the airport, close to industrial or commercial centres, at major exhibitions, on key business commuter routes and at railway stations and airports. Outdoor advertising can promote industrial products and business services, as well as consumer goods. Even the best sited posters are glanced at for less than 10 seconds but of course may be seen by several hundred thousand people during the course of the poster's life.

The medium tends to be very popular in some countries, with a waiting list of up to one year quoted for Belgium (100,000 advertising sites), a very high penetration compared with the size of the country. In the Netherlands, rail sites are controlled by one company (Alrecon) which also has a monopoly (with another company Talsma) on bus shelter panels. The largest general contractor is Publex, who control 60% of the country's 70,000 poster sites. France has around 175,000 sites spread among four main contractors including the rail network. Almost half of West Germany's poster sites are controlled by one contractor (Deutsche Stadte Reklame) and 70% of the sites are large size (3.6 x 2.6 metres).

Large posters also predominate in Greece, with the main contractor Union controlling 55% of the country's 24,000 sites. Italy has many contractors and 78,000 sites, including small poster sites and vehicle panels. In Portugal the main contractor is Red Placa, with some 80% of the 2,500 available sites (mainly large format 3 x 4 metres). In Spain the industry is highly fragmented: 40,000 sites, of which 80% are very large format (3 x 8 metres), the remainder are mainly 3 x 4 metres. There are nearly 100 contractors, some of them working within a consortium called Roseo.

Outdoor advertising is a highly specialised business and requires the services of a local advertising agent who knows the medium well and who can negotiate the best positions and prices from contractor or site owners. The medium then accommodates either a permanent or semi-permanent display – which can even be moving or three-dimensional – or accepts printed posters which have a finite life. Booking periods can be from a few days to longer periods, usually in blocks of 7, 10 or 14 days according to local custom.

Other outdoor media include aerial advertising, using static balloons or banners trailed behind light aircraft, such as those seen over large stadia in Italy just before a football match. Again specialist local advice is required to ensure that the proposed advertising method is allowed by law.

Moving vehicles are of course used to carry advertising. In addition to vehicles painted and signwritten in the firm's own livery, some large vehicles are designed to take changeable posters or van sides. These can be produced using 'decals' which are printed using high precision methods onto flexible plastic films. These are then affixed to the vehicle. They will withstand mechanical washing but can eventually be removed when required. Regional promotions can incorporate the use of (additional) vehicles carrying such signs.

Cinema advertising

It used to a be a general rule that a country with a strong television service had a weak cinema, and certainly there is evidence of falling attendances in many West European countries. However, cinema survives by appealing to a largely young audience (over 4 million per week in France) and cinema advertising using films or slides can be used either regionally or nationally as part of consumer promotional campaigns. The numbers of available cinemas are as follows: Belgium 400, Denmark 300, France 3,500 (Paris 670), West Germany 3,000, Greece 350, Italy 900, Portugal 350, and Spain 2,350 (UK has 700 cinema screens, including those in multiple venues).

Radio and television

Despite the advent of satellites (discussed below) and the fact that national radio and television programmes can be received across borders, Europe's television and radio services are most conveniently considered on a country-by-country basis. Advertising is handled by agencies experienced in the sector, and there may be opportunities for using both radio and television through public relations – news announcements, guest appearances, etc., again handled by people experienced in these tactics. The broadcast media in each country are summarised in the following paragraphs.

Belgium Broadcasting is controlled by the government, with two French and Flemish speaking television channels, one each of which accepts advertising. A further 9 foreign channels are accessible and cable television reaches some 90% of the country's 3.5 million households. There are national (no advertising) and regional public radio stations, and around 200 commercial stations who accept some advertising.

Denmark One public TV channel and a second channel started in 1987 which accepts some advertising, reaching 2.2 million households. Some commercial radio starting in 1989.

Netherlands 5.6 million households receive three TV channels, all with limited advertising permitted, except on Sundays. There are 5 national radio stations, 3 of which accept advertising. Several foreign television and radio stations can be received.

France The country's main public channel TF1 is now privatised and covers the whole of France. There are 5 other main channels (Antenne 2, FR3, La Cinq and M6 and Canal-Plus), and most of France's 19 million households can pick up foreign stations as well. All accept advertising. Radio is divided between the state-run France Inter and FIP (very limited public service advertising) and over 1,000 regional/local commercial stations. In addition RTL (Luxemburg), Europe 1 and other foreign stations achieve wide coverage. There is some cable television in Paris, Lille, etc. – some 30 cities, which carries advertising.

West Germany The two main television networks, ZDF, which is national, and ARD which is divided into 9 regional stations, between them reach some 25 million households. Advertising has to be booked several months in advance (in September for the following year), is restricted to certain times (mainly between 17.30 and 20.00 hours) and separate for each regional station. No advertising is allowed on Sundays. There are 15 state-owned radio stations which carry advertising (not on Sundays).

Greece Under 3 million households have television, which comprises two state-owned channels ERT-1 and ERT-2 with limited, restricted advertising. There are 30 commercial radio stations, including those run by the two national radio/TV networks.

Italy Chaos reigns. Italy's 19 million households can receive 3 state-owned channels (RAI 1, 2 and 3) and up to 350 commercial TV channels, including broadcasts from other countries. The situation with radio is even more fragmented, with over 2,000 radio stations whose transmissions frequently overlap. Advertising is possible on all these media but extreme caution is advised.

Spain Two main state television channels reaching 24 million households, plus three regional channels covering north west (Galicia), northern (Basque) and north east Spain (Catalonia/Barcelona) controlled by the regional governments. Additional private channels are forecast and in addition there are some 500 radio stations. Advertising is limited.

Portugal Two state-owned television channels reach 3 million households but only RTP1 reaches the whole country. The second channel covers only the capital Lisbon and surrounding areas. Limited advertising is allowed on both. There are 3 national radio channels, plus a further 500-plus unofficial/private radio stations. One of the three national radio channels (Radio Commercial) is expected to be privatised and some of the other stations legalised.

As will be seen from the above brief survey, national television and radio broadcasting within Europe is hedged-in with restrictions at the national level (including bans on certain types of product/advertising) and at the opposite extreme is liberalised to a degree that makes much of the media unreliable as an advertising medium, particularly in Italy. Advice should be sought from competent local advertising agencies and caution generally exercised.

In addition to the national television services there are satellite broadcasts either existing or planned. They include TDF1 (France, 4 channels), Astra (Luxemburg, 16), Tele X (Scandinavia, 2), Olympus (Italy, 2), BSB (UK, 3) and TV SAT-2 (replacement of SAT-1,

Germany, 2). By 1990 it is expected that some 30 new channels will be available to advertisers wishing to reach a wider European audience.

Direct marketing

This branch of promotion involves establishing a direct relationship with the end customer, who is reached either by the use of printed media which are sent by post or hand-delivered; and/or by telephone. In the various sections on the promotion of services and capital goods, it was suggested that direct contact can be made with potential end customers in the business-to-business sector, through use of trade directories and other sources. Mail-order selling also makes use of customer lists built up over years of trading or resulting from responses to other forms of advertising. Consumer direct marketing is an extension of all of these activities.

Using printed media – coupons, leaflets, etc. – direct marketing includes postal and hand deliveries, as well as direct response advertising in other media. Telemarketing is used to make contact with consumers, either selected at random or from directories and lists, and a further extension is the use of customer response devices such as tele-shopping using a home based videotex service through which the householder can place orders direct with the supplier.

The direct marketing industries have grown in countries which have or have had restricted television advertising, and curiously are also growing in countries with an over-abundance of media (including TV) where costs are rising and the audience is harder to pinpoint. Mailing houses and list brokers are able to provide more or less well-researched lists of prospects, who can then be approached by post or telephone. For regional or local mass distribution (e.g. for a store opening) the services of the local postal administration can normally be used, and/or special companies employed to hand-deliver leaflets to housholds within a defined area.

Advertising agencies, many of whom have direct marketing divisions, can be approached for specialist advice in this area.

Handling your own media relations

When your advertising budget is very small or non-existent, press relations (including radio and television) can be used to bring information about your product or service to the attention of the readers of European newspapers and magazines. As already noted, particularly at the specialised trade and professional level, these publications generally have small editorial staffs and rely to a great extent on PR material sent to them by outsiders. So when your competitor's name appears constantly in the trade press, remember that there is no magic formula involved; it is simply a question of keeping editors informed about your own products and services.

If you can afford a public relations consultant, he or she will learn about your products and hopefully prepare the sort of material that editors like to publish. Quite often, however, good writers are unable to grasp complex technical subjects, while many technicians make poor writers. So using an expert is a good idea if you are prepared to give the time to brief him thoroughly, allow him to attend trade shows, visit your factory, go and see clients and generally get the feel of what your business is all about.

All this activity of course costs money. PR consultants usually work on a retainer, with a monthly fee calculated on the likely amount of work that needs to be done. Exceptional items, like attending an overseas exhibition for several days, would be charged extra. Good consultants are not cheap, and an average rate might be around £400 per man day with items such as printing, photography, bulk mailings, etc., charged extra. It does not matter much if the consultancy you choose is large or small, as you end up buying the services of individuals. It is the quality of the person who looks after your account that matters, rather than the size of the management staff (for which you are paying albeit indirectly). Many good technical PR consultancies are quite small, even one-man bands. They represent good value.

If you decide to go it alone, there are a number of books and courses in do-it-yourself press relations. The backbone of the small-budget PR programme is invariably press relations and the techniques include preparing and issuing press releases, feature articles and photgraphs. A press release embraces hard news, and can include a straightforward announcement of a new or modified product or service, the opening of a new factory or depot, the appointment of an agent or sales person, and other items of company news likely to interest the readership of trade and technical journals.

The art is to present the facts contained in your press release in a logical way (who, what, when, where, why, how!) leaving the superlatives to be added – or not – by the editor. As a result of receiving your material, an alert editor may telephone for further information or arrange to meet you or visit your premises, in order to gain material for a longer piece about your company. Alternatively, you can invite editors to your new product launches and factory open-days. Such events are known as press visits and while they often send panic into the hearts of company managers, they are relatively simple to organise both at home and in Europe.

Within your own trade or specialisation, the exporter will already have an idea of the principal trade journals. Many of these noted in the section on the press are international in their distribution and content and are printed in English. Others with a more European or national bias should be brought to your attention by your agents and distributors. These specialised magazines form the basis of your press list. To them can be added more general business journals, those covering export activities and certain radio and television services. The BBC's overseas division broadcasts news and information about British companies to a wide audience abroad and material can be sent to them. In addition, copies of your press release can be sent to local and regional radio and television stations in Europe, particularly if you are planning to open a factory or distribution centre in the area. Here the journalists' interest will be primarily in aspects such as the new jobs that will be created locally.

These considerations will give you some idea of the possible content of your news announcements. Journalists are above all seeking an 'angle' on a story, something that will grab the attention of their readership. By emphasising certain aspects of your operation – such as job creation, a training programme, sensitivity to the environment, for example – you are more likely to gain interest than if you simply send out a standard press release describing your new product or service.

Planning a press event

When the occasion demands it, it is possible to invite the press to come to you. We have already mentioned the factory visit, and this is appropriate if, for example, it forms part of an opening ceremony at which a local dignitary will officiate; or if your building or process line are particularly interesting and innovative, and the processes complex. In this case the journalists will appreciate the opportunity to visit the plant, meet company officials, ask questions and prepare lengthy news stories.

When organising a facility visit, it is not necessary to spend large sums of money on lavish entertaining. Journalists spend their life going to such functions and, despite popular belief, their loyalty cannot be bought for the price of a drink. What they do need is well prepared background material and photographs, which form the basis of a press information pack; and a well planned programme that enables them to accomplish a day's work that will provide them in the end with usable copy for their publications, in time for their press deadline.

One of the most acceptable formats for a typical press visit is a mid-morning arrival, with coffee; a series of formal briefings followed, if appropriate, by a tour of the premises; lunch, with an opportunity to meet and talk to company personnel; and departure planned for early afternoon. Most events fit into this type of programme, which is well accepted by press people; breakfast meetings, riverboat trips, tours of local nightclubs are the exception rather than the rule.

There is no guarantee, however, that journalists will turn up to your proposed press event. Trade journals are chronically under-staffed and editors have to weigh up competing claims for several organisations. To ensure a better chance of success the following tips are suggested, based on many years experience of organising such events:

- As soon as you have a date in mind, telephone around to a few key journalists, to gauge their initial interest. You will soon get a feel whether they are enthusiastic about visiting you, and whether the date clashes with something more important happening elsewhere.

- Check that your proposed date does not clash with another competing event, such as a major trade exhibition or other important local event that journalists are bound to cover.
- Avoid the later part of the week (Thursday, Friday) and other times (if you can find out) when many of the journals are going to press. At these times staff are confined to their offices for last minute editorial changes and the arrival of late news. Best days are Tuesday and Wednesday, and away from press days – but there are always exceptions, so take soundings first as suggested.
- If you are dealing with foreign media you will need to speak the local language or have your agent or local PR consultant do this preliminary work for you. These locally based people will already have established contacts with certain journalists and can more comfortably make the initial approaches on your behalf.
- Once the date is settled, send out invitations. If you are planning a large-scale event a printed invitation and accompanying letter are needed. For a smaller event a personal letter will suffice. Ask for an acknowledgement in either case, so that you can gauge numbers attending (for catering, staffing, etc.).
- If your company's operations are new or likely to be unknown to the journalist, send some background material along with the invitation. Also send a programme of the day – journalists like to know when they can expect to get away, in case they have another event to cover. Send a location map and details of transport arrangements (e.g. pick-up at the local station or airport) if appropriate.
- Some people advise telephone follow-up prior to the event. If the numbers responding are satisfactory, this is probably not necessary unless some key journalists are missing from your acceptance list. In this case, check that they received your invitation.
- Do not hustle journalists. They resent this and may say 'Yes' to your invitation simply to get rid of you.
- Do not expect 100 per cent turn-out on the day. There will be some missing faces for reasons beyond your control. Send them a copy of the press pack, with a note saying you are sorry they missed your event and invite them to a private visit.
- In order to avoid embarrassing lack of numbers or where only a handful of journalists are expected, you can combine your press

day with a visit by company officials, customers, local dealers, distributors, agents, etc. Some companies worry about mixing press and customers but such concerns are often not justified. If a major in-company event is also taking place (such as a sales conference) a useful compromise is to invite the press to join you for part of the day only, for example a few hours either side of lunch. After their departure the in-company activities can continue.

- An appropriate ratio of staff to visitors is required. Clearly staff should not overwhelm the visitors by their numbers, but neither should the press and other visitors feel neglected. Staff not directly involved in meeting the visitors should be told of the event and firm guidelines laid down for such things as the timing of the factory visit (not during the lunchbreak, for example). If the event includes a plant opening or equipment commissioning, all staff should of course be involved in the accompanying official ceremony as part of the programme.

- Senior company people need to be on hand for interviews and to answer questions, pose for photographs, etc. They should not be allowed to disappear back to their offices when they feel like it.

- The press information pack should include: a programme of the day's events, with timings; names and details of main company people; full text or outline of major speeches (this saves mistakes and a lot of arduous scribbling); general company and product background, such as press releases and leaflets. All this should be in the appropriate language.

- Photographs should be available in the press pack or offered (using a display at the reception area, for example). Black and white photographs are more generally required, and colour can be offered.

- Photography (and filming/TV coverage) on the day can be disruptive to other visitors, and it may be advisable to offer separate opportunities for photography – for example, early morning before the official event begins, when staff have more time.

- Keep to your schedule. Even the best planned events tend to over-run so that allowances should be made at the planning stage. You should also 'walk the event' by means of a full rehearsal with all those involved, in time to iron out any problems – e.g. what to do if it rains and there is a one hundred yard gap between the factory and the area set aside for lunch?

- Plan and rehearse all presentations, with slides, audiovisuals etc., and have back-up equipment available. Use a public address system if necessary and simultaneous translation for non-English speakers.

- Learn to relax and keep a sense of humour. Disasters and embarrassments occasionally happen at the best planned events. Try not to panic and pass them off with a good humoured apology.

- Finally, ask yourself if your planned event is really necessary? It is not good form to summon the press (assuming they will come) to a press conference to announce something that could have been put into a press release and sent to them. Unless you are a major company or government department, this approach will not work. The press visit will succeed if you have something worthwhile to show, such as a new building, production line, machine or equipment demonstration.

9 Transport and distribution in Europe

Examining the distribution alternatives

The move into Europe presents the United Kingdom manufacturer with a number of new problems in the areas of distribution planning and physical distribution, which are considered in this chapter. Several different approaches are possible, depending upon whether you are concerned with the sale of capital goods, consumer products or industrial and business consumables. Distribution will involve the handling of goods by greater or lesser numbers of middlemen (importers, wholesalers, distributors, etc.) and will reflect the marketing and selling arrangements already established by means of agency agreements and other methods of selling to Europe discussed in Chapter 5 and elsewhere.

Capital goods

The exporter of capital equipment is often able to rely on direct sales from the United Kingdom, where initial contacts are fostered by a network of local agents. Agents call on likely customers in the course of promoting the interests of usually a number of principals. Once an initial contact has been made, it is likely that sales staff or sales engineers from the UK-based company will become increasingly involved. They will prepare a price schedule, possibly outline engineering drawings if the product is not standard, and generally liaise with the customer and the agent to determine precise requirements and propose amendments and modifications. Eventually, a 'sales visit' becomes inevitable, and assuming all goes well at this stage and during subsequent visits which are invariably necessary, an order is eventually placed by the customer and a manufacturing and delivery schedule agreed.

Stock items will normally be available for delivery within a matter of days or weeks, while larger, specially designed pieces of equipment may have to be fitted into a manufacturing programme stretching months – and in some cases years – ahead. Final delivery will be a relatively simple process, when the capital item is transported to the end customer's premises. This is followed by a period of installation, trials and commissioning which normally form part of the sale contract.

As will be seen, aside from the intervention of a local agent at the start of the sales process, the sale/delivery of capital goods places the UK manufacturer for much of the time in direct contact with his end customer in Europe. Sales of capital equipment are likely to be fewer than for other types of goods, and of higher value. Much of the selling will be to precise specification worked out between the customer and the supplier, with several meetings required between technicians from both sides. This is in addition to the commercial negotiations which will be running in parallel, to determine price, delivery and terms of payment, and other elements such as training and after-sales service. The stages in the sale of capital items will be familiar to exporters of these products.

As the level of business increases, a decision might be taken to stock spares and industrial consumables locally, with limited warehousing – possibly even servicing – provided by the agent and his staff. This is an alternative to handling after sales service direct from the United Kingdom, although many companies do adopt this approach. Service engineers are despatched to all parts of Europe and urgent spares sent by one of the express or air courier services. This allows for the manufacturing location to be almost anywhere in Europe, provided there is reasonable access to transport facilities.

Consumer products

Other types of goods – consumer products and some business consumables – will normally require the establishment of a more sophisticated distribution network. Its length and components can vary. We have already noted in earlier chapters that as a result of the concentrations of retailing that are evident in much of Europe, many consumer goods can be sold and delivered direct to the European retail outlet, such as a hypermarket, supermarket or department store. Other consumer goods may pass through a wholesaler en route to the retail outlet and this distribution method is traditional in certain areas such as fresh meat, fish, fruit, vegetables, etc. However, the power of the retailers is eroding this distribution method, with many such items now delivered to the supermarket or department store by the manufacturer.

Retail selling by the manufacturer to the end customer is used in some special situations, for example, by the petrol companies who own chains of garages and by brewers operating tied or managed licensed premises. These arrangements allow direct control by the manufacturer of prices charged to the consumer but this near-monopoly situation is increasingly under attack by government and consumer groups, concerned about the limitation of choice and price competition.

In the area of business-to-business sales, while some items – such as capital goods – may be sold direct to the business or organisational consumer, others may have to pass through a network of agents and distributors. In selecting the channels of distribution, the manufacturer has to examine the requirements of the marketplace and choose those that are appropriate to the needs of the eventual consumer, the retailer, the product itself and the activities of the competition.

In any examination of consumers, it is necessary to determine their number, concentrations, average frequency and value of their purchases. Also where they shop and how often. The retailer for his part is concerned to meet his customer's requirements by relying on frequent deliveries and stocking a wide range of alternatives, while at the same time being concerned about stock turnover, shelf-life and the perishability of goods. He will also be monitoring – together with the manufacturer – the performance of competing suppliers in meeting these criteria.

Different products from the same manufacturer may be subject to varying distribution arrangements. Exclusive brands might be sold only to selected outlets, and more popular brands or own-label products pass through a different distribution chain. Differing methods may be adopted at the various stages of the product life cycle, from its establishment in a new market, through to maturity and eventual obsolescence.

Some products may lend themselves to only one of the forms of distribution, which can be described as exclusive, selective or intensive.

Exclusive distribution: A prestige, generally higher margin product would be sold through a number of selected outlets only; consumers are relatively few in number, selective in their purchasing, willing to seek out the product and the retailer, who in turn offers a high level of service and personal attention. Examples of products that can be sold in this way include top-of-the-range cars, designer clothes, exclusive watches and jewellery, speciality food and drink items, 'designer' lighting and furniture.

Selective distribution: More run-of-the-mill items such as furniture, shoes, clothing, home computers can be sold through a larger number of selected outlets. Here the object is to widen the market, which is neither an exclusive niche nor mass consumer. However, it may be difficult for the manufacturer to establish a clear identity for his product.

Intensive distribution: A no-holds-barred approach to the mass market, where volume sales/profits are paramount. Examples of products suitable for receiving this treatment include groceries, household items, magazines, all of which are common daily requirements, which the consumer expects to find available in the widest possible range of outlets without experiencing the need to shop-around.

Relations between manufacturer and distributor

As already noted the aspirations of the manufacturer may not always accord with the demands of the distributor. As a result the manufacturer will have to tread a delicate path between satisfying his own company's requirements and the needs and aspirations of members of his distribution network. Among the problems that will require solution at the planning stage are pricing and purchase terms. The UK manufacturer's idea of the final price may not accord with the retailer's view, or the price levels of the competition. Some adjustment upwards or downwards may be necessary. (It is generally felt that British manufacturers underprice their goods for Europe, allowing distributors to make excessive profits as retail prices are increased in line with competitor items. This subject is explored more fully under Pricing in Chapter 10.)

Payment conflicts may occur when the manufacturer is concerned to seek the most prompt methods of payment, with minimum discounts and the shortest possible credit period. The distributor/retailer for his part will be looking for maximum discounts and extended credit. Differences may also arise over the frequency of deliveries, the amount of notice given by the distributor to the manufacturer of his need for additional supplies, and over marketing methods. Whereas the manufacturer wants to offer bulk deliveries, un-mixed consignments, regular orders and standardised products, the distributor will invariably be looking for specials and one-offs, extended and split deliveries, goods on consignment and sale or return, and the maximum flexibility in ordering and stocking.

Conflicts also arise over the methods of marketing. The manufacturer may favour the widest possible distribution in order to capitalise on the market, whereas the distributor may demand exclusive rights and a controlled territory that effectively keeps out competitors. The distributor will demand maximum advertising support, when the manufacturer is concerned to control his promotion budget. There will inevitably be conflicts over allocation of display and shelf space inside stores and supermarkets, much of this related to the amount of consumer advertising the manufacturer is prepared to undertake.

Ideally, in attempting to resolve these conflicts, the manufacturer should try and avoid the dominance of one distributor or retail outlet, and early on in the planning process try to iron out potential problems such as pricing, product promotion, discounts, payment terms, size and frequency of deliveries. Retailers in particular are able to apply enormous pressures. For example, despite their insistence on bar coding of a wide range of consumer products (which cost the manufacturers large sums of money in redesigning and printing labels and packs) retailers have not responded with widespread installation of electronic checkout systems – as a result they say of their high costs.

Some considerations after 1992

Much of this book is concerned with the increased ease of doing business that will be a feature of Europe up to and after 1992. Some of the greatest benefits will occur within distribution and transport and they are considered briefly in the following section. Some of them will affect the exporter's distribution planning and accordingly some possible alternative strategies are discussed.

Effects of the Euro-Tunnel

Clearly, the Euro-Tunnel is going to have a profound effect on transport and distribution between the United Kingdom and the rest of Europe. Scheduled for opening in 1993, the full benefits will unfortunately not be enjoyed immediately by Britain largely as a result of delays in planning and constructing the improved road and rail links that will connect London and the regions with the Tunnel. At the time of writing, a major road improvement programme has been announced by the Government but arguments are still continuing about the precise route that the rail link should take. Invariably construction will not take place until well into the 1990s.

Among the major road improvements announced (in May 1989) are widening of the M25 London Orbital route which is currently subject to heavy daily congestion, negating its value as a bypass route from the north and west towards the Channel ports and the Tunnel entrance. In addition a programme of upgrading to four lanes will be applied to much of the M1, part of the A1, M6, M3, M4, M23 and M20. A serious problem for drivers on the M25 from north of the River Thames is using the existing Dartford Tunnel. Delays of several miles are not uncommon in either direction, due to the requirement to collect tolls and the sheer volume of traffic. Although a privately funded road bridge is under construction between Dartford and Thurrock, this will also be funded by tolls and similar traffic congestion may ensue.

Although traffic forecasting methods are demonstrably unreliable, it is known that road traffic in Britain has risen by 35% since 1980 and motorway traffic doubled during the same period. Forecasts are for an increase by 2025 variously calculated at between 80% and

140%. Because the present situation is described as 'urgent' the government is hoping to reduce the time taken from planning to opening of new or improved roads from the present average of 13 years to just four. Whether this will be achieved remains to be seen, but what is clear is that it will be at least 10 years before any radical improvement in Britain's trunk road system will be seen.

All this is in marked contrast to the mainland European road building programmes, most of which have been under way for several years, and which will force British manufacturers to consider locating their major distribution facilities outside the United Kingdom. A further worrying aspect is the shortage already of suitable land sites for warehousing in Britain's over-crowded south east corner, due to both environmental considerations and neglected infrastructure.

Apart from these problems, road journey times from the United Kingdom to Europe should theoretically be reduced making attractive the option of using your own transport or independent road carriers. Increasing competition from the Tunnel should also lead to improvements in the existing ferry and hovercraft services. These will include more frequent crossings and improvements in Roll-on/ Roll-off and container facilities at the Channel docks. Because of the design of the Channel Tunnel – a rail link that carries vehicles rather than a straightforward road tunnel – it remains to be seen how in practice journey times for the Channel crossing will be reduced, compared to an improved ferry and hovercraft service. The exporter will, of course, retain the option to consider the other Channel ports in Belgium and France (for example, Le Havre) as well as the more obvious short route via the Tunnel.

Another major benefit of the Channel Tunnel should be faster rail links between Britain and Europe for both passengers and freight. Unfortunately, Britain once again lags behind her Continental neighbours in providing the necessary high speed links from the Tunnel to London and other parts of the country, again in contrast to France's rapidly expanding TGV rail network. Journey times will eventually be reduced for both people and goods, making the journey to Brussels or Paris equivalent to those to Birmingham or Manchester. At present 90% of UK rail freight is accounted for by bulk commodities, much of it in trainloads, but if British Rail and their European counterparts can develop services such as the popular Red Star parcel network and more containerisation, then rail freight may have a place in the exporter's distribution programme.

Air transport

The use of air freight services overcomes many of the problems associated with road and rail transport. This is not to say that Britain's principal airports are without their difficulties, including congestion at peak times, but there are encouraging possibilities. First is the greater use of Britain's provincial airports, outside the greater London area, both for freight and passengers. Business travellers from the Midlands and north of England have complained for many years about the annoyance and frustration of having to travel to Heathrow or Gatwick for many overseas connections, and cannot understand why these two airports continue to be expanded to the detriment of the provinces. Hopefully, pressure from the consumer and the progressive freeing-up of air transport during the 1990s will lead to the creation of more passenger routes and European freight services that will enable direct flights from Belfast, Birmingham, Manchester and Scotland to the European capitals and other business centres. Under the 50:50 rules whereby flights on the same route are divided equally between national carriers, high levels of wastage and over-capacity are currently passed on to the customer in the form of artificially high fares. The Commission's proposals, if adopted, will help promote greater efficiency and reduce costs.

Within Europe, several major airports are being designated as key transport centres. Paris's Charles de Gaulle has reserve capacity for both passengers and freight, and improvements already in hand include direct links to the TGV rail network. Rome Airport has expansion plans up to 2000, with the construction of a new cargo centre, and new passenger terminals and car parks. Frankfurt is over-loaded, due to the absence of a second alternative runway, and already passenger traffic is being diverted to Munich (300 kms. away) rather than to Cologne. Amsterdam's Schiphol already has almost continuous night arrivals and take-offs.

On the freight side, there is already evidence of greater cooperation between the established airlines and forwarding agents, partly as

a reaction to the success of many express and courier services (discussed below). Freight spends four times as long on the ground as it does in the air, so that any reductions in delays caused during pick-up, clearance and distribution can dramatically improve the total time taken for a package to travel from the exporter's factory to its final European destination. Some European airports are now re-structuring to capture greater shares of the freight market, offering round-the-clock facilities for freight handling. Brussels airport which is ranked eighteenth in terms of passenger traffic is now fifth in terms of freight handled. Major freight expansion is also taking place at Amsterdam, Cologne and Luxemburg, giving the exporter a useful range of alternative destinations in the densely populated regions of northern Europe.

Air express and courier services

Much of the airlines' reaction has been in response to the success of the specialised air courier services. Express services involve the use of light aircraft, including single engine propeller aeroplanes, to pick up and fly small consignments to and from local airfields closer to the exporter and his customer. Research shows that daily volumes of under half a tonne can justify the establishment of regular express services of this type. Already manufacturers of small high value items, such as electronic or engineering components, find that they can distribute to the whole of Europe from, say, Scotland whereas reliance on other means of transport would virtually rule this out in the face of local competition.

One of the fastest growing areas of freight transport are the European express freight services. They offer a range of services, including the use of air couriers who personally accompany consignments, and those that use priority freight services (specialised freight forwarders). In addition there are a number of integrated carriers, who use their own road vehicles and aircraft, and special door-to-door services offered by the scheduled airlines. A 1987 estimate was of around 5 million express freight movements within the EEC, with major companies including DHL, IML, Securicor, TNT, United Parcels and World Courier.

There is increasing cooperation between the express companies and Europe's national postal services, and relaxation of customs requirements and freedom of movement of goods within the Community will all further improve prospects for these companies and their users. Principal customers of the express services have been identified as the financial institutions, engineering and construction companies, professional services, oil and shipping, electronics and manufacturing, as well as the carriage of essential import/export documentation and goods. One can see scope for their greater use by all manufacturers of comparatively high value, low volume consumer and industrial requirements.

Because of the already large volumes of freight handled by the specialised carriers at great speed (sometimes with only minutes to spare between connecting flights), freight operations are increasingly being computerised. Real-time systems are widely used to trace and locate consignments, vehicles and containers; to process orders and monitor stock levels; and in warehousing and inventory management. Direct links to airlines' computerised systems by freight agents will also speed the movement of freight within Europe. The exporter may have to consider streamlining his own distribution operations to take advantage of these developments.

Finally, the exporter may have to look carefully at how to improve his transport and distribution services in response to the growth of just-in-time delivery methods. The philosophy behind this approach is ridiculously simple: goods are delivered to the warehouse or factory strictly as close as possible to the moment at which they are required for use. This means that stock levels are kept to an absolute minimum, with consequent savings on storage space. At the same time, the onus for accurate and timely deliveries of often vital components or stocks is put upon the supplier. Like retailing, this is further evidence of the major customer's ability to dictate delivery terms to his supplier, who in turn is obliged either to go along with the system or go under.

Physical distribution management

As we have already seen, the European exporter is faced with a number of options when evolving a transport and distribution policy. We have examined some of the transport alternatives and some the post-1992 factors which will influence your choice for Europe. Among the most important of these will be deciding whether to provide local distribution facilities in Europe, and where and how they should be operated.

Distribution management frequently involves trade-offs between costs and customer benefits. One of the most common is between the (lower) cost of trunking goods over long distances, against the increased benefits that may arise out of establishing a network of local warehouses. The latter normally results in faster deliveries, shorter lead times, availability of buffer stocks, ability to assemble a mix of products – all contributing to increased customer satisfaction.

The question of lead times will depend upon the customers' own requirements and how well the supplier is able to respond. He will also be influenced by the actions of his competitors, the anticipated shelf life of the product, average and peak sales volumes, availability of alternatives if stocks run low, and so on. As we have seen, while the customer will invariably be looking for shortest lead times, frequent deliveries and small orders, the supplier for his part is anxious to reduce costs by providing bulk deliveries at less frequent intervals. Incentives may be offered in the form of additional discounts to major purchasers, willing to buy in bulk, and an identical delivery schedule will not necessarily be applied to each and every customer.

Local European warehousing

The advantage of local European warehousing is that goods can be stored closer to the local market, so relieving many of the headaches associated with ensuring deliveries to key customers on time. Even though Europe is being increasingly opened up for the free and fast movement of goods and vehicles, lorries and vans can still be subject to delays especially over comparatively long distances. Breakdowns or accidents can occur, drivers may be sick or absent, industrial action may close important transport routes. All these problems can largely be avoided by establishing a local warehouse, closer to the customer. Such a warehouse can also carry a wider range of the manufacturer's goods and even operate as a cash and carry depot for smaller customers to whom it may not be economical to undertake deliveries.

A number of techniques can be employed to help choose the ideal warehouse location. They include use of a gravity model, which is now more often simulated on a computer. This method first establishes where the largest concentration(s) of customers exist, and then calculates their average daily or weekly demands. The 'weight' of their demands will pull the model towards the optimum location of the centralised distribution depot.

While such models may assist in selecting the 'ideal' location, other considerations will have to be borne in mind. They include:

- the availability of suitable land and/or buildings at an economic price, either for lease or sale;
- access roads suitable for handling frequent movements by heavy vehicles (up to 40 tonnes);
- sufficient turning-space for long articulated vehicles;
- proximity to points (ports) of entry from the United Kingdom;
- proximity to road links with the rest of the market;
- proximity to customers;
- availability of suitable staff locally.

The action of setting-up a European warehouse operation represents a major commitment by the UK manufacturer. Some of the corporate and fiscal implications are discussed later (in Chapter 10); and as was noted earlier (in Chapter 5) in addition to taking over a green field site, the exporter may consider working with a local agent or distributor who already owns facilities, with a view to profiting from an established sales and distribution network.

Whether seeking a green field site or considering using the facilities operated by an established distributor, a number of factors (aside from the commercial aspects) will influence the choice of location. We have already noted the lack of suitable UK distribution sites from which the exporter can launch a drive into Europe. A further disincentive, as noted, is the uncertainty surrounding the Channel crossing. Even with the advent of the Channel Tunnel delays and congestion may occur, and alternative ferry services can be subject to cancellations due to bad weather or industrial action.

Almost as important are the psychological barriers the exporter may face when confronting a mainland European customer. Because of Britain's physical separation from Europe, and the difficulties of ensuring uninterrupted supplies of goods, buyers may be reluctant to commit themselves to a distribution system that relies purely on UK warehousing. The exporter who can offer distribution from a mainland European site has both practical and psychological advantages.

How to choose the right location

There are a number of information sources that the British exporter can consult in his search for the ideal warehousing and distribution location. As already noted in the guidelines listed above, you should have a reasonably clear idea in your mind about what you are looking for – size of site, handling facilities required, vehicle access, staffing levels, etc., – and the location of your most important actual and potential customers. You may also be used to shipping your goods through a particular Channel port and already have good commercial links with freight forwarders, transport companies, handling agents, possibly even some limited warehousing and storage. Unless you are contemplating a complete break from existing arrangements, all these factors will tend to narrow your range of options.

If the exporter is at the stage of seeking agency representation (including warehousing and distribution) you should refer again to Chapter 5. For help with physical location you can make use of information sources such as Central Government planning agencies, regional planning agencies, Chambers of Commerce, British Embassies in Europe, consultants and UK and European estate agents. There are also a number of published guides. All these sources of information and help are considered in the following paragraphs.

An excellent source of up to date information about Europe is available in *Corporate Location Europe*. This is a quarterly publication, available free to companies considering locating in Europe. In addition to general articles, for example about Europe's main ports or property prices in the main centres, the magazine contains much detailed information about individual regions, enterprise zones, financial incentives, etc., that make it invaluable for the businessman. Several Chambers of Commerce and regional enterprise initiatives are listed either editorially or in advertisements. Additional single country supplements are regularly published, which discuss property location in considerable depth, as well as offering guidance on employment regulations, salaries, taxation and the intricacies of buying or leasing property.

Another good general source is the *Property Director*, published occasionally by the Institute of Directors. An issue of May 1989 contained general articles about property in Europe and included a useful list of British estate agents working in the main European capitals.

The national governments of each European country all have departments dealing with territorial planning (such as France's DATAR) and they, together with regional initiatives (around 150 in Europe) and local Chambers of Commerce, can also offer information and advice. It should be noted that all these bodies, however well intentioned, exist to attract investment to their particular region and it is a truism that the worst areas offer the best incentives. In his search for an ideal warehouse location the exporter should not be unduly influenced by the availability of generous financial incentives, if other considerations would make him decide against that particular site. In practice, most companies find that while financial incentives are acceptable they do not become an overriding consideration when selecting a location.

The fiscal incentives offered by European national governments are also increasingly less relevant as country boundaries become submerged. However favourable existing tax regimes may be before 1992, they will become less important as taxation is harmonised throughout the Community. In the area of VAT, for example, the Commission's proposals to approximate rates between countries are designed to nullify the advantages of cross-border shopping (including activities by wholesalers) which would distort the operation of the free market. The exporter should therefore, as always, think European rather than nationally when looking for a business location, basing his decision on geographical rather than national considerations. In this sense, it is quite feasible to consider a location in, say, northern France, from which you could service markets in Belgium, Luxemburg and Germany, as well as France.

By visiting the regions and bypassing the central government(s), the exporter will see for himself what is on offer in the areas of his choice. The regional enterprise initiatives and Chambers of Commerce in Europe are themselves active in promoting and constructing facilities, and the ownership and management of existing transport infrastructure (including ports and airports). Many of these are already being developed as warehouse and distribution centres (see below) and offer the advantages of bonded warehousing, entrepot facilities and all forms of transport.

Several of Britain's Embassies in Europe also produce detailed notes on their territories, and commercial counsellors are aware of local sites and developments that may be of interest. They can and should be consulted.

A number of British firms of estate agents are also active in Europe and among the specialists who can advise on industrial and commercial properties are:

Healy & Baker	Paris, Brussels, Dusseldorf, Madrid
Jones, Lang, Wootton	Paris, Amsterdam, Brussels, Madrid
Richard Ellis	Paris, Amsterdam, Brussels, Madrid
Debenham, Tewson & Chinnocks	Amsterdam, Brussels, Frankfurt
Gooch & Wagstaff	Amsterdam, Rotterdam, Frankfurt

Plant Location International, based in Brussels, can also advise companies on the location of manufacturing and warehouse operations.

A central European location

Although some costs are lower in the further extremities of the European Community, these advantages may be outweighed by the additional transport costs and the hazards of being located too far from the main markets. As was indicated in Chapter 2, European centres of population are well defined and run in a broad arc extending from Britain's north west and Midlands, through Greater London, and on into Southern Holland/Northern Belgium, the Rhine/Ruhr conurbation, and south to the industrial areas of northern Italy. The only major conurbations outside this broad population band are Greater Paris, Madrid and the area around Naples.

Consequently, although costs may be lower in Spain, Portugal,

Southern Italy, Ireland and parts of Britain (Wales, the West Country, North East, North West, Scotland) none of these are particularly favourable locations for a centralised European distribution facility. It is likely therefore that the final choice will be between Netherlands, Belgium, France and Germany.

The Netherlands benefits from the availability of the major ports of Rotterdam and Amsterdam and the increasing number of freight services based at Schiphol Airport. It has excellent road links north towards Denmark, east into Germany and south to Belgium and France. Sites are well developed and already available, many of them built around the ports. Rotterdam, the world's largest and busiest port, is continually being improved and developed. It has an efficient customs service, and an established network of freight handlers, forwarders, transport companies and warehousing of all types. Current investment includes improved road and rail links. Holland's rival port of Amsterdam benefits from closer proximity to the country's major financial and commercial centre, excellent communications and several incentives for industries locating in the port area. English is widely spoken throughout The Netherlands. Average warehouse rents are around Df 1.60 per square metre.

Belgium offers the advantages of established ports (notably Antwerp and Gent), and excellent road and rail links to the Netherlands, Germany and south into France. Despite the presence of the European Commission and other Community institutions in Brussels, commercial rents are not exorbitant in or near the capital. They reduce considerably in the industrial zones around the ports and in the industrial area near Liege and elsewhere in the south east. Rents are from BF2,000 per sq metre down to BF1,000 per sq metre per year. Flemish and English are widely spoken in the northern half of the country, and French and English in the south. Brussels is bilingual (Flemish and French), with English widely spoken.

France With its central location within the Community probably offers the widest choice of potential sites for the UK exporter. Already the areas around the Channel Ports of Calais and Boulogne are proving popular with British companies, and extensive industrial and warehousing developments are already available. Unlike Britain's south east area, the Nord/Pas de Calais region is not expensive – despite the house buying activities of the British. The Channel Ports enjoy excellent road links with the main north/south autoroute to Belgium and the rest of France, and east (via Lille or Rheims) to Germany. Various grants and loans are available to encourage establishment here as well as in several of France's Provinces.

Greater Paris nonetheless remains a popular location, partly because of its base of 12 million consumers. There are major industrial developments at Charles de Gaulle and Orly airports, and close to the Paris ring roads. Warehousing in the Paris region is around FF400 per square metre reducing to FF200 in the Provinces. The port of Le Havre is undergoing extensive development, much of it aimed at attracting non–European investment (for example from the USA) to the industrial/warehousing sites in its hinterland. With the advantages of regular Ro-Ro ferry services from the United Kingdom, British exporters could consider Le Havre, with a view to having easy access to Paris and south towards Bordeaux/Toulouse and Spain via the main A10 autoroute.

West Germany presents a number of options to companies seeking warehousing and distribution facilities. To the north Hamburg is emerging as an important rival to the Belgian and French ports, and in addition to its traditional cargo handling activities, there are plans to develop the surrounding area to provide facilities for storage, break-bulk and distribution. Despite its northern-most location, Hamburg offers good road connections with Denmark, east to Berlin, and south to the rest of Germany, Holland and Belgium. Elsewhere within West Germany, the Rhine-Main area around Frankfurt is the most central location and a popular centre for distribution – again due to excellent transport links in all directions. Dusseldorf is also emerging, with some Japanese companies already located there. Further south, Stuttgart and Mannheim give access to the southern German market, including the prosperous Munich area; and to eastern and south-eastern France.

Packing and packaging

Goods destined for the European market may require some adjustments in packing and packaging to take account of the longer distances and extended shelf life involved. As well as the retail pack, many goods travel in 'outers' which offer a degree of protection during handling and transit. There may be a need to protect the product against the possible effects of sunlight, damp, infestation, excessive heat, breakage, vibration, evaporation or spillage. However, many of these hazards are being reduced due to the increased use of containers, particularly where a full load can be provided by the exporter.

During distribution, the outer pack needs to be durable and comparatively easy to handle and store. The outer pack should not be so voluminous or weighty that it cannot be manhandled as required. It must be designed to accept bar coding, as many wholesale systems exist which rely on machine readable codes for distribution and warehouse management. The outer can sometimes be designed to act as a product dispenser at the retail outlet. Examples of this approach include bottles of mineral water which are frequently packed into boxes of one dozen; the upper part of the outer pack is then torn away, making a useful display of a product that might otherwise not command prime shelf space (due to its high volume and low price).

The package designer has many materials from which to choose including paper, board, plastics, films, foils, cloths, wood and glass. The final choice is guided by its appropriateness to the product, desired shelf life, image, cost, typical usage and what is customary. However, a number of conflicting national regulations may override these considerations. For example, while many European supermarkets require most liquids to be packed in PET plastic bottles, countries like Denmark can insist on the use of returnable glass bottles in the interests of conservation. Liqueur minatures are now supplied to airlines in plastic bottles, whereas this type of packaging would not appeal in other retail outlets where miniatures are bought as a novelty or gift item.

While appropriateness and custom may influence the packaging designer's choice, quite often established products are supplanted by innovative packaging. Milk bottles have been largely replaced by cartons and shaving sticks by aerosol creams. Shampoos now come in sachets and tea in bags. Even fresh produce frequently arrives on the supermarket shelf washed and packaged.

Product labelling is a final important element in packaging, at both the wholesale and retail levels. In addition to proclaiming the product's brand name, packs must contain information about the size, weight and contents; information or instructions for use; warnings against misuse; identifying marks and (bar) codes; and sometimes money-off coupons, special promotional elements and instructions for storage and display. Much of this may have to be printed in more than one language.

European consumer and safety legislation will increasingly influence pack design in areas such as child-proof closures, tamper-evident packs, and the use of biodegradable and environmentally friendly materials.

There is also a growing requirement for packs that incorporate measures to deter counterfeiting by the use of special materials such as security inks, holograms or other devices. Pilfering is another problem during distribution, and some wholesale packs are now designed to disguise rather than proclaim their precise contents.

Use of containers and vans

The need for security and speed are prime considerations that influence the choice of containers as a means of transporting bulk loads from the United Kingdom to Europe. As already noted their increasing use has led to a reduction in the robustness/cost of outer packs. Containers are available in a variety of sizes, and most are designed for combined road and rail usage. Airline containers are specially shaped to accommodate the design of the aeroplane's cargo hold, but are otherwise transferable.

Facilities exist for packaging part loads where the exporter cannot command use of a full container shipment.

Containers can be conveyed on the exporter's own transport, or use can be made of covered vans – particularly where door-to-door deliveries are required. The continuing growth in the use of Roll-on/Roll-off ferries and Hovercraft, as well as the Channel Tunnel, will encourage many exporters to use road transport direct from their

UK factory or warehouse to the European destination. The choice is between running one's own fleet or using contract transport, but either way speed, security and flexibility are assured.

Transport operators offer a wide variety of services, including warehousing and break-bulk, and specialised services such as refrigerated containers and light van services for delivery of low volume/high cost items such as fashion clothes or computers. Many offer regular scheduled services, with journey times of only two or three days from the United Kingdom to almost all parts of Europe.

Within the constraints of the various remaining transport regulations and occasionally congested routes to Europe, the UK based exporter should be able to service his Continental operations with the same speed and efficiency as his domestic market. As has been shown, a wide range of differing approaches are possible although research and planning at each stage remain essential.

10 Facing up to Europe: Strategies for 1992

A policy for Europe

This book has been all about facing up to the challenges presented by the new, open European market after 1992. However, although the date of 1992 – or more accurately 1 January 1993 – looms large in the minds of both the government and many industrialists, the process of removing barriers to increased trade is already well under way. As has become apparent many of the initiatives being taken today by the Commission are an attempt to implement at last the letter as well as the spirit of the original Treaty of Rome. This Treaty envisaged as early as 1957 the free movement of goods within the Community, the free movement of individuals, the freedom to sell services and the free movement of capital.

The fact that it has taken so long to reach this stage is due partly to the economic uncertainties of the last thirty years, and to the weakness of many of the European institutions, including the European Parliament, and perhaps some of the people working in them. What is now coming about is due largely to the determination and foresight of a few key individuals within Europe. For her part, Britain's attitude to Europe has at best been ambivalent, and as stressed earlier, although geographically Europe has always been Britain's closest foreign market, it has traditionally been passed over in favour of links with the former empire and colonies. Indeed, it is only in recent months that government aid has been extended to include Europe, whereas before exporters were largely expected to find their own way and pay their own costs. It is only since the launch of the 1992 initiative that many grants and other forms of assistance are available for European research, marketing, quality control, etc., that before were only offered to exporters considering more distant overseas markets.

It is not surprising that in such a climate, British manufacturers are not clear just how to react to the sudden rush of official pre-1992 propaganda, and there are signs that discussion of 1992 may already be producing an adverse reaction among business people. Those who have been selling to Europe for years may be tempted to sit back in the belief that their existing structure and procedures will be enough to let them survive in the new market; others are so bewildered by the threats of increased competition, a mass of new legislation and the imagined Europeanisation of British institutions, that they are either vehemently opposed to the European concept or hoping it is a local difficulty that if ignored will go away. Neither view is realistic.

The speed with which new legislation is being implemented has taken many observers by surprise. In the areas of border controls and fiscal harmonisation (excise and VAT), the acceptance of Member State's technical standards and professional qualifications, the right of establishment and cross-border research and cooperation, the Commission has moved with astonishing speed. And it is these actions that as we have seen have important implications for business. Alternatively, the cost of not going ahead with the Common Market has also been spelled out extensively.

So, where does the UK business person make a start? The first step may involve a radical change of attitude towards Europe, together with the acceptance that, like it or not, the Common Market programme is going ahead and will impact on your business. Accordingly, it is as good a time as any to take stock of company strengths and weaknesses, to look at where you are going, to examine your product offering and consider how it could possibly be adapted for the new European market.

General information about Europe can be gained from books (such as this one), conferences, outside consultants, government sources, Chambers of Commerce and trade associations; but a detailed analysis of your own business is something that is best handled internally – possibly using expert outside help. Financial assistance for this sort of excercise is offered by the Department of Industry under their Enterprise Initiative programme.

Even if you are already exporting to Europe, it is a good idea to put together a special 1992 project team, which can operate alongside and in cooperation with your existing marketing, sales, production and product development departments. It may well involve many of the same people. This team should be headed by a senior person within your organisation, who has both a real commitment to Europe and the authority to make – and implement – decisions. He should be backed up with similar top-level people from each of your organisation's key departments.

Precise tasks and targets can then be assigned to the team members, under each of the major headings – production, product development, purchasing, marketing, sales, finance, etc. Team members would undertake their research and report back to regular meetings of the full group, where individual findings can be discussed and decisions taken on the next stage of your overall European Plan.

The team member in charge of production may, for example, be charged among other things with looking at your product range, production lead times, stock-turn, delivery performance against competitors, commitment to quality and how this is monitored. In reviewing production processes, you might also look at optimum utilisation of existing plant and machinery, the skills and experience of existing staff, the availability of additional staff if required, the company training programme, the inflow of apprentices and trainees – all with a view to assessing whether your company could cope with an upturn in business as you expand into Europe.

Taking stock

This process of self assessment will also include an examination of your company's core production technologies ('what are we best at?') and whether these can sustain the company over the medium and longer term. Has there been sufficient investment in machinery, using the latest technologies? Are design and manufacture incorporated? Are you making fullest use of economies of scale, just-in-time delivery, competitive purchasing? Are alternative policies worth considering such as contracting-out all or part of manufacturing, assembling more or fewer components, radically altering existing methods of manufacture and supply?

None of these aspects can of course be examined in isolation. Closely related to these findings will be assessments of existing products and how they can be changed and adapted for the wider European market. Among the key questions to ask are:

- Can development can take place in-house or a (European) partner be sought?
- How should this be achieved: through joint R & D, through sub-contracting, to acquiring licenses for new products or new technologies?
- What assistance is required to understand and implement European standards?
- Can local technical colleges and universities be of assistance, what about your trade association, have you considered one of the European research programmes?
- How will all this activity be funded?

Because the Common Market will encourage two-way trading, the British based manufacturer now has an opportunity to review his purchasing policies. New sources of supply will be opened up, and part of the team research in this area will involve identifying potential new European suppliers by attending trade exhibitions; obtaining catalogues, samples, prices; visiting potential suppliers; cross-checking technical standards.

Much of this book has been concerned with market research, marketing, sales and distribution, and appropriate team members will be concerned with the specific tasks of identifying:

- new customers, how many, where they are located, how they can be reached;
- buying patterns, how the purchasing decision is reached, anticipated lead times, activities of competitors;
- availability of market information and specific market research;
- patterns of distribution, packaging requirements, frequency of shipments;
- existing distribution methods and how they may need to be altered;
- sales promotion, product literature, advertising, public relations, product launch, problems of language and translation;

The company's financial expert will be concerned with the key questions of resources needed to sustain your company's move into

Europe. All the changes proposed have financial implications and the company accountant will need to identify any requirement for additional financing, potential sources, the need for improved financial management, the effect on cash-flow, the impact of extended credit, exchange controls (where they exist), currency management, pricing for the European market, tax implications and the effects on profitability.

These lists are not meant to be exhaustive but they indicate the wide range of topics that will require investigation, evaluation, decision and implementation by the 1992 team, in order that the company can evolve an overall European policy. A useful checklist is contained in the DTI's Single Market brochure, and many of them are considered further in the following sections.

Building a European team: the personnel problems

Many companies facing the kind of re-assessment outlined in the preceeding paragraphs find that, possibly for the first time in the organisation's history, there are serious gaps in the quality and availability of personnel who can take on the responsibilities of facing up to the new market. The problem is not confined to Britain, but is probably more serious particularly among small and medium sized companies that are still managed by their original founders and owners.

It is well known that many British companies of this type are managed by largely self-taught people. Some owners went into business straight from (usually secondary) school, largely without obtaining any formal qualifications. A recent NEDO survey (by Professor Charles Handy of the London Business School and others) found that only 24% of British managers had a degree, against 85% in Japan and USA. And although the MBA is rapidly gaining in popularity, existing schemes are producing only 1200 graduates per year in Britain, against 70,000 in America – plus a further 240,000 with bachelor degrees in business.

In France increasing numbers of younger managers are passing through the Grandes Ecoles, nearly half of them engineers and one-fifth as managers. In addition a further 20% of managers under

35 have received bachelor or masters degrees in business. A survey of the directors of Germany's hundred largest companies showed that over half had earned a doctorate and that most managers do not join a business until they are aged 27 or older, after having received extensive formal education.

When it comes to managing export activities, the lack of formal training is even more acute. This is partly due to the absence of suitable university level courses, although recently some full and part time programmes have been initiated in languages and European studies. As noted in Chapter 2, Britons are generally worse at speaking foreign languages than mainland Europeans. In France, for example, nearly half of the managers in export departments regard languages as the prime qualification (followed by marketing) for their job. But they too suffer from a lack of formal 'export training' with 70% confessing to having picked up their knowledge on the job. (These problems are discussed in *Exporter Plus* by Alain-Eric Giordan, an excellent guide to setting-up and running your export department.)

Overall the greatest gaps appear to be in:

- knowledge of languages;
- knowledge of the individual countries and markets;
- selling and negotiating skills;
- technical and product knowledge;
- export documentation and procedures;
- marketing and promotion;
- transport and distribution.

All these skills can be learnt.

In assembling a European team, both for the initial planning and assessment stages and later when operational in the market, the British exporter will therefore probably be faced with a number of personnel problems. One solution is to recruit from Europe and already there are signs that some five hundred white collar vacancies a week are being filled with people from across the Channel. There is, however, a slightly larger movement in the opposite direction, as European companies also try to plug the gaps in their own organisations.

Staffing European operations

Among the alternatives that can be used to staff European operations are using British managers (who transfer abroad), using locally based managers or using personnel from third countries outside Europe or drawn from a number of countries within Europe. The use of expatriate British staff means that managers sent to work in Europe enjoy unparalleled knowledge of the company and its products, but may lack language and marketing skills, which of course can be learnt. They are also relatively costly to employ as the European remuneration package will have to include the provision of assistance with housing and schools for children, and higher salaries to compensate for the inconvenience of living abroad and possible loss of a wife's earnings. Living standards and therefore costs in Europe are generally higher, so adding to the expatriate's salary expectations.

Unless he is left in place for some considerable time, and perhaps not even then, the resident British manager will rarely gain total insight into the workings of a local economy, something that only a resident national can. Nationals of the country concerned bring with them not only this local knowledge of the market and the business/political climate, but their network of contacts in business and government, fluency in the foreign language and possibly experience in the manufacture and distribution of the same or similar products. Although they will expect to earn the equivalent salary of the British manager, the cost of employing local managers is less in real terms than the typical expatriate remuneration package. However, some difficulties of communication, monitoring and control may occur. Some local managers tend to run their operation with an alarming disregard for head office policy and may be reluctant, for example, to part with detailed information on customers and other contacts, in case they are sacked or decide themselves to move on. In close knit communities they may also have difficulties in running-down operations and dismissing staff, should either be necessary, that would be less of a problem for the man from head office.

Many of these problems are compounded when nationals from a third country are deployed locally. While they bring undoubted skills learned in the international market place, they too may lack detailed knowledge of the local conditions. Cultural and linguistic clashes may occur, particularly where several nationalities are employed: old enmities die hard! Such mobile international executives may regard each posting as an essentially temporary assignment, affecting their attitudes to the market and to the longer term future of the company. However, they can be usefully employed to start up or re-vamp a European operation, to be taken over gradually by local managers as the business becomes more established.

Integration of your European team

When European agents and distributors are used, they will require constant support in the field from head office personnel, who will need to be linguists and of the calibre necessary to understand and exploit the dynamics of the local market. Such people are difficult to find, they generally command high salaries and require the back-up of similarly experienced people based at the UK office who can channel information rapidly and effectively to and from personnel in the field.

Can a European team be grafted onto an existing export department structure? Much will depend upon the hierachy of responsibility in an area where a number of organisational models are commonly used. Where the existing export department forms a separate division of the company or group, there may be minimal liaison by the department with production and product development divisions, so offering few chances to influence the design or adaptation of new products for the European market. Where the export office of a group of companies is highly centralised, there is sometimes even less contact between production occurring at a number of different manufacturing units and overseas sales departments.

Where companies are divided by function from the chief executive down through production and marketing management of different countries and regions, there may be even less direct vertical contact between an individual market and someone at main board level. This means that markets can be neglected, production may be switched to favour 'important' markets and again products and strategies cannot be tailor-made for Europe. Where overseas divisions have traditionally been left on their own, it may be difficult to alter their policies and outlook and rapidly implement a dynamic pan-European strategy.

Division by product presents similar problems, as several product divisions may be attempting to serve the same market and opportunities for a concerted, cooperative approach are diminished. Strategies may not be coordinated and as a result sales lost. Effective communication between divisions is particularly important, both at the informal levels and through such channels as sales meetings, company newspapers and the mutual sharing of sales information. If a company is succeeding in selling, say, capital equipment through one of its division, then this information is invaluable to sales people selling other products within the same market, as it inevitably breeds confidence in the overall performance of the group.

While none of the above options is ideal, the most effective solution seems to be division by region, with possibly some additional sub-division by product if necessary. What this means in practice is that:

- Europe is seen as a single market.
- Within the market are a number of regional variations, which for convenience can be considered on a country-by-country basis.
- Products are developed/adapted for the whole European market.
- Regional product variations can be introduced without detriment to overall production or marketing strategies.
- Promotion and marketing can be coordinated within the whole market, with less reference to international boundaries. (A recognition that both people and media overlap national borders.)

It can be seen from the above that some internal reorganisation may be necessary in order to achieve the maximum benefit from the Single Market. Added to this is the need to provide sufficient numbers of people of the right calibre who are engaged in market research, marketing, promotion and selling. It is not enough to add a vague European responsibility to an already overworked executive responsible for other duties as well within the United Kingdom. Apart from very small companies, this approach simply will not work. Given the size of the major European markets, a company wishing to gain the maximum benefit from France, West Germany, Italy or Spain must be prepared to provide a similar level of manpower and resources in these countries as they do in the United Kingdom. You cannot expect to achieve meaningful results simply by relying on the part-time efforts of an overseas agent in each territory.

Staff training

Before leaving the question of staffing for Europe, the British exporter may need to take stock of the personnel implications at other levels within his organisation. Despite high levels of unemployment in Britain during the last decade, around 65% of companies still report skill shortages in some key areas. Not only is there a lack of young people coming into the job market, due to low levels of births occurring during the 1970s, but many training programmes have been run down. During 1988 only 8500 apprentices were trained by British industry, the lowest for many years. Engineering suffers from a bad image, high turnover and lack of new recruits – who prefer the world of finance or the professions. In information technologies, companies already reported skill shortages of around 20,000 in 1989, with the figure expected to exceed 50,000 within five years.

The lack of investment in training in Britain contrasts with schemes in, for example, France, where the employment of youngsters between the ages of 16 and 18 is not allowed unless they are allowed to attend college one day a week; and in Germany where most are educated up to the age of 18 and factory-based apprentice schemes abound. The British company looking seriously at the European market will need to investigate all the available education and training schemes and see how these can be applied to his company. These will include part-time and day-release courses, undergraduate sponsorship and assessment of the training needs of more mature employees anxious to learn new skills. Already there is evidence of companies having to recruit older people (a sensible and welcome trend), including part timers. Many courses such as part-time MBAs and distance learning packages such as the Open University and the Open College are being tailored to the needs of people returning to work or considering a mid-life career change. The prudent employer will be attuned to these trends and willing to consider a range of alternative recruitment and employment strategies that will increasingly be a feature of the 1990s.

A response to Europe: joint ventures and acquisitions

As has been noted continuously throughout this book, the advent of the Open Market in 1993 will bring considerable benefits to the British exporter in terms of the ease with which business can be conducted in Europe. Unfortunately, these benefits will also be available to Britain's competitors who by 1989 had already shown themselves to be more adept in understanding and exploiting the potential of the European market. The mainland European's inherent sense of community, the ease with which he crosses national frontiers and speaks a second or third language in addition to his own, all make him a formidable business rival to the traditionally insular Briton. In addition, there are a number of areas where the United Kingdom allows greater entrepreneurial freedom for the 'foreigner' and one of these is in international takeovers both from within and outside the EEC.

Recent figures show that about 500 mergers or takeovers are occurring annually within the Community, more than double the figure of 1984, and growing by about 100 each year. During the period 1984-87 British companies made around 400 acquisitions in Europe, and two hundred British companies had been bought by European firms. Considerably more (over 1,500) European companies – including British – have themselves been acquired during the same period 1984-87 by companies from outside the Common Market, notably by the Americans, Japanese, Scandinavians and non-EEC Europeans (Austria, Switzerland), some no doubt in preparation for 1992.

The comparative ease with which British companies can be taken over has been a source of alarm in some quarters, following well publicised cases such as the acquisition of Rowntrees by the Swiss-based Nestle company. This should be viewed in the context of the larger numbers of available British quoted companies (around 2,500) compared with the rest of Europe: 460 in West Germany, 400 in France, 330 in Spain, 300 in Denmark, 275 in the Netherlands, 250 in Italy and only 200 in Belgium. In addition, as we have seen when discussing the principal industries in Europe, there remains considerable state involvement in some sectors in Italy, France and Spain and intimate and long-term involvement in companies by banks in West

Germany and the Netherlands. There are sometimes national and political objections to takeovers of companies by outsiders. All these factors can inhibit the acquisition of European companies by British firms.

Despite this, mergers, acquisitions or joint ventures remain valuable routes to European expansion. How does the British businessman go about finding a suitable partner? Clearly, a knowledge of your own industry sector and the principal European companies within it are obvious sources of potential trading links. Years of trading with a European partner may lead eventually to more or less formal talks about possible closer cooperation. Although there is not the detailed analysis of companies that is a feature of UK stockbroking (because of the smaller number of European public companies) some information may be available through banks and British and European stockbrokers.

Trade directories may also provide basic information on turnover, number of employees and perhaps names of directors. These are compiled from annual company returns and as a result may not be entirely up to date. Official filing requirements vary from country to country and timescales are not always adhered to. There are also disparities in the amount and type of information that have to be disclosed, and disparities in accounting and auditing practices. Only limited information may be provided about shareholdings in publicly quoted companies, even less for those that are family owned and controlled. Methods of valuation, for example of stock or fixed assets, vary between countries and until they become subject to a possible takeover, many European companies may never have had the occasion to assess their true worth.

Because of these obvious difficulties, the European Commission has been active in promoting measures for company harmonisation, as well as the procedures for orderly takeover of 'foreign' companies and the gradual removal of exchange controls. However, some national restrictions on foreign ownership may continue, in so-called sensitive areas, among them defence, airlines and the media.

Advantages and disadvantages

Having identified a suitable European partner, discussions may lead to the creation of a joint venture, local manufacture or partial or total takeover. There are advantages and disadvantages inherent in all these approaches.

Joint ventures are popular not only where a majority foreign shareholding in a company is not allowed, but where they enable two, or sometimes more, like-minded partners to come together for their mutual benefit. They reduce the amount of investment required by each party and can enable the exporter to profit from available expertise in manufacturing, distribution, local market knowledge, etc. If the level of investment is equal, decision making is vested in both parties. This may become a source of conflict. Where only a minority stake is held by the British investor, he clearly does not have control and potential problems need to be ironed out in advance or the agreement modified.

The British partner, if he is providing manufacturing expertise, will excercise considerable *de facto* control over the European venture partner. However, product quality will require continual monitoring, and agreement reached on such questions as transfer pricing of components and the precise extent of the market to be covered by the joint venture operation. In return a viable European base can be created in this way.

A more limited form of involvement is an arrangement for *local manufacture or assembly*. There are a number of advantages including flexibility to cope with fluctuating demand in a newly created or unpredictable European market, and the ability to adapt existing products to suit local requirements. There is usually limited financial investment. If the agreement is between two EEC member companies, no problems should arise over the issue of 'local content' of the finished products. The principal concern of the British partner will be in monitoring quality and ensuring the profitability of the venture.

The greatest degree of control arises from the outright purchase of an existing European operation by *merger* or *takeover*. It enables the British exporter to establish a foreign presence rapidly and acquire local market share and an existing workforce and other facilities. Some rationalisation may have to take place in order to offload unproductive parts of the operation. These activities, together with any associated reductions in the workforce, will require careful and sensitive handling if local goodwill is to be maintained.

Arriving at a purchase price for a European going concern is extremely difficult, among other things as a result of varying accounting practices. These may make it difficult to assess the value of buildings, fixed assets, stocks, work in progress and future orders, as well as goodwill and any accumulated tax losses. Complete honesty and frankness will be required by both sides during the takeover process. It may take time to earn the trust and respect of the potential European partner, and this will invariably be backed by undertakings linked to future performance and guarantees as to the accuracy of statements made during the acquisition process. If the European directors are to stay on, at least for a time, part of the purchase price can be deferred (an 'earn-out' arrangement) in order to retain their interest in promoting and managing the firm to maximum profitability.

Negotiations to buy a European company will invariably be protracted, requiring both stamina and commitment by all parties. Being open about your intentions for the future of the company – and sticking to your promises – will go a long way towards alleviating doubts and fears among staff who will undoubtedly be concerned about their jobs. This is not a time when you will want to lose key people to your competitors.

In larger takeovers there will undoubtedly be consultation with the appropriate trade unions. Some countries require the establishment of a works council, even in small companies. In Germany this is mandatory for companies of more than 20 employees, in the Netherlands above 35, Spain 50 and Belgium 100. Works councils generally have the right to be consulted about major reorganisation and impending dismissals. European social legislation may extend these requirements to other countries.

The final option for the British company is to acquire a greenfield site in Europe and *start operations from scratch*. Such a move enables complete control over the choice of location, including those favoured with grants and incentives, and all the advantages associated with a presence in the local market. However, the investment will be larger and the time taken from initial plan to implementation may be lengthy. In addition to building new premises (if an existing structure is not taken over), the European operation will have to be equipped and gradually staffed before production can begin. Time will be needed to recruit and train new people, and it may be many months if not years before the operation is profitable.

Fiscal implications of the European operation

A British company (or individual) planning to do business in Europe should be aware of the tax implications of his proposed strategy. Professional advice must be sought in complex cases, such as setting up an overseas company, merger or acquisition. This section outlines briefly the taxation implications of dealing with Europe from the simplest level of direct selling or branch office, through to a fullscale physical and possibly fiscal presence in Europe. The present position and future changes in the VAT regulations are also discussed.

As was shown in Chapters 5, 6 and 7, it is possible to sell capital equipment, consumer and business-to-business goods and services more or less directly from the United Kingdom. In some cases a local sales agent may be employed, who is paid by commission on sales, possibly with the addition of a retainer. Sales visits are made to the European country by the British exporter as and when required, and these efforts may be supplemented by setting up some kind of local European sales office. From the tax point of view, the costs of promoting sales in Europe will in principle be fully deductible in the UK. These will include expenses associated with sales visits, producing promotional materials and all travel, hotels etc. while the UK exporter is in Europe. Goods or services would be supplied from Britain and invoiced from the UK office. This sort of operation does not create a 'taxable presence' in the European country, under the terms of the present double taxation agreements between Britain and each Member State of the EEC.

Moving up a degree the UK exporter may decide to establish or make use of a local branch or sales office in one or more mainland European countries. Although generally judged on a case by case basis by the foreign tax authorities, the establishment of a local office (which can include some warehousing, storage of display materials, spare parts, etc.) does not give rise to a fiscal presence in the country concerned. Accordingly the profits arising out of such activities should not give rise to taxation in the European country. The sales income generated will of course be added to the company's UK turnover, and profits taxed in the normal way in Britain. The cost of running the branch office would be deductible against UK income.

The main criteria for avoiding taxation in the European country include the notion of doing business *with* the country as opposed to *in* it, and practical evidence of this would be the acceptance and fulfilment of all orders from the United Kingdom (and not the local office), and eventually invoicing the goods or services rendered from the UK (not from the local office).

Once the European branch office is set up with authority, among other things, to accept orders, then a permanent fiscal presence is established in the European country. At this stage the British company becomes increasingly subject to local laws and taxation. The local company is in effect a separate entity from its British owners, and will pay tax on the profits accruing from this local activity – both in the European country and in Britain. Under the dual taxation agreements, tax paid abroad will be credited against UK liability to tax, with the effect that tax is only paid once. However, regardless of whether the tax rate in the European country is higher or lower than in the UK, relief is allowed only at the relevant UK rate. As a result the company may end up paying more tax overall than if its operations were wholly based in the United Kingdom and European sales were conducted through a local sales office. Corporation tax rates in West Germany can be as high as 56% (reduced to 50% in 1990) and in France 42% – against the level of 35% in Britain (1989).

As already mentioned, a further option for the British exporter is to establish or acquire a separate European company. This company is then fully subject to local laws and taxation. A local witholding tax may also become payable on dividends and monies repatriated to Britain - but again double taxation agreements apply. Professional advice should be sought about this and other matters relating to the establishment of branches, subsidiaries and separate companies in Europe, and the laws relating to mergers, takeovers and acquisitions.

Profits arising out of licensing and franchise agreements with European partners are also taxable when these reach the United Kingdom, and relief may be obtained on taxes (such as witholding tax) already paid in the European country before these profits were repatriated to Britain. No fiscal presence otherwise occurs in the European country.

Harmonisation of taxes and VAT

Rates of corporation tax vary within Europe, the highest being in West Germany. In addition some countries – including Germany, Italy and Portugal – apply local taxes on business profits, but their overall effect is mitigated as they are deductible from the final tax bill paid to the state. The European Commission wishes in principle to harmonise tax rates. Their reasoning is that this will discourage the notion of tax havens whereby companies will seek to set up operations in countries with the most favourable tax regimes, so perhaps working against other policies for regional development and redeployment. They also favour greater approximation of the basis for taxation, for example, by agreeing what activities are or are not tax deductible, and by establishing common accounting conventions. The practical effects of these measures are to enable companies interested in making European acquisitions to know that when valuing a European company they are more or less comparing like with like, according to a common set of rules. The rights and duties of directors are also likely to be spelled out, together with agreed penalties for fraud and mismanagement.

Another interesting development is that of the European Company, which will work alongside the European Economic Interest Grouping. The idea of the European Company is to enable the creation of a supra-national entity, which would not be governed by the rules of any one Member State. It would instead be subject to a set of European norms. There have been a number of problems agreeing these new rules, in such areas as works councils which are common in Europe but appear to alarm some British employers. Taxation proposals would include the ability to offset profits and losses between activities in each of the Member States, so partly doing away with the necessity for double taxation agreements.

The European Economic Interest Grouping is an idea designed to help the formation of partnerships and joint ventures. Under this arrangement tax would be paid by each partner in his own country, according to the profits earned and allocated to him. (Partnerships between individuals in Europe still remain subject to the general rule that each partner pays tax in his own country, according to his share of the profits. In this way they replicate the rules applicable within the United Kingdom and other Member States for the treatment of partnerships where each member is individually assessed and liable for his own tax.)

As noted in Chapter 2, rates of personal taxation continue to vary between Member States, although with some minor variations average take-home pay ranges between 75% and 85% of income, when family benefits are included in the calculations. Wage levels of course vary more widely, between the more prosperous northern European countries and the south. These factors will have a bearing when recruiting and employing local personnel but otherwise should not concern the British exporter unduly.

The harmonisation of the principal indirect tax – VAT – is of interest, however. The proposal is that this should take a number of forms. First would be the approximation of VAT rates between countries, from the lowest or Zero-rated items up to the highest, with the upper limit to be determined by Member States. This would be known as the standard rate. A reduced rate of between 4% and 9% would also operate throughout the Community after 1992. Agreement also has to be reached on abolishing the zero rate where it applies and possibly replacing it with the reduced rate.

The idea of harmonisation is to discourage distortion in trade, whereby goods might be bought and sold across national borders to take advantage of lower rates of VAT. Another important proposal is for an end to the practise of zero rating goods and services 'exported' from one Member country to another. Instead they would be charged at the appropriate rate at the point of export (i.e. the country of origin principle). The recipient of the goods or services would then deduct the VAT paid on the imported goods when making his VAT return. In this way European sales are treated exactly like domestic transactions.

However, because VAT rates between countries may vary (even with harmonisation) a further Commission proposal envisages a central European VAT clearing house to avoid excessive VAT losses or gains by individual Member States. It has been calculated that without this sort of system, Britain and France would lose most, and West Germany and the Benelux countries enjoy the greatest gains. This process of harmonisation and centralised settlements would again reduce the likelihood of abnormal commercial transactions between companies in different Member States.

These changes will have a number of effects, including two parti-cularly worthy of note. First, the virtual elimination of tax-free sales at ports and airports. It is well known that duty free prices are excessively high: the prices charged in duty-free outlets do not equal the standard retail price (in a High Street shop) minus the duty and VAT. They are much higher. Second, while VAT will be charged on exports to countries within the Community, exports outside Europe will continue to be zero rated.

With regard to excise duties on items such as cigarettes, alcohol and petrol, the Community has proposed limited national freedom to impose rates, again with the object of minimising distortions of trade – cross border shopping again.

Customs duties within the Community will of course be abolished as part of the Single European process, and the simplified Single Administrative Document (SAD) used. Customs duties on trade from outside the Community will continue, but procedures will be streamlined and measures adjusted in light of the Community's obligations under existing arrangements such as GATT and EFTA. Agreement will have to be reached on the level of 'local content' of goods assembled from items imported into the Community from outside. Examples include Japanese cars assembled in a European plant from components made in Japan.

Finance, prices and payments within Europe

As we saw in Chapter 1, among the wider-ranging benefits that will result from implementation of the Single European Act after 1992 are freedom of movement of capital within Europe and the opening-up of financial institutions. The latter should result in cheaper banking services for users, as greater competition is introduced into the system. The proposed common market for financial services will allow banks the right of establishment in any Member State, where they would be free to offer their full range of services, subject to the national regulations of the country in which they are operating. They would also be able to offer cross-border services, for example, a loan from a German bank to a customer in Spain.

Among the benefits of these measures claimed by the Commission are a reduction in the cost of banking services to customers as a result of greater competition, and, more importantly for the European exporter greatly simplified procedures for making payments and collecting monies owed. These measures are in turn related to the gradual removal of all exchange controls, and the integration of the European currencies into the European Monetary System.

Anticipating fluctuations in the exchange rate is a permanent headache for export managers and accountants, faced with the need to set a price for (capital) goods that will be delivered several months or years ahead of the time the order is accepted. It is of course possible to hedge against future exchange rate fluctuations, or indeed price goods on the basis that prices may have to be re-assessed in the light of rates prevailing at the time of delivery. This second solution may not be acceptable to the customer for obvious reasons, while the first requires considerable resources and expertise.

Another option is to price goods in the local currency. This can benefit the British exporter while the pound is weak against European currencies such as the D-mark (enabling him to increase profits) and offers the advantage for the customer of a firm price, payable in his own currency. However a major devaluation can adversely affect the British exporter. Avoidance strategies include separating-out items such as transport or installation, which could be paid for in local currency, while the balance of the invoice is calculated in sterling.

Many of these difficulties could be avoided by wider adoption of the Ecu as a unit of European currency for the pricing of goods and services. As noted elsewhere the Ecu is composed of a basket of the major European currencies (originally excluding the Spanish peseta and Portugues escudo) which are assigned a value. This is periodically reviewed either every five years, or more often if fluctuations occur that are greater than 25% and a review is requested by any one Member State.

The use of the Ecu is in turn allied to integration within the European Monetary System which is designed to keep fluctuations within an agreed band, and full participation in the exchange rate mechanism, which has long been opposed by the British Conservative government.

However, there is growing evidence of more widespread use of the Ecu for European transactions such as loans and mortgages, and it seems likely that a European central bank will eventually have to be established if only to meet the demands of business for faster and more flexible transaction and settlement systems.

When it comes to pricing his goods or services for Europe the British exporter has to weigh up a number of considerations. Travelling in Europe you rapidly become aware of the generally higher levels of salaries and some prices, particularly in the north. However, some services like hotels and restaurants are cheaper, compared with UK prices, even in areas where high salaries are also earned. Some comparisons between UK and European prices have been studied, among others by the Henley Centre for Forecasting. They found that items like wine and mineral water cost more in Britain, while beers, liqueurs and spirits and chocolates cost up to 30% less. Some British machinery and equipment cost 20% more, but in some sectors could be nearly 20% less than the equivalent from a European manufacturer.

These price variations are difficult to understand and in some consumer areas reflect differences of taste and culture. Europeans may regard chocolate as an occasional, luxury item which is expensively packaged and purchased as a gift; whereas in Britain chocolates and snack foods generally are a popular, fairly down-market purchase. The final retail price will of course also be affected by the varying rates of VAT within Europe while these remain in force.

In arriving at a European price for his goods, the British exporter has to take into account the extra costs of selling in Europe, such as promotion and delivery, packaging changes, together with a margin of profit – all this as well as keeping an eye on competitive, perhaps locally produced, goods. It is possible to enter and dominate a market purely on price, while some highly successful companies are able to maintain market share as well as charge premium prices for their goods and services.

It is generally felt that British companies charge prices that are too low, in the belief perhaps that this is the only way to enter a difficult market. This may reflect a lack of faith in their products or service, poor salesmanship or their inability to hold their own in negotiations with potential foreign purchasers. Where low prices are charged ex-UK, agents and distributors can make additional profits as the final price is raised to bring it into line with local levels.

Certainly some buyers have enormous power, for example in the retail sector, but the exporter should evolve a consistent policy on European pricing and stick to it. If you sell your goods or services on low price alone, take that away and you lose your sole advantage over the competition. Whereas by emphasising the superiority of your product, the range and depth of research that went into its creation, its appropriateness to the buyer's needs and the level of after-sales support you are prepared to offer – clearly you have a number of weapons in your negotiating armoury that help you to sell product benefits rather than apologise for the high cost.

A good salesman will also be familiar with local retail prices for similar goods and as far as possible with the margins offered or expected by competitors. His knowledge will be acquired by judiciously studying the local market, with his agent if appropriate, and being prepared to negotiate from a position of familiarity with every aspect of the selling/distribution chain.

In setting European prices the exporter must be mindful of Common Market regulations designed to prevent unfair competition resulting from dumping and industry cartels. Dumping is the practice of selling goods at prices considered to be below their true cost, in order to dominate a market. Examples have included electronic equipment, such as computer printers, where the suppliers were accused of selling them at below manufacturing cost. A cartel on the other hand groups together related suppliers who between them agree to share a market and exclude competitors. Both activities are prohibited under Common Market regulations and are subject to fines and other sanctions. The Commission and national governments also keep a watchful eye on transfer pricing between companies who have manufacturing facilities in a number of countries, in order to discourage price manipulation by companies taking advantage of differences in national taxes and duties.

Exporting is sometimes regarded as a hit or miss affair when it comes to actually being paid by the foreign customer for the goods or services delivered! The arrival of a foreign payment is sometimes seen as something of an unexpected windful rather than the routine settlement of an outstanding debt. It is true that exporting may also have a significant effect on the company's cash flow. Certain delays may occur in shipment, clearance, delivery of goods, all of which may result in delays in payment. However, the exporter needs to be firm about both about the amount of credit offered and the time allowed for payment of invoices.

In terms of the amount of credit information available and geographic proximity, Europe rates highly as an 'export' market and the British businessman should take all the normal precautions he would adopt when supplying a domestic customer. Credit services such as Dun & Bradstreet offer some European coverage but as noted in the section on acquisitions, financial information about companies may not be as readily available as in Britain or it may be presented in a form that makes interpretation difficult. Many business relationships are built on trust, but when in doubt the exporter should propose terms of business that ensure the minimum of risk.

After all, business is about supplying goods and services at a fair price and being rewarded for your efforts by reasonably prompt payment of your invoices. In the European context, if you suffer a bad debt as a result of non-payment, this effectively negates everything you have done so far towards studying, evaluating, researching and entering the new European market of 1992.

Good luck!

Appendix: Main sources of further information and help

(Please note that all Central London 01- numbers will change to 071- after May 1990)

DEPARTMENT OF TRADE AND INDUSTRY

Main Office: 1-19 Victoria Street, London SW1H OET
Exports to Europe Branch – Enquiries 215 5549 or by Country (to obtain country booklets, reports etc.)

Belgium, Luxemburg – 215 5486
Denmark – 215 5140
France – 215 4762
West Germany – 215 4796
Greece – 215 4776
Italy – 215 5103
The Netherlands – 215 4790
Portugal – 215 5307
Spain – 215 4260

1992 Hotline – 200 1992
(general enquiries, literature, copies of *Single Market News*, details of Spearhead Database, etc.)

Statistics & Market Intelligence Library
(same address) – 215 5444 (open Monday-Friday)

Regional Offices: North East – Newcastle upon Tyne
                   North West – Manchester and Liverpool
                   Yorkshire & Humberside – Leeds
                   East Midlands – Nottingham
                   West Midlands – Birmingham
                   South East – London, Cambridge, Reading,
                     Reigate
                   South West – Bristol
                   Scotland – Scottish Office, Glasgow
                   Wales – Welsh Office, Cardiff
                   Northern Ireland – Industrial Development Board
                     for Northern Ireland, Belfast

Small Firms Service – Dial 100 and ask for Freefone Enterprise, for connection to your nearest branch

CENTRES FOR EUROPEAN BUSINESS INFORMATION
(established by European Commission in partnership with local organisations, offering help to Small Businesses):

South: Department of Employment, Small Firms Service – 730 8115
Midlands: Birmingham Chamber of Commerce & Industry – 021-454 6171
North: Northern Development Company – 091-261 5131
Scotland: Strathclyde Euroinfocentre, Glasgow – 041-221 0999
Further centres are being added.

BOTB FAIRS & PROMOTIONS BRANCH
Dean Bradley House
52 Horseferry Road
London SW1P 2AG
212 7676

Information about Overseas Fairs also from local Chambers of Commerce and Trade & Professional associations.

BRITISH STANDARDS INSTITUTION
Linford Wood
Milton Keynes MK14 6LE
Information on British Standards – 0908 221166
Technical Help to Exporters Service – 0908 220022

EXPORT DOCUMENTATION
Simplification of International Trade Procedures Board (SITPRO)
Almack House
26-28 King Street
London SW1Y 6QW
Enquiries 930 0532

RESEARCH AND DEVELOPMENT/EC PROGRAMMES
DTI Ashdown House – Enquiries 215 6618

EXPORT CREDITS GUARANTEE DEPARTMENT (ECGD)
London HQ – 382 7777
Regional offices in Cardiff, London City, Croydon, Belfast, Birmingham, Bristol, Cambridge, Glasgow, Leeds, Manchester; or through major Banks.

COMMISSION OF THE EUROPEAN COMMUNITIES
UK Library and Information Office
8 Storeys Gate
London SW1P 3AT
222 8122

EUROPEAN PARLIAMENT
Information Office
2 Queen Anne's Gate
London SW1H 9AA
222 0411

Both the COMMISSION and the PARLIAMENT have a library (telephone to check opening times) and numerous reports, publications, directories, the OFFICIAL JOURNAL, and background information, much of it free.

BRITISH EMBASSIES IN EUROPE

Belgium – Brussels (2) 217 9000   Fax 217 6763

Denmark – Copenhagen (31) 26 46 00   Fax 43 14 00

France – Paris (1) 42 66 91 42   Fax 42 66 95 90

West Germany – Bonn (0228) 234061   Fax 234070

Greece – Athens (1) 7236 211   Fax 7241 872

Italy – Rome (6) 475 5441/475 5551   Fax 474 1836

Luxemburg – Luxemburg City (no area code) 29864 Fax 29867

The Netherlands – The Hague (70) 64 58 00   Fax 60 38 39

Portugal – Lisbon (1) 661191, 661122, 661147   Fax 676768

Spain – Madrid (1) 419 0200   Fax 419 0423

Details of Consulates in other main cities can be obtained from the British Embassy.

PERMANENT REPRESENTATION OF THE UNITED KINGDOM, BRUSSELS

The office of the UK Permanent Representation includes several specialists with wide knowledge of the Commission and its policies, and can arrange introductions where required. Located opposite the Commission's own Berlaymont Building at:
Rond-Point Robert Schuman 6
B-1040 Brussels
Belgium
Telephone (2) 230 62 05

MAIN BRITISH CHAMBERS OF COMMERCE IN EUROPE

France   – Franco British Chamber of Commerce
                    8 rue Cimarosa
                    75116 Paris   (1) 45 05 13 08   Fax 45 53 02 87

Germany   – British Chamber of Commerce in Germany
                    Heumarkt 14
                    D-5000 Cologne 1   (221) 23 42 84

Italy   – British Chamber of Commerce in Italy
                    via Agnello 8
                    20121 Milan   (2) 876981

The Netherlands   – Netherlands-British Chamber of Commerce
                    Bezuidenhoutseweg 181
                    2594 AH The Hague   (70) 47 88 81

Spain   – British Chamber of Commerce in Spain
                    Plaza Santa Barbara 10
                    28010 Madrid   (1) 410 7064   Fax 410 4605

Some of the above Chambers also have regional Offices.

Index